Architectures of Time

Architectures of Time

Toward a Theory of the Event in Modernist Culture

SANFORD KWINTER

The MIT Press
Cambridge, Massachusetts
London, England

This book was set in Adobe Garamond
by Graphic Composition, Inc., Athens, Georgia
and printed and bound in the United States of America.

Library of Congress Cataloging-in-Publication Data

Kwinter, Sanford.
  Architects of time : toward a theory of the event in modernist culture / Sanford Kwinter.
    p. cm.
  Includes bibliographical references and index.
  ISBN 0-262-11260-4 (alk. paper)
  1. Modern movement (Architecture) I. Title.

NA628.M63 K89   2001
724'.6–dc 21

                                                              00-045085

CONTENTS

To my mother,
who taught me how to use tools

The essays that make up this study were written between 1984 and 1989. They were substantially rewritten in 1990 to incorporate scientific material that could not be included in the original manuscript and that focused on the demise of classical mechanics in late nineteenth-century physics, particularly in the work of Ernst Mach, Henri Poincaré, Ludwig Boltzmann, and Max Planck. That revised manuscript with its accompanying notes and documents was lost in transit between Cambridge and New York in 1991. Though the Getty Center for the History of Art and the Humanities, where the majority of the work of revision had taken place, was unimaginably generous in taking on and completing the task of reconstructing the lost research from library records, the actual task of rewriting the book represented a path I could not retrace myself, quite simply because I was no longer committed to its specific thesis. While preparing the material the first time around, I had already been realizing that the significant transformation in twentieth-century epistemology in which I was interested could not be understood simply in terms of the disturbances and theoretical adaptations taking place within the world of physics, but involved a far more systematic shift in style, method, and explanation than could be readily perceived from within the boundaries of its now narrowing paradigm. The "time problem" (could time yield to scientific investigation, or was it merely a chimera?) was clearly an inheritance from nineteenth-century physics, but this did not mean its impact could be grasped properly from within a purely physical framework.

It became clear to me during this period of research that the irreversibility principle (or the *non*symmetry of space-time) introduced by the science of thermodynamics (and statistical mechanics) and by the theory of evolution did not represent a mere *part* of physics, but rather referred to a broader field of labile phenomena into which the world of physics fits itself as but a single component. The study of rules of organization of large ensembles, of global and general behaviors, and of intuitable processes in apparent semifree development had begun to take precedence over the numerical formalization of microscopically reduced and isolated systems. The problems of "mechanical explanation" and field theory was, for example, more directly and speculatively treated in embryology than in the quantum mechanics of the period, and it was in fact the problem of "organism" that most deeply affected early twentieth-century metaphysics (Bergson and Whitehead) and, soon after, philosophical aesthetics. The closed, controlled, mechanical world of physics was giving way to the approximate, active, and qualitative world of *biology* as a model of both scientific and metaphysical explanation.

This shift in twentieth-century thought toward a biological model and toward its more systematic offspring, information theory, became the subject of a subsequent book project entitled *Soft Systems.* The decision to publish the present book in its originally intended form is a response to a clear and emerging interest among designers and architects in the problem of time and its relation to form. This work is meant as a contribution to an already fecund field of contemporary speculation and experimentation—to my mind, the design discipline's greatest current hope for systematic renewal and continued relevance—a field, however, that is not always as attentive to the nuances of historical understanding as it is enthusiastic about what it charmingly imagines to be its own discoveries. The advent of the computer in our laboratories and studios has certainly made the shape and form of time amenable to human manipulation and intuition in a way that has not been the case within rational disciplines since the dawn of the modern era; but without as broad and historical an understanding of the time problem as possible, these exciting developments are at risk of falling into formalistic parody or mere embellishments and celebrations of market logic in frictionless freefall. The following essays at best constitute an implicit encouragement to others to extend as far into the future as possible what is most exciting in design speculation today, by reaching back into the past and connecting contemporary thought and research to as broad a series of historical developments as can be found or invented.

The themes developed below concern the relation of certain vitalist or immanentist models to the specific philosophical, scientific, and aesthetic modernisms that emerged in the early twentieth century. The advent of thermodynamics (the seat of the modernist resurgence of the time problem) serves as a general and implicit backdrop for the study, which deals principally with Albert Einstein's theory of relativity (1907), the technical writings of sculptor Umberto Boccioni (1910–1914), the influential townplan schema of the architect Antonio Sant'Elia (1912–1914), the philosophy of Henri Bergson (1896–1922), and the writings of Franz Kafka (1904–1924). In physics, the demise of absolute time is shown to give way to a theory of the "field," effectively superseding the classical notion of space as a substratum against which things occur, and consequently giving rise to a physics of the "event." Nowhere were these two concepts of field and event so profoundly, and so early, deployed as in the theoretical writings of Boccioni and more importantly, in the visionary architecture of Sant'Elia. Nor was it a coincidence that such a modernity—so radical as to have overturned the laws of classical physics—should have been at the root of futurism, aesthetic modernism's first, and only absolute, avant-garde movement. Sant'Elia's massively complex scheme is the first to give concrete expression—aesthetic or otherwise—to the new notions of time and space developed by nineteenth- and early twentieth-century physical science. It is also the first schema within aesthetic modernism to have elaborated a theory of nature in which the ground or first principle is seen to reside nowhere else but at the level of its effects; that is, it was the first to have embodied the principle of an *immanent cause*.

The last two essays develop these same themes but move away from the thermodynamic model to consider the closely related one of Bergsonian *durée* or virtuality. The objects analyzed in this context are the literary works of Franz Kafka. Here I attempt to show that Kafka's works, despite appearances, manifest a coherent cosmology, but that this cosmology can be understood only in relation to a certain type of movement—and therefore time—that underlies it. This movement belongs to the realm of what Bergson called the intensive; here movement is caught up in *qualitative changes* of state, differentiations, and especially individuations ("qualities" cannot be divided without changing *in nature;* "quantities" change only *in degree*). It is only this type of movement that can account for the appearance or creation of "the new," even if this novelty is of the most troubling and unforeseen kind. Kafka's world is one in constant (qualitative) temporal flux, even if its appearance is one of (quantitative) spatial stasis. In fact, it is literally defined in terms of metamorphosis, singularity, and flight. Finally, it is precisely this peculiar (Kafkaesque) instability of Being that I try to identify as the positive, even affirmative principle throughout the works.

Readers with a more pressing and abiding interest in design issues than in literary aesthetics and philosophy are invited to skip chapter 4 entirely, as well as the sections of chapter 5 that precede "Milieu and Event."

ACKNOWLEDGMENTS

This book would not have seen its way to publication if not for the persistent, patient, and often well-timed encouragement of several people who helped overcome my embarrassment at the insoluble imperfections of the work's form and ideas. Primary among them are Jeffrey Kipnis, Jonathan Crary, Mark Rakatansky, Lars Lerup, Michael Bell, and Peter Eisenman. To Peter Eisenman in particular I am grateful for having produced at his own risk a type of work that continues to make mine possible. John Johnston, Molly Nesbitt, Marjorie Perloff, and Albert Pope read portions or versions of the manuscript and gave important and especially imaginative feedback that helped me find new ways to understand this work and to become reconciled to its unusual final shape. Daniela Fabricius ministered with humbling clarity to the final stages of the book's preparation, did a considerable amount of the final photo research, and helped design the cover. Ana Miljacki and Peony Quan did much legwork on the photos as well and kept things cheerful long after I alone was able to. Matthew Roush found the image of the free solo climber. The Getty Center for the History of Art and the Humanities provided a critical period of peace and distance in 1990 during which the present project took on a vastly different shape. Though the book before you no longer reflects those changes, my tenure there served as an indispensable reminder of how accelerated intellectual work can become within an uncommon old-world environment of formal respect and where one is freed of the pressures of administration and mere production. I am grateful to all my collaborators at ZONE over the years for having helped to produce the type of environment in which transdisciplinary work is finally beginning to be seen as a necessity and a norm and not merely an exception or a descent into untidy generalism. I would like to thank my colleagues at the Rice School of Architecture for providing, in what is certainly among the most congenial and civilized university departments in the country, an atmosphere of unqualified support and openness. The Social Sciences and Humanities Research Council of Canada provided support in the years in which I was writing and teaching art criticism in New York and in which the ideas in this book were developed. I would like to express my gratitude to Judy Feldmann for her firm yet infinitely light touch in the editing of the manuscript and to designer Erin Hasley for getting me everything I requested and for understanding implicitly the tactical necessities and advantages of restraint. I would like to thank Larry Cohen and the MIT Press for a fifteen-year relationship that has been uncommonly tolerant, respectful, and fun.

I am indebted to Brian Boigon not only for his friendship but for his originality, his madness, and his unflagging faith in the world. They were among the things that enticed me away from a career in comparative literature in the first place. It was Bob McNulty who first brought me into the architectural fray with an invitation to speak at the Skidmore, Owings, Merril Foundation in Chicago in 1987. Part of that paper has been integrated into chapter 1. To Mack Scogin and Michael Hays I owe perhaps the biggest debt of all: they were the first to have taken a chance on me by offering me my first job at Harvard's Graduate School of Design when such an act was truly but an act of faith and audacity. The design world has been my chosen home ever since. To Bruce Mau I owe a type of debt that few writers will ever have a chance to incur let alone to repay: the opportunity to work out and to apply one's ideas in the concrete realm of design with a fearless and inventive collaborator. Many of the ideas in the present book found direct and methodical application in the design of our first book at Zone, *ZONE 1/2 The Contemporary City.* A more detailed theoretical account of this and subsequent collaborations is forthcoming. Kerri Kwinter and Adam Brooks sustained me morally and physically through a prolonged period when my health alone could not. Their generosity was boundless and among the many transformations it permitted was one most dear to me: I became an ex officio family member and favored friend to Theo and Taia. Finally, I would like to thank my parents who, when I was still young and dangerous, found the courage to cut me a far longer leash than their own world of mores and good sense could ever have prepared them to do. I thank them for the lesson to do things differently and for their conviction in backing it up with both risk and implicit belief.

Architectures of Time

1.1
Surfer, 1960s. Photo: Dr. Don James.

1   The Complex and the Singular

Reality . . . is a perpetual becoming.
It makes or remakes itself, but it is
never something made.
— HENRI BERGSON

WHAT WOULD IT CHANGE in our arts, our sciences, and our technics if time were conceived as something *real*? Though over a century has passed since the first tremors of this fundamental question began to make themselves felt in philosophical and scientific debate in the Western world, the problem stubbornly remains, either largely intractable or willfully ignored. What is it about time's relentless fluidity, its irreducible materiality, that the modern mind finds so impossible—or repellent—to think?

"But Western Being," the voices of our institutions will protest, "*is* time, and has been so since the very dawn of modernity"—since the advent of rationalized accounting practices, the discovery of universal mechanical laws and constants, the application of systematic techniques for governing populations, the rise of humanistic disciplines and experimental method, the birth of the Cartesian or modern "self." But the forms of time expressed in these seemingly disparate historical developments are not, strictly speaking, "real" at all, but only chimeras of an emerging and very specific instrumental culture; they are, in a word, *abstractions*—ingenious tools contrived to distribute the senseless procession of events in nature within an external, thinkable space of measure, management, and mastery.

But nature itself is wild, indifferent, and accidental; it is a ceaseless pullulation and unfolding, a dense evolutionary plasma of perpetual differentiation and innovation. Each thing, it may be said, changes and arrives *in time,* yet the posture of externality that permits precise measure and perfect mastery can be struck and assumed only in space; one must first withdraw oneself from the profuse, organic flux in which things are given, isolate discrete instants as projected frozen sections, and then interpolate abstract laws like so much mortar to rejoin these sections from the new perspective. But the very gesture that carries thought away from the "event" and toward the "thing" abstracts and spatializes time in the act of instrumentalizing it; it subjugates the contingency and volatility of time by reconstituting it external to phenomena as a finitude and a regularity: it becomes a technique of measurement embodied in economic axioms and algebraic laws.

Real time is more truly an engine, however, than a procession of images—it is expressed only in the concrete, plastic medium of duration. Time always expresses itself by producing, or more precisely, by drawing matter into a process of *becoming-ever-different,* and to the product of this becoming-ever-different—to this in-built wildness—we have given the name *novelty*. Yet exactly what is novelty, and from where does it come? What might thinking about it make possible in this world, in this civilization whose deepest religious and philosophical beliefs, and whose social and political institutions, are committed precisely to reducing, eliding, or denying the continual mutations and insistent mischievousness of unmasterable innovation and the wild becoming that drives it?

We might say that novelty is simply a modality, a vehicle, by or through which something new appears in the world. It is that ever-fresh endowment that affirms a radical incommensurability between what happens at any given instant and what follows. What has made it a problem for thought—and its problematic nature predates our own modernity, reaching back to the time of the Greeks—is the way it is seen to introduce a corrupting element or impure principle into the pristine and already full world of "Creation." The offending element here is no other than the principle of change, for in cosmological thought, change is either recognized as a first principle or not accepted to exist at all.[1] All change is change over time; no novelty appears without becoming, and no becoming without novelty. But more important, setting out to think about novelty, or "the new," might provide a way to revive our presently atrophied capacities of acting—practically, ethically, and politically—in this world, a world whose scope and complexity have effectively passed beyond grasp or measure. It is, in other words, our capacity actively to engage the *processes* of contemporary reality, a capacity that by most accounts is today so menacingly at stake, that might itself be brought into relief here, grasped, interrogated, and perhaps transformed.

The era of cultural production we are traversing is unarguably one of impoverishment and mediocrity—in art, philosophy, literature, even architecture, though to a lesser extent—an era whose inaugural segment was marked by reaction, an era in which innovation itself seemed all but to have collapsed and which neurotically lauded itself for a "criticality" that was little more than the impulse, which would normally discharge itself through the assembling and invention of new capacities, ensembles, and functions, become corrupted and turned inward as "critique." In the domain of architecture—the first to have declared its "postmodern" emancipation from avant-gardist modernity—this tendency to mediocrity was expressed, and only barely masked, by a decade of submission to the cult of historical styles, and subsequently to myriad, but often hollow neo- and antimodernist intellectual postures ("strategies" such as

1 This statement applies of course to systematic philosophy and classical science, not to the continually self-updating pseudo-axiomatics of Christian theology and Western capitalism.

collage, deconstruction, and the crypto-formalist revivals of computer-aided modeling). Though the parochialism of these especially recent developments is often obscured by the virtuosity of their results, they have never managed to hide their fundamental aimlessness, the inevitable result of cultures whose intellectual activity has become severed from its foundations in social, historical, and economic life.

Yet a return to the "critical" modes of the preceding period is no acceptable solution. For it is in periods like those that architects and artists, as well as writers and thinkers, are able to see the world only in the terms of a (real or imagined) oppressor's conventions—indeed of conventions *tout court*—for they have lost the thread, one might say, of their own reality or perspective, their own politic, their own "world-building." Critique is always a critique (and therefore an elaboration) of what exists already, implicitly reconstituting this preexistence as a static thing (both in its referential and *re*presentational forms). Clearly all critique is of representations and is, as many of its own most rigorous practitioners have claimed, at bottom no more than an elaborate *re*-representation. But what concerns us here is the concept of time that one finds bound up in these wedded practices of critique and representation. What type of intervention do these two practices actively effect in the world, and what type do they passively imply?

The two relationships—between representation and reality on one hand, and critique and representation on the other—may be understood according to the classical morphogenetic model that is determined by the relationship of the *possible* to the *real*. I use the technical term "morphogenesis" here in no gratuitous sense, but because it is precisely the problem of "the emergence and evolution of form" that I am proposing to discuss, and because it is precisely this problem that is indisputably at the heart of all formal aesthetic practice in general, and design practice in particular.[2]

How does one characterize the morphogenetic model of the possible in relation to the real? To begin, "possible" finds itself invariably placed in opposition to "real" as if it were some type of earlier stage; it has on its own, therefore, no reality in the strict sense, but takes this on only at a later stage, through the process of realizing itself. How does it do this? Two controlling rules or operators must in-

---

2 The term "formal" is used here not in the poor sense as in "formalistic," but in reference to the largely unthought dimension of all active patterning processes in the universe, comprising linguistic, social, political, and biological *behaviors* and *forms,* in addition to aesthetic ones.

tervene here to relate the two states or realms: The first is resemblance, the second limitation.[3] *Resemblance,* because what is real always conforms to, or matches, the image of the possible—the possible presents the preexisting *image* of the real whose attractive forces realize it. The possible—though it is but a phantom entity—is nonetheless a true and faithful copy. Second, *limitation,* because although anything whatever can exist as a "possible" (a phantom or image) clearly not everything that is possible can be realized. Were it the case, the world would become saturated in a clamoring instant and historical time would be annihilated altogether. Everything would not only happen at once, but would indeed already have "happened."

To these two operators of resemblance and limitation, then, something clearly must be added, something that actively filters and constrains what can pass into reality. Here we find the only trace of a time-principle borne by this model: Something divides into successive stages the passing of preformed phantom images into concrete reality. Reality, according to this model, would still be nothing but a picture of possibility *repeated,* and the world of possibility would be no more than an unchanging storehouse of images existing from time immemorial. This theory of appearance or morphogenesis supposes a sad and confining world already formed and given in advance. Yet this static view of things has dominated nearly all aspects of Western culture from the time of the Eleatics, though most significantly throughout its modern scientific culture. According to Henri Bergson, this fallacy—that there exists a "realm of possibility" underlying the world of actuality—is the one upon which Western metaphysics is based. Both the deep-seated mechanism of our scientific traditions and the implicit finalism of our theological, historical, and political traditions find their roots in this fallacy.

It is through the development of this argument that the problem of novelty takes on its full importance. For the very same principle that "corrupts," transforms, and diminishes Forms, evolving them toward disuse, decrepitude, and disappearance, also *gives,* produces, and creates. No object in nature—be it organic,

---

3 See Henri Bergson, "The Possible and the Real," in *The Creative Mind* (New York: Philosophical Library, 1946), *Introduction to Metaphysics* (New York: Philosophical Library, 1961); and Gilles Deleuze, *Différence et répétition* (Paris: PUF, 1968) pp. 272–275, *Le Bergsonisme* (Paris: PUF, 1968), chap. 5. See also the arguments of Alfred North Whitehead concerning the "Fallacy of Misplaced Concreteness," in *Science in the Modern World* (New York: Macmillan, 1925), chaps. 3 and 4.

mineral, or entirely abstract or immaterial such as an idea, a desire, or a function—escapes the perpetual onslaught of differentiation according to which objects are continually becoming different from themselves, undergoing transformation. It is true, that change may and ought to be seen as a type of movement—the flow of matter through time—but even the simplest mechanical movement of the classical translational type resisted scientific and philosophical assimilation until very late in our history. For "transformation" and "invention," I wish to show, are also twin and inseparable functions. Both are quality-producing processes that describe the coherent flow of matter through time, and it is time, and only time, that makes the new both possible and necessary.[4]

To think in this way, however, means developing a radically different theory and regime of morphogenesis. The so-called emergence and evolution of form will no longer follow the classical, eidetic pathway determined by the possible and the real.[5] Rather, it will follow the dynamic and uncertain processes that characterize the schema that links a *virtual* component to an *actual* one. What is most important to understand here is that unlike the previous schema where the "possible" had no reality (before emerging), here the virtual, though it may yet have no actuality, is nonetheless already fully real. It exists, one might say, as a *free* difference or singularity, not yet combined with other differences into a complex ensemble or salient form. What this means is that the virtual does not have to be realized, but only actualized (activated and integrated); its adventure involves a developmental passage from one state to another. The virtual is gathered, selected—let us say *incarnated*—it passes from one moment-event (or complex) in order to emerge—differently, uniquely—within another. Indeed *the actual does not resemble the virtual,* as something preformed or preexisting itself. The relation of the virtual to the actual is therefore not one of resemblance but rather of *difference,* innovation, or creation (every complex, or moment-event, is unique and new). Thus the following should be clear: realization (of a possible) and creation (through actualization-differentiation) are two intrinsi-

---

4 In *Creative Evolution,* Bergson argues the need for a science or "mechanics of transformation" of which our "mechanics of translation" would become but a particular case (New York: Henry Holt and Co., 1911), p. 32. Alfred North Whitehead, drawing a similar distinction, claimed in 1925 that "biology is the study of larger organisms; whereas physics is the study of the smaller organisms") (*Science in the Modern World,* p. 103). For Whitehead even the physico-chemical world could be understood only in terms of the (prehensive) "events" it undergoes, and to which it gives place.

5 Cf. Bergson's critique of Platonic and Aristotelian *eidos* in *Creative Evolution,* pp. 314–329.

CHAPTER I

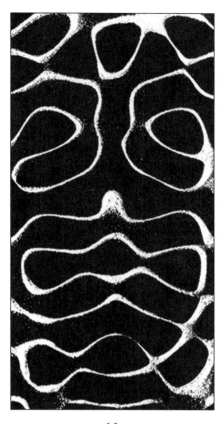

I.2

Hans Jenny. Kymatic: *Wellen und Schwingungen mit ihrer Struktur und Dynamik*, 1967.
Basel: Basilius Presse AG.

*In these Kymatic images by Hans Jenny, standing waves are generated by sinus tones emitted across steel plates by crystal oscillators (in much the same manner as Ernst Chladni's eighteenth-century **Klangfiguren**). A mixture of sand and superfine lycopodium powder forms the outlines of the resultant shapes as it is transported across the plate surface into virtual troughs between the more highly activated areas of the field. One can discern a specific and uniform underlying pattern or texture "beneath" the resultant figure that is a joint property of the metallurgy of the sounding plate and of the tone that moves through it. This underlying pattern is itself never reproduced, but remains **virtual**. The **actual** pattern (the sand-lycopodium figure) always expresses a variation or development of its virtual form—built on the template but continuously variable and varying. Both the actual and the virtual structures are legible in the same image, though their ontological status remains perfectly distinct.*

cally distinct and irreducible processes. The first programmatically reproduces what was already there, formed and given in advance, while the other *invents* through a continuous, positive, and dynamic process of transmission, differentiation, and evolution.

The crux lies here: Actualization occurs *in* time and *with* time, whereas realization, by limiting itself to the mere unfolding of what preexists, actually destroys novelty and annihilates time. In the first instance time is real; in the second it remains artificially derived and abstract in relation to events. In the one case time is a dynamic and perpetually activated flow, in the other, the result of an externally built-up succession of static images. Morphogenesis occurs either as a mechanical process of translation fixed once and for all and external to the specific morphogenetic moment-event, with its highly particular and unreproduceable conditions—or else, it is the very principle of life, that is, perpetual instability and therefore creation itself, and wedded to the ever-evolving particularities of time, or what one could call, in homage to mathematician René Thom, the minute and ceaseless procession of catastrophes. Clearly, if time is real, then the principle of morphogenesis (novelty) must be sought *in time,* within a mobile and dynamic reality riddled with creative instabilities and discontinuities.

Can there, then, be an ethics of material culture free from the bureaucracy of critique, of the negative, of the spatial-visual, and of the static? Can there be a politics of form based on the productive, the positive, the mobile, and the new? Might concepts such as "novelty" and "movement" still be politicized and placed at the heart of cultural production? Clearly, the concept of "new" as it is used here is deeply indebted to modernist philosophies—that is, philosophies that are bound up chronologically with those same movements whose claim at another level to "newness" is so often reviled by contemporary critical cultural practices and theories. I use such a concept both without apology and without taking sides in this debate—its purpose is to underscore why it may be interesting and fruitful to reject the very terms and conditions in which such a debate is posed.

The late nineteenth-century prescription to remake oneself *absoluement moderne* was inseparable from a more systematic and generalized historical need to discover—or to invent at any cost—a principle of absolute novelty and a correlative river of time to bear it along. For Nietzsche, the punctuated violence of the *Unzeitgemäßliche,* or the untimely, was wedded to the infinite spiral—not circle—of eternal recurrence, in order that the Will to Power might circulate freely, unfettered by the sclerosis of a false memory tainted by "morals." Bergson's enlightened vitalism may certainly be seen as a development of Nietzsche's radical "biological philosophy," albeit in a more temperate, systematic mode. Bergson's principles of an ever-individuating élan vital and of becoming, both cast and unfolded within an irreducible actualizing duration, would resurface nearly a century later combined with those of Nietzsche to produce Deleuze's philosophy of difference, and Foucault's philosophy of power/knowledge and philosophy of will. These philosophies each develop in their own way the principle of a mobile ground of continuous production of the real as the basis of history and life. They reject the static field of eidetic Forms and representations as so many sources of illusion, bad faith, or at the very least, as hostile to movement and arresting of an irreducible *living* dynamism that drives existence from within.

To approach the problem of "the new," then, one must complete the following four requirements: redefine the traditional concept of the object; reintroduce and radicalize the theory of time; conceive of "movement" as a first principle and not merely a special, dismissable case; and embed these latter three within an all-encompassing theory and politics of the "event." This presents us with five areas of interrogation: novelty, the object, time, movement, and event. We can consider the problem of novelty only by confronting the question of determinations or causes: What makes something new emerge? Where does that which did not exist before come from? How does it continue to persist in being? and especially, What is its relation to matter?:—for clearly the "new" is significant only to the degree that it is concrete, And finally, how does that which is just a pure difference take on a body? These questions apply with their own urgency and specificity to the social and perceptual field—the realm in which objects and architectures of all types are assembled and circulated.

The question of the object may well be even more complex than the previous. On one side it calls for a systematic investigation of physical theory: What is an object's relation to the space immediately surrounding it, to its own component parts, to the other objects with which it is combined; what are the forces—both historical and physical—that traverse it, compose it, and bear it along; and what are the adjacent activities and behaviors it makes possible, the so-called meaning systems it partakes of, the spaces and temporalities it carves up (one thinks especially of technical objects and their correlative "modes")? On the other side, it forces to the surface the corresponding panoply of questions regarding the status of the subject as well.

The problematization of *time* entails a challenge to the primacy of the role of space, and the reintroduction of the classical problem of *becoming* in opposition to that of Being. With movement is introduced the larger problem of dynamical and evolutionary systems and complexity, and the more remote question of a "middleness" that is opposed to essential or foundational beginnings and ends. (Since movement can be caused and modified only by other movements, the problem of origin and initiation must either be reconfigured or pass away.) Next emerges the problem of nonlinearity and indeterminacy (what is cautiously referred to as "deterministic chaos"), understood not only as a heuristic and cosmological model but also as an ethos. And finally, in the "event" it may be possible to discover a vantage point from which all action is understood as political in the positive (i.e., not critical) sense—because after all, in both the social and subjective realms, politics is arguably nothing more than the production of new possibilities.

What follows will proceed schematically to develop two pathways along which design thought and practice might move today—pathways that would have as a role to restore to architecture specifically the active, and not merely reactive, role it once had in shaping cultural and social life. This will be done without forgetting or denying the fundamental fact that is often seen to hamper social and cultural activity today: the perception that the world is finally composed of systems so extensive, so dense, and so complex that it is no longer a question of representing them in their totality/globality—through images, concepts, theorems, or maps, all spatial models that today arguably have fallen into disuse—but rather of engaging these systems at certain specific and local points along their lines of deployment or unfolding. It is as if today one were forced into a new type of intellectual and cultural warfare, forced to accept the mobile and shifting nature of the phenomena that make up our social and political world, and by this same token, forced to discover within this slippery *glacis* of largely indistinct swells and flows, all the ledges, footholds, friction points—in short, all the subtle asperities that would permit us to navigate, and negotiate life, within it.

The first pathway entails a revision of the concept of the object. Here architecture may be said to have a natural and privileged role, owing first to its natural function as an institutional, social, and instrumental operator (it must not be forgotten that within every concrete architecture is embedded an abstract institutional "machine"); and second, because once we accept this machinic role and the behavioral (motor) modalities it regulates and entails, it is impossible not to consider architecture in an expanded sense as a technical object, subject to the same rules and dynamics as all other technological historical development.

The second pathway attempts to conceive of movement as a first principle—though it secondarily both engages the theory of time (treating time as something *real*) and develops a theory and praxis of the "event." This will be done in allusive adjacency to a body of recent developments in physics and experimental mathematics—those proposing the use of new types of geometry (phase space, fractals, attractor dynamics, scaling), new types of algebra (nonlinear equations, recursion, genetic algorithms), and new types of modeling tools (principally the interactive cathode ray tube and the desktop microcomputer).

These last developments are particularly important, first, for having reoriented contemporary science toward the consideration of dynamical phenomena or dynamical morphogenesis, toward geometries or patterns that are not static but appear only *over time;* second, for their role in the study of complexity—the study of phenomena no longer in analytic isolation but as embedded within a rich and unstable milieu of multiple communicating forces and influences; and third, for having introduced into popular discussion the technical concept of "singularities," referring to those critical points or moments within a system when its qualities and not just its quantities undergo a fundamental change. It is possible that this latter development alone—the incorporation of *qualities* into the numerical continuum of mathematics—is as radical in its implications today as was the renunciation of qualities at the end of the sixteenth century (Kepler, Galileo), the decisive event—itself a historical singularity—that gave rise to modern scientific method. The concept of singularities provides us with the chance to revise our understanding of the role of time and the event in both historical and physical processes.

Let us begin with the first pathway revising the concept of the subject. Among the important developments in design discourse over the last few years has been the architectural profession's discovery of the appeals of an intellectual cosmopolitanism that had for several decades already come to characterize many of the other humanities disciplines. The architectural object today nonetheless remains strangely unmolested by this putative but still superficial cross-fertilization of disciplines. One important reason for this has to do with architecture's strange and problematic relation to history. Is architecture simply a branch of traditional art history—the history of movements and styles, the successive aesthetic solutions through which epochs, cultures, and entire civilizations express their indomitable "will to form"—or does it, by virtue of those intrinsic characteristics outlined above, belong to history in another way? If architectural thought and practice is to break out of narrow academicism on one hand, and aestheticism on the other, it must conceive of itself as belonging to a different series of developments—to what recent parlance sometimes calls the "history of practices." This approach is already opening architectural thought and practice to a new series of relations, both historical-theoretical and material-practical, indeed to a *field* of relations in which many of the accepted unities of classical architectural thought are coming to lose their sovereign and constitutive status. Architecture would then be seen in its full proximity and intimacy with the system of forces that give shape and rhythm to the everyday life of the body. Thus the object—be it a building, a compound site, or an entire urban matrix, insofar as such unities continue to exist at all as functional terms—would be defined now *not by how it appears, but rather by practices:* those it partakes of and those that take place within it.

On this reconception, the unitariness of the object would necessarily vanish—deflected now into a single but doubly articulated field (relations, by definition, never correspond to objects). What comes to the fore are, on the one hand, those relations that are smaller than the object, that saturate it and compose it, the "micro-architectures" for lack of a happier term, and on the other, those relations or systems that are greater or more extensive than the object, that comprehend or envelop it, those "macro-architectures" of which the "object," or the level of organization corresponding to the object, is but a relay member or part. Furthermore, these particular clusters of action, affectivity, and matter—what I am calling "practices"—correspond less to formed and distinct objects than to *a specific regime* (of power, of effects) that for a given time inhabits the social field. A regime can be said to impose a configuration on such a field insofar as it organizes, allies, and distributes bodies, materials, movements, and techniques in space while simultaneously controlling and developing the temporal relations between them. There is nothing forced in characterizing these two planes of relations as "architectures"—they are every bit as material, as constructed, and as imperious as any building. Nor is the building or object conjured away or repressed, as some will want to claim, but is rather reconceived as a hinge produced at (and producing) the intersection of these two systems of articulation. It would therefore be a mistake, I would argue, to limit the concept of "architectural substance" to building materials and the geometric volumes they engender and enclose. Just as the meaning of a sentence differs depending on who is speaking, to whom it is addressed, the time and place in which it is uttered, the infinitely complex interplay of will, desire, and systems of legitimation, as well as on these same conditions applied to the referents of each and every element of the sentence, so any proper understanding of architecture must also confront *its* character as an *illocutionary event,* or at the very least as an element inseparable from and in constant interface with the world of force, will, action, and history.

In his book *Discipline and Punish*—today commonly recognized as the canonical analytical work of this type—Michel Foucault demonstrated in considerable detail how the domain of "architectures"—*social* technical objects—forms the principle hinge or conductive relay permitting abstract, incorporeal (i.e., discursive) formations of power to enter and permeate the adjacent material realm of human flesh, activity, and desire. Architecture's proper and primary function, it could be said—at least in the modern era—is the instrumental application of mastery, not only to an external, nonhuman nature, but to a *human*—social, psychological—nature as well. This method in no way excludes a guerilla architecture of subversion and resistance, such as the active "resingularizing" of the familiar and precoded, amplifying the transformative power of the contingent through an ethics of flexible, or "opportunistic" vigilance, or tapping the history-producing forces of the emergent and untimely. On the contrary, this vision of the technical world as a constellation of *active* agencies (rather than fixed or sedimented constructs) invites intervention as a détournement of moving, flexible processes.

No genealogy of the body in relation to Western architectural mastery is possible, even today, that does not begin by reviving, at least in passage, the convention of Vitruvian man splayed out and mathematically embedded in a reticulum of regulating lines like a proud trophy honoring the Idea and geometric exactitude. This familiar image still stands at the ceremonial head of a complex and many-stranded procession through Western history in which the histories of the body itself, of architecture, and of the even more basic "will to order" are inseparable from one another. The role of mathematics especially must be underscored here, in its relation to the anexact formalism of the sensuously and infinitely varying body: the Vitruvian hammerlock of quantitative-numerical reduction appears here as the forerunner of a relation that would grow only deeper, a deepening that would be made possible only by diversifying and reinsinuating itself in ever new institutions and practices.

Among the most significant developments in the history of Western modernization was the emergence of the European monasteries of the early Middle Ages, in particular (as Werner Sombart, Lewis Mumford, E. P. Thompson, David Landes, and others have argued) those of the Benedictine order. There, for the first time, a periodic system of bells was used to punctuate the day—seven bells corresponding to the seven canonical "hours" or devotional periods—contributing immeasurably to the already staggering discipline and regimentation of monastic life, all the more notable in an era still centuries away

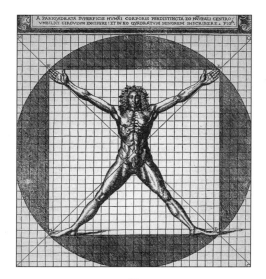

1.3
Vitruvian Man

1.4
N. Audry, *Orthopaedics,* 1749

from the appearance (in Europe) of the first mechanical clocks. This development represents the insertion of a new "template" or plan at three levels of cultural organization: (1) at the macroscopic, geopolitical level, these routines activated a wide range of adjacent processes through the broader social-historical function of the monastery, whose ostensible task was to provide for the welfare of souls and to supply sanctuary—in effect, however, and more pragmatically, its function was to provide a capture or *refixing point* for the human overflow that had been set precariously adrift by the chaotic, destabilized conditions of post–Roman Empire Europe; (2) at the level of the formation of collective subjectivity, one witnesses the first institutionalization of the Christian contempt for the body and its unruly affects and sensations, all of which are forced to submit to a rigid, even protomechanical aridity, regularity, and rule; and (3) at the level of behavioral morphologies or "motor patterns," one notes the incipient mathematization of the day and the body's temporal activities (meals and sleeping schedules in addition to the devotional activities), reinscribed by a complex system of spatial organization that includes the monastery walls, the distribution of cells, common rooms, meditation yards, and so on. These latter are, after all, the medium and vehicle through which the action of the bell and the intervals it scoops out of the continuum of duration are made to penetrate into, and reorganize, the bodies they seize.

The monastery, then, is nothing if not a prototype clock; yet the clock and the advent of homogeneous, mechanical-numerical time are rarely considered as more than incidental technical devices, and, even when they are recognized for the cataclysmic effect they have had on every aspect of Western culture they are certainly not commonly thought of as being the province of architects or architectural thought. Yet the clock appeared in culture, initially as a form of pure rationality and as a pure *function,* at once invisible and inseparable from the continuum of bodies, behaviors, building-apparatuses, and the social life that they carved up. If an independent clock mechanism was abstracted later from this empirical arrangement of elements (naturally monks figured prominently in the subsequent development and specialization of this new technology), it was only to affect the body/architecture continuum in an ever deeper and more generalized way. For example, the clock was soon transposed from the monastery to the town marketplace (from the domain of private faith to that of commerce, an invisible but active connection that Western capitalism has never sought to sever); and when the modern clockface was invented, it allowed time to be dissociated ever further from human events, at once spatially projected in vision and displayed in a marvelously rationalized notational form.

It is all the more curious, therefore, that architectural thought in the last two decades should have seized so willingly upon another "device"—Jeremy Bentham's *Panopticon* and the associated role of the mathematical *quadrillage* (sectoring or gridding)—despite the fact that it was never built and exists, as Foucault himself has clearly underscored, only as "a figure of political technology that may and must be detached from any specific use." This same tradition of design philosophy remains nonetheless unwilling to accept the general role played by architecture in the history of technique, and that which technique plays in the history of architecture. Yet the issue is more extreme than this: technique itself, I am arguing, must be seen as an inseparable link in the continuum joining architecture and all other aspects of design to the world around it (to bodies and human motor-fields in particular), for technique is the foundation of all overcoding, indeed, technique is the architecture of architectures.

The clock may be said to have made possible not only the historical renascences of the fifteenth and sixteenth centuries, but the whole of what we call the modern world—by introducing the use of quantitative methods for ordering and correlating the episodic fluxes of nature into the cultural equation. It is well known how these methods came to be generalized in painting, science, cartography, music and economics. Interest in mathematical proportion, anatomy, rational orders, and so on was also revived at this time in architectural and aesthetic discourse and practice. Yet historical thought, applied to material culture in general and to architectural culture in particular, has not fully confronted these developments as processes of *longue durée*, bound up with the evolutionary production of *new* domains: the universal optical theory of space; the evolution of battlefields, their science and design; the triadic nineteenth-century assemblage of the city, the factory, and the mines; the formation of the modern domestic household and the bureaucratic workplace. Indeed management—or rather *logistics*—may well represent the preeminent, and perhaps only real, modern architectural "object," albeit an object with a mutable and elusive shape.

Before turning to the twentieth century, we must pause for another moment to consider Bentham's Panopticon and Foucault's analysis of it. What we have presented before us is the plan, or at least the idea, of a building in which we are supposed to understand there to be expressed a total and abiding vision that a society produced for itself—a vision *that never came to be incarnated in the building in question* but that was inserted rather into the social body all the more effectively and surreptitiously at a level, or number of levels, at which architectural objects in the classical sense simply do not appear. For this very reason Foucault provides a self-motivating, capillary action theory of the social field, a microphysics of power corresponding to a micropolitical domain. It is a characteristic of Foucault's analysis to direct attention at each turn to an always different level of reality—away from the plane of (obvious and therefore misleading) *objects* and toward a more fundamental and complex plane of *relations*. The Panopticon, his argument clearly suggests, may already have been the last time that the constitutive relations of a society would be articulated at this particular, and traditionally architectural, level. The implication is not that the discrete and unitary building or building-complex had or ever could become dismissably trivial or obsolete; rather it is that the constituent body of relations that determine it is simply no longer to be found at this level. It is one of the central tasks of Foucault's study to develop—to flesh out, as it were—the new microphysical continuum where architectural and human multiplicities mingle as if two modes of a single substance.[6]

If it is possible to conceive of architectural practice and the field of architectural objects in intensive and extensive (or micro- and macrophysical) terms rather than uniquely at the level of formed objects, then what I am calling *practices* and *techniques* fall squarely into its domain. If the Panopticon—insofar as it represents a technique rather than a building—could figure as an emblem for an entire epoch and as an intensifying relay for that era's power-effects, what figures, it might be asked, serve analogous functions in the twentieth century? Clearly, one must resist the habit of thought that would propose the midcentury Gulags or concentration camps themselves. Indeed the real meaning of these sinister architectures can be found only in the macroscopic systems of which they are a part—the insidious, bureaucratic, molar, political formations whose microphysics is still surreptitiously evolving (or else is once again even in Europe overtly and barbarously being explored).

But where, for example, would one situate such a banal technical object as the loudspeaker, an apparently mundane appliance that played such an important role in both Hitler's and Mussolini's rise to power in the 1920s and 1930s (long before it successfully revolutionized musical aesthetics through the electroacoustic

6 The work's last three chapters (those that follow the one on Panopticism) are those to which the attention of architectural and design thought would most fruitfully be turned today. With the example of delinquency, for instance, one witnesses the direct and invisible incarnation of a complex motor-spatial ordering mechanism in the social sphere *without the mediation of objects*. Here again, the actualization of virtual forms is apprehensible only in a temporal continuum. See Michael Foucault, *Discipline and Punish, The Birth of the Prison* (New York: Pantheon, 1977).

1.5
Loudspeaker, 1930s

experiments of the 1950s and '60s). The loudspeaker's electrical amplification of the voice made possible the staging of vast, live aural spectacles, the amassing of unprecedented crowds of people, which gave literal and palpable expression to the concept of "mass culture" and "mass movement." The logistical achievement that underlay these spectacles was redoubtable, and the extension of military techniques of planning and control to the civilian multitudes was undoubtedly but a felicitous side-effect from the viewpoint of the ascendant fascist regimes. Leni Riefenstahl's documentary film of the 1934 Nazi Party rally at Nürnberg rhythmically intercuts from crowd to marching army and back, underscoring the progressive annihilation of the distinction between military regimentation and civilian life. What it must have felt like to have been among all those other bodies, grouped, organized, and maniacally disciplined into precise geometric configurations, resplendently arrayed between Albert Speers's liquid columns of light, riveted by the literally electric voice of the Führer, is a feeling that today we can only imagine—and tremble. But the loudspeaker brought with it other developments as well: the capacity to appeal to the masses bodily and in person (here an electric technology serves to *create* literal contact with the interlocutor, not to diffuse or destroy it); the capacity to appeal to those sectors of the electorate who do not or cannot read; and the capacity to appeal to baser and more common sentiments in a contagion-prone setting, a technique that invariably favors demagoguery and hysteria.

The loudspeaker is but a single element in a century of exhaustless innovation and complexity, yet it arguably had a greater effect on, and may reveal more about, the workings and aspirations of an entire social and political conjuncture than perhaps any visionary building of the era—Vladimir Tatlin's Monument to the Third International, Le Corbusier's La Ville Radieuse, or even Italy's Mussolini/Piacentini EUR-city notwithstanding.

The ultimate site of all political and social mechanisms, and the power-effects they engender, is today often said to be the collective or individual body. Yet as Foucault's study shows, the literal body has for a long time ceased to be the *immediate* site of these. If power seizes the body it does so with an increasingly sophisticated *indirectness*—an indirectness in which architectural and design practice is always implicated in the deepest possible way. As design practice and thought are deflected away from the traditional and largely "aesthetically" constituted *object* and simultaneously reoriented toward a dynamic macro- and microscopic field of interaction, an entirely new field of relations opens itself to the designer, theorist, or artist.

A nondogmatic approach to this "field" and to the politicization of design practice today would be to consider all architectures as technical objects and all technical objects as architectures. By technical objects, I mean simply this: that around each and every object there may be associated a corresponding *complex* of habits, methods, gestures, or practices that are not attributes of the object but nonetheless characterize its mode of existence—they relay and generalize these habits, methods, and practices to other levels in the system. Thus it is not in the object that analysis ought to be interested but in the complex, and if indeed it is to practices and to the life of the body that we wish to open architecture up today, then we must be vigilant and rigorous in keeping the two entities conceptually distinct.

Each of the three technical objects or architectures presented above (clock, panoptical system, loudspeaker) shares one important feature with the others: each is part of a more or less generalized Western technical apparatus of mastery—an apparatus whose power derives from its capacity to vanquish time by spatializing it. How paradoxical, one may think: the origin of the clock as the *demise*, rather than the invention, of time! But the clock, we must remember, did not produce time, it merely standardized it and permitted, or rather *forced*, it to be correlated. The clock reduces fraught, immanent time to a single transcendent time, it relates all events to a single, "thin" duration that is general—the same for everyone, for all processes, and so on—not specific or local. Clock time fixes in order to correlate, synchronize, and quantify, renouncing the mobile, fluid, qualitative continuum where time plays a decisive role in transformative morphogenetic processes. What is more, real time is not a unitary strand distributing homogeneous units of past, present, and future in a fixed empirical order, but is rather a complex, interactive, "thick" manifold of distinct yet integrated durations. Events belong to a class known as "emergent phenomena"—the product and expression of sudden communicative coherences or "prehensions" (Whitehead) of converging qualities inexplicably interweaving and unfolding *together,* even though they may originate at vastly different temporal and phenomenal scales.

The modern process of reduction and spatialization began in the Benedictine monasteries of the Middle Ages and was definitively and substantially reinforced in the fourteenth century with the invention of double-entry bookkeeping practices. Soon after, the invention of linear perspective and the rise of quantitative methods in science completed the epistemological hold of space over time. By the seventeenth century the modern system was in place, and from that time it would remain merely a question of increasingly fine tuning. Everything that needed to be mastered—after all, capitalism needed a comprehensive system of global correlation, where time could be transformed into standardized units of value, units of value into goods, and goods back into time—could be mastered by spatialization and quantification. Time, forced now to express the false unity and rationality of all being, ceased to be real.

By their very nature, temporal phenomena cause disturbances and irregularities—what scientific experimentalists call "noise" in regular, linear, quantitative systems. They pollute data with continual fluctuations and instabilities. They are untrackable by conventional linear equations because mathematicians have not discovered how to give equations autonomous flow or "life"—the capacity to absorb or be sensitive to unforeseen changes in material conditions. Indeed, classical linear equations are often compared to clockworks—they are set in advance and continue to run out their program according to conditions that held only ideally at the moment the initial programming took place. They cannot, and do not, receive additional input regarding changing conditions—they cannot even be reliably updated by input they themselves generate or gather up.

What is needed—but which is by definition impossible—are time-sensitive equations. These would be less like clockworks and more like engines that carry their own independent, mobile reservoirs or motive sources with them, along with second-order servo-devices (governor, gas pedal, or steering assembly) to manage the shifting information fluxes of communication and control. Whereas a clockwork or a linear equation can transmit only a prior or initial motion along a predetermined path (from the possible to the real), a non-linear equation or servo-device is able to produce novel motion and pattern-breaking and to update itself from within its trajectory—it remains, in fact, perpetually sensitive to its surrounding milieu.

Scientists first became aware of this problem in the nineteenth century, particularly through the science of thermodynamics, when it became necessary to track the flows of heat through a continuum of matter. As changes of state and *qualitative* transformations began to impose themselves as significant problems for scientific investigation, matter increasingly came to be seen as active, and space as plastic, flexible, sensitive, and organic. James Clerk-Maxwell used partial differential equations as a means to begin to plot these movements. Einstein borrowed these same techniques in 1905 when developing the field concept in relativity theory.[7] But these were still reductionist methods that just happened to suffice to solve the specific problems at hand. *Real* time (and movement) remained a problem, for nobody knew how to construct an organic equation that could flow along with the phenomena and chart all of their moment-to-moment transformations. Indeed, there were actually two problems. A human tallyer with paper and pencil could certainly attempt the task (at least experimentally), but he could certainly never reckon quickly enough; nor could he ever account for the avalanche of interactive complexity (nonlinearity) that would be introduced in the first billionth of a second.

From the moment a system is understood as evolving over time, what becomes important are the transformations it undergoes, and all transformation in a system is the result of energy—or information—moving through it. As energy courses through a system it induces three general types of transformation: (1) It imports information from outside the system. (In addition to changes provoked internally within the system, this also transforms the external milieu in such a way as to affect the type of information it will, in subsequent stages, channel into the system.) (2) It exports energy from within a system to its ambient milieu, producing this same double effect now in asymmetrical reverse. (3) *It transports information from certain levels in the system to other heterogeneous levels*—producing morphological events that are often dramatically unpredictable with respect to location, causal sequence, and magnitude of effect.

---

7 Einstein himself liked to describe space-time as a "mollusc."

1.6
Steam Engine at Crystal Palace

Any model that would attempt to account for the behavior or patterns in such systems must continually account for the millions of interdependent transformations occurring within the system at a given moment. The equations must perpetually feed information back into themselves, information that can be made available only *in time,* not in advance, and *across* temporal scales, never within a single temporal plane. That classical mathematics, and its corresponding tradition of Western technics, should need now to become time sensitive is an ironic reversal of its deeply spatialist history. But let us return to these dynamical or complex systems. I have said that what characterized them is that they cannot be understood by their spatial relations of configuration alone, but only through the events and qualities—transitions of phase or state—produced as a result of the flows of energy and the informational gradients that move through them. Values are perpetually redistributed throughout such systems, but the specific behavior of this "cybernetic" redistribution is neither determinable in advance nor entirely random and continuous. There exist parameters, limits, border or catastrophe states, and these always gather in basins around singularities.

If time is real, then the world itself represents a complex, infinitely entailed, dynamical system or fluid manifold. As a manifold or flow phenomenon the world comprises not pregiven, ideal Forms but metastable shapes floating in a river of ever-generating differences. But there are differences of two kinds: There are random, or uncombined (incoherent) differences, which emerge and pass without leaving a trace; and there are those that are "singular" and give rise

1.7
Preston, England; Cotton manufactory.

to potential or real morphogeneses within and across a system. A simple example is when the molecular phase transition of boiling water (conversion into
gas) is combined with a mechanical piston-and-pressure-chamber matrix to
form a steam engine. The steam engine, rising let us say, upward through the
world-system to the next level, combines with an economic flow reaching its
own critical point (conversion to organized industrial capitalism) and is then
combined with the cotton gin to produce a more complex entity: mechanized
labor. This third-level machine-complex now combines with others of identical type to produce a mobile, non-site-specific (because no longer dependent on
naturally occurring streams, wind patterns, or ground-level real estate) production system—an early industrial (manu)factory—and this combines with the
nineteenth-century social organization of the English town, giving rise to the
first industrial urban centers, which in turn draw huge population flows from
the countryside, as well as flows of capital and primary materials from remote investor, market, and supplier countries and regions. Each perturbation
generates instabilities in the system one level up, which, once resolved, transmit the instability in turn to the next higher level. (In truth these cybernetic systems are computationally very powerful and do not require such step-by-step

procedures.) This "processing" continues until the system has either damped out the original perturbation entirely, or else has "used," "exfoliated," or "geometricized" it in order to transform its global dynamics in toto. Thus a singularity describes specifically that type of difference, in a world of perpetually engendered differences, that is produced at some point along a particular flow and that may be *combined* with another flow to induce a difference at another scale or level in the manifold.

To understand the precise mechanics of how a form may be "time- and difference-generated"—or *actualized* in the jargon of the present argument—consider the example of the domestic ice cube versus the free-form snow crystal. Is time *real* for the ice cube in the same way as for the snow crystal? How do their respective forms arise? In the former case a cubic slot is prepared and preformed in plastic or metal and filled with water. It is placed in an environment where cold is able to penetrate it from the outside, first fixing its boundaries in conformity with its geometric receptacle, later simply filling out its interior. Every ice cube resembles every other just as it resembles it own mother mold. There is no real time to be found in this system, as almost nothing is permitted to flow (save for heat, though along a rigidly controlled gradient); everything is locked into a static spatial system that reproduces a pregiven form. All the aleatory conditions, all of chance, hazard, all virtuality and sensitivity to other disturbances and changes in the environment—all wildness and openness—are scrupulously (i.e., by design) eliminated.

The snow crystal is different. Its genesis is dynamic and can be situated initially at the convergence of three distinct fluxes: mica and mineral particles; a moisture-saturated field; and a thermal flow of heat exchange. One does not know in advance where or when such a crystal will begin to nucleate or form, but one knows it will emerge—apparently spontaneously—from a flux or convergence of flows, not in a prepared form or space. The form of the crystal, however, is not fixed from the beginning—it is merely an incarnated singularity, a speck of dust-ice, that has been carried to a new level where it interacts with higher-order flows—gravity, wind, barometric pressure, humidity, other silicate dust, water, crystals, and thermal and even acoustic flows, plus electrical and magnetic gradients. All of these conditions vary continually in relation to themselves and affect the snowflake's trajectory. The crystal does carry some fixed information along with it—its preestablished molecular structure, developed within a rigid tetrahedral lattice of hydrogen and oxygen atoms, determines the even formation of hexagonal plates with six "inflections" or surface asperities. This apparently "regular" architecture produces a dynamically *ir*regular space, causing certain regions on the

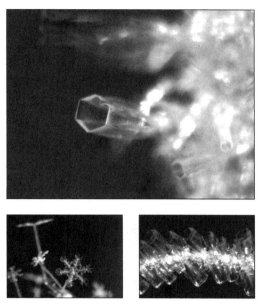

1.8

*Free crystal growth is a product of both complex nonlinear dynamics and specific constraints: geometric instabilities of water, air, temperature, and saturation gradients. Each design perfectly expresses not only the state of one of the universe's neighborhoods during a specific interval in time but also the snow crystal's own particular historical trajectory within it. Because the snow crystal is literally the product of "time," in it **growth** and design are one.*

hexagonal matrix to catch more than their share of the external weather conditions.[8] The resulting build-up takes place disproportionately on these humps, so that the snow crystal will always have six sides.

Of course this inflexible part of its "program" may be said to transcend time; yet this aspect is hardly what is compelling about snow crystal morphology. What is interesting is that despite its partially fixed matrix no two results are ever alike. Each is different because the crystal *maintains its sensitivity* both to time and to its

8 These inhomogeneities are activated only by the particle's *movement* in time; the crystal inaugurates its *becoming* through a "symmetry-breaking" operation, or the introduction of an initial informatum of difference that frees the crystal from the monotonous regularity of the tetrahedral lattice and triggers a cascade of self-structuring pressures through the system. Processes of this type, and indeed the concept of "weather" in particular, were introduced into aesthetics by Marcel Duchamp and later systematically elaborated by John Cage.

complex milieu. Its morphogenetic principle is active and always incomplete (i.e., evolving)—the snowflake interacts with other processes, across both space and time; it belongs to a dynamical, fluvial world. As the snow crystal falls it absorbs, captures, or *incarnates* all the chance events, all the fluctuating conditions (magnetic, gravitational, barometric, electrical, thermal, humidity, speed) and builds them, or rather *uses them,* to assemble itself, to form its structure or edifice. The snow crystal creates itself in the middle of, and by means of the convergences of, flux. Thus snow crystal morphogenesis is less the result of specific, punctual external causes than a sympathetic but critical insertion within, and the subsequent "cybernetic" management of, already present flows. This analytical model—based on developmental pathways, dynamical interactions, singular points, and qualitative movements in abstract, sometimes multidimensional space—arguably furnishes a far richer theory of "site" than most currently employed in orthodox aesthetic or architectural practice.

It would not be inappropriate to liken this approach to the artful shaping of a surfer's trajectory on the sea. Unlike more traditional (hunter-warrior model) sports, surfers do not conceive of themselves as exclusive or "prime motors" at the origin of their movements; they rather track, from within the flows, a variety of emerging features, singularities, and unfoldings with which they can meld. This style of "soft" intervention—primarily perturbation or inflection—is certainly emerging today with increasing frequency in a variety of domains—art, politics, mathematics[9]—though sports may well offer the most startling and salient examples. Since the early days of surfing (whose origins go back to the 1950s), one notes the appearance of other airstream sports such as skysurfing (carving freefall aerial trajectories between airplane and earth with a resistance board strapped to one's feet), deltaplaning, hang- and paragliding (motorless, "low-," or archaic "tech" sports), in which the principle is to slip oneself into moving columns of air,[10] to create formal and temporal intensities by gliding, weaving, and hanging—tracking and combining flows by apprehending and appropriating hydro- and aerodynamic singularities.

In more immediately adjacent domains there has also been an interesting proliferation—and fusion—of "cousin" board sports that deploy the same fluid

9 Interventionist art, earthworks, hacking, terrorism, sampling, vogueing, "experimental" mathematics, computational biology, etc.

10 On the shift from the motor model in contemporary sports and society, see Gilles Deleuze, "Mediators," in *ZONE 6 Incorporations,* ed. Jonathan Crary and Sanford Kwinter (New York: Zone Books, 1992).

"streaming" techniques combined with a rigorous ad hoc engagement of the surrounding milieu—namely, skate- and snow-boarding. As in surfing, the primary qualities valorized in these sports are fluidity of movement, intuition (a quiet body harmoniously in step with its milieu—"in unity with the wave"), and innovation ("rewriting the rulebook," "exploring uncharted territory"),[11] though because these unfold in a solid landscape, the environing terrain too must now be made to pulse, flow, and break. This involves the selection and identification of "hits" (incidental barriers, obstacles or breaks) and "lines" (trajectories of particular velocity or shape) in the urban continuum or landscape—a staircase, half-pipe, railing, pool, or any incline or gap for a skater; and note the total promiscuity of the (early '90s) snowboarder who indifferently "skis" or "worries" trees, rockfaces, fences, logs, buildings, and service equipment, transforming any found space into a smoothly quilted interlock of disparately textured, twisting, quality-emitting, sequenced surfaces. The extension of the streaming ethos to landscapes and motorfields of *solids* may easily be identified as the primary engine of transformation of both technique and style in all sports of the last thirty years (track and field, basketball, tennis, martial arts, cyclo/motocross, dance).

These developments are perhaps most acutely exemplified in one particular sport that has also recently taken on a contemporary—some would say, postmodern—dimension: rock-climbing. Today, according to a new concept of purity and rigor, certain rockclimbers will attack a mountain with *no tools whatever.* The morphogenetic principle of the climbers' space is no longer susceptible to forms imposed from outside (the "assisted" ascent). The free-soloists must flow up the mountain, flow or "tack" against the downward gradient of gravity—but also must become hypersensitive tamers and channelers of the gravitational sink, masters at storing it in their muscles or making it flow through certain parts of the pelvis, thighs, palms, and this only at certain times; they must know how to accelerate the flow into a quick transfer that could mean the difference between triumph and disaster, to mix and remix dynamic and static elements in endless variation—for it is not enough to prevail over gravity but rather be able to make

11 "Shane Dorion turns the ultra-vertical lip-pierce into the cool and casual float. Not only is the modern-day surfer fusing sports—surfing, skating, snowboarding—but also manoeuvres. Cutback rebounds become 360s, reentries become reverses, and as we see here, lip smackers become floaters." Jamie Brisick, "Young Guns on the North Shore," in *Warp,* v. 1, no. 2, spring 1993. For a surprisingly sustained debate on the ascending role of novelty vs. the descending one of power in the surfing world, see also Matt Warshaw, "Power Outage," in *Surfer, The State of the Art: A Special Issue,* v. 34, no. 7, July 1993.

1.9
Photo: Simon Carter, Onsight Photography

it stream continuously through one, and especially to be able to generalize this knowledge to every part of the body without allowing it to regroup at any time—transcendent and unitary—as a spatialized figure in the head. Thus the body too must be broken apart into a veritable multiplicity of quasi-autonomous flows—conditions on the mountainface vary critically from centimeter to centimeter—no climber could afford a strategic command *center* that programmed the body to behave globally in response to fixed or, god forbid, *average* conditions. Every square centimeter represents its own interdependent dynamical system continually cross-referencing with the others, but *locally* in relation to its own "micro-site-specificity."

Yet it is the mountainface itself whose flow is the most complex, the most intractable and problematic of all. The mineral shelf represents a flow whose timescale is nearly unfathomable from the scale of duration represented by the electrolytic and metabolic processes of muscle and nerves—but even at this timescale—nanometric in relation to the millennia that measure geological flows—singularities abound:[12] a three-millimeter-wide fissure just wide enough to allow the placement of one segment of one finger, and anchored by sufficiently solid earth to permit but eighty pounds of pressure for, say, three seconds but no longer; an infinitesimally graded basin of sedimentary rock whose erratically ribbed surface (weathered unevenly by flows of wind and rain) offers enough friction to a spread palm to allow strategic placement of the other palm on an igneous ledge a half meter above. This very rock face, until recently considered virtually slick and featureless—an uninflected glacis even to classical pick and piton climbers[13]—now swarms with individualized points, inhomogeneities, trajectories, complex relations. The site is brimming over with interweaving forces and flows—though without these the face's asperities and differences would fall back into a true near-featurelessness—and the climber's task is less to "master" in the macho, form-imposing sense than to forge a morphogenetic figure *in time,* to insert himself into a seamless, streaming space and to subsist in it by tapping or tracking the flows—indeed to stream and to become soft and fluid himself, which means momentarily to recover real time, and to engage the universe's wild and free unfolding through the morphogenetic capacities of the singularity.

12 The art of Robert Smithson of the late 1960s and early '70s developed this type of singularity beyond that of nearly any plastic artist of modern times. In literature, and in the more classical arenas of painting and sculpture, this program as we will see can already be discovered in the work of Franz Kafka and in the Italian Futurists respectively.

13 Cf. "Les Procédés artificiels d'escalade," in Gaston Rébuffat, *Neige et Roc* (Paris: Hachette: 1959), pp. 72 infra. Even a cursory pass through any of the great manuals of classical mountainclimbing is sufficient to note that this "ethic" that I have called recent and new has always been an integral part of the Alpinist's tradition, and that what is taking place today is a shift in emphasis. Witness the legendary Rébuffat: "There is an intimate pleasure in communicating with the mountain, not with its grandeur or beauty, but more simply and directly, with its sheer materiality, like an artist or artisan with the wood, stone or iron that he works." Rébuffat goes on to evoke the "rediscoverable kinship" between granite, ice, and flesh (p. 14).

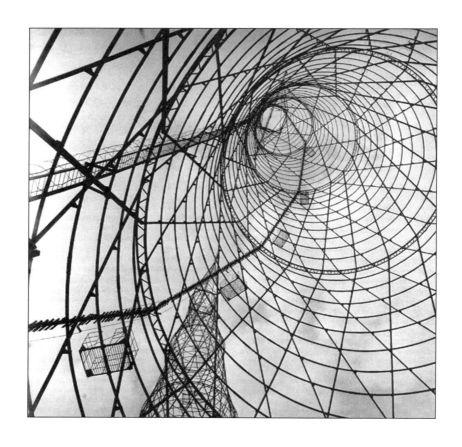

2.1
Vladimir G. Suchov, *Electrical Towers,* c. 1922

Modernist Space and the Fragment

*What is real is the continual **change** of form:*
form is only a snapshot view of a transition.
— HENRI BERGSON

Modernism and Modernity

THE PHRASE "MODERNIST SPACE" is used here to serve as a more modest decoy for what is the truly intended subject of the following chapters: the problem of "modernity" itself. Unlike many standard treatments of the subject today, the present one seeks to cast the problem of modernity as a philosophical problem and not primarily one of historical periodization.[1] According to this approach, "modernity" would need to be distinguished from any of the various historical modernisms whose empirical aspects—whether the result of social or aesthetic avant-gardes or else technical or scientific revolutions—are at best complex, contradictory, and indeterminate. What they have in common cannot be discovered on this empirical level but only at the more abstract plane of relations that underlie them and that form what might be called their "conditions of possibility."

It is to this level that the following analyses are directed. For embedded within most modernisms there may be discerned something deeper and more nuanced than the mere, apparent "break with the past." What is more, it is at these moments that the very notion of "past" and of historical time generally nearly always undergo a subtle, sometimes imperceptible, but nonetheless fundamental transformation. It may even be said that it is only in the fleeting but marvelous density that characterizes the actual instant of such "breaks" that modernism and "modernity" may be said ever to coincide. For the philosophical, or ontological, problem of modernity, as I will try to develop it, can perhaps be shown to reside in some specifiable condition that actually renders possible such breaks, transformations, or changes. If these historical breaks involve more than just a break with a past (a previous epoch, regime, or paradigm) it is because they often imply, somewhere within their intricacy, a more irregular and untimely break with a far

---

1 The spectrum of approaches here is rich and wide, running from Oswald Spengler to Daniel Bell, Paul de Man, Ernest Mandel, Matei Calinescu, Jean-François Lyotard, Frederic Jameson, Ihab Hassan, etc. An extensive bibliography may be found in Matei Calinescu, *Five Faces of Modernity: Avant-garde, Decadence, Kitsch* (Durham: Duke University Press, 1987).

more expansive tradition, metaphysic, or worldview. In short, the concept of modernity that will be developed here would need to be understood as a reverse stream that is present *virtually* (but relatively rarely actualized) throughout history, emerging here or there as a kind of counterhistory or counterpractice. Modernity, then, clearly must be more than a mere, benign synonym for "new" or "contemporary," for the problems it raises conceivably can be addressed to any work in any historical period. What's more, its function as countermemory connects it with those elements in a given culture that necessarily go beyond a dialectical relation with a previous historical period, or with an allegedly hegemonic ideology. It is precisely for this reason that the modernisms, at once deeply entrenched in the social and existential crises of the nineteenth century as well as the more sanguine, emancipatory humanisms of the post-Renaissance period, might comprise less the object than the site of a more fundamental yet always emergent modernity.

A distinction must therefore be made between the "critical" task of many *modernizing* or avant-garde movements and the more fundamental project of modernity, whether avowed or not, of a "transvaluation of all values." The first project addresses at best the specific institutions and systems of representation in which history and power have become incarnate; the second addresses their very conditions of possibility. Insisting on the distinction between them makes it possible to see beyond the exaggerated "critical" project of the modernisms toward a preliminary descriptive ontology of modernity itself.

Modernity and Time

Such a conception of modernity is admittedly problematic, especially as I have said, in its relation to time—its roots, dispersed throughout history may be linked to thinkers such as Lucretius, Bruno, Spinoza, Vico, Nietzsche, and others—but it is precisely in its relation to *time* that its complexity can and ought to be apprehended. Though undeniably heterogeneous in many ways, these thinkers can be said to share a common task: the attempt to think Being free of any transcendent unity and without reference to anything outside itself as its cause or ground. In other words, it is, in its first instance, a *structural* repudiation of the concept of transcendence, ultimately determined in each case by the specific historical conditions in which it arises, that characterizes the notion of modernity that will be developed here, though always and necessarily in relation to the counterflow of *tradition* whose time and space belong to late Greek and early Christian cosmology.[2] These latter, strictly derived forms of time—eschatological, primordial, "historical"[3]—will be seen to give way to increasingly sophisticated theories of immanence in which time no longer remains spatialized in order to furnish the stable ground or backdrop for phenomena, but meshes inextricably with them, and forms the new rule of their endless and aleatory proliferation. Thus space too will be shown to undergo an exactly analogous emancipation from its metaphysically determined relations (body/nonbody, inside/outside, center/periphery, whole/part) as it weds with time to become intensive, dynamic, or continuous.

In short, by the end of the nineteenth and the beginning of the twentieth centuries, the world was no longer constructed in quite the same way as it had been and its elements would no longer combine as they once did. Thought was now forced to move beyond its abode in the philosophy of transcendence—for too many of the sacred emblems of this tradition such as God, Nature, and Truth had by now been sacrificed to the "modernizing" processes of the nineteenth century[4]—and there arose, amid the vertigo and malaise, a fundamental ontological change that would have important effects on the nature of knowledge, perception, and representation. Nothing was any longer considered absolute and every element was capable of reorganization, redistribution, and revaluation. Space and time no longer carried with them their fixed categories of intelligibility, nor did they distribute their contents in quite the same ordered way. What is more—and this was the most unthinkable thing of all—they would no longer remain separate from one another, but had merged to create a new field, one that would characterize the rest of our century, yet for which a properly solid map never emerged and will certainly never exist.

Fragmentation vs. Multiplicity

If it is true that early Greek cosmological thought centers around the problem of the One and the Many, then our own modern era, with its fixation on the social and epistemological complexities that bear on the relations between totality and

2 The present definition makes no attempt to situate or understand "modernity" beyond the most rigorously local Western context to which it is, by definition, indigenous.

3 By "history" I understand the magical substratum through which events allegedly communicate with one another and in relation to which they are said to occur.

4 Industrialization, rationalization, urbanization.

fragmentation constitutes what could be called a kind of "neo-Hellenism."[5] For the Greeks, it was the task of accounting for the phenomenon of change that became the central problem, to explain or reconcile the "corruptive," transformative effects of time in relation to the doctrine of essential and immutable forms. Time ultimately had to be abolished from the ontological schema as an effect of mere illusion (Zeno, Parmenides, Plato) in favor of a theory of participation of Ideal Forms in their imperfect, worldly reflections (copies). Things—the Many—were, if chaotic, at least reassuringly "participated" by the One—the latter conceived as a static, timeless plenitude. But the banishing of time, and the elision of the problem of change, meant that Greek thought would no longer try to think the Many, or the Multiple, in and for itself, that is, free of a reassuring totality that existed *in another domain.*

It is a cliché that bears repeating at this time, that our own modernity is inseparable from the self-conscious project of "thinking outside of metaphysics." What this entails, of course, is an attempt to think phenomena—the Multiple, or the profusion of events and things—independent of an external, totalizing, foundational schema. But it is just at this moment, as the stabilizing *grid* of transcendence dissolves and is drawn away, that Forms themselves vanish and remerge into the chaotic flux of unstable aggregates and events.

Much of our (modernist) culture clung exuberantly to this new world, but often only as a radical, new form of totality that was comprised no longer of oppressive, passé, or falsely consoling forms but of *fragments.* This gesture came to represent nothing less than an apparent rebirth of matter and meaning, for suddenly anything seemed again possible, the old laws no longer applied, the new

---

5 The immense power of Nietzsche's modernizing gesture in the history of thought is explicit in the radicality of its genealogical method: to descend *against the grain* of history and Western thought to those moments when transcendence (dialectics, morality) was first introduced into man's being by way of Socratism and Christianity. Nietzsche, like many after him, allies himself with the pre-Socratics, Homer, and the tragedians. See especially *Philosophy in the Tragic Age of the Greeks, The Birth of Tragedy Out of the Spirit of Music,* and the *Genealogy of Morals,* bk. 3, no. 25. The anti-Platonist theme is central to the theory of modernity being developed here. This tradition of Nietzschean modernity seems to reproduce this gesture of descent and return as if by programmatic necessity. See Michel Foucault's espousal of the sophists and Gilles Deleuze's strategic use of both stoicism and sophism, in Michel Foucault, *L'Ordre du discours* (Paris: Gallimard, 1971) and "Theatrum Philosophicum," in *Language, Counter-Memory, Practice,* ed. D. F. Bouchard (Ithaca: Cornell University Press, 1977); Gilles Deleuze, *The Logic of Sense* and appendix, "The Simulacrum and Ancient Philosophy" (New York: Columbia University Press, 1990).

ones were yet to be invented; all was polyvalency, possiblility, and promiscuity. But this exuberance of experimentation was seldom separable from an almost universal anxiety of loss, of disenfranchisement and disorientation. Fragments after all were shards, ruins—at best, brave traces of a past or future plenitude. Fragmentation and its attendant spectacle of polyvocality was perhaps an incomplete consolation for a world that would never again serve as a home.[6] Yet are we not still far from the Greek world of happy immanence where delight in phenomena and appearance was everything? Can our own "condition," typified and expressed through the modern emblem of the "fragment," ever be conceived free of the nihilism embedded both in myth and memory, a nihilism by whose agency we define ourselves (and our world) *always in relation to what we are not* (and never were)—that is, *unitary and constant beings*? Fragments, for the moderns—though still for us today—are too often "thought" in terms of a world and a Wholeness to which they no longer have any relation. Is it not possible, however, to restore to the fragment that which is properly its due, to develop it in the element of its positivity, as a specific characterization of matter within a continuous, fluctuating, and time-imbued multiplicity?

It is precisely this project, this tendency, that I have sought to characterize, on the one hand, as constituting the work of "modernity" itself, and on the other, that I have sought, descriptively as it were, to embody in the present study. The best way to embark on such a descriptive project, it seems to me, is conceptually to isolate, even partially or provisionally, certain moments and elements or even aspects of moments and elements within historical modernist culture where this "modernity," understood as a specific approach to the fragment and multiplicity, appears to emerge.

Time, Space, and Force

The apparently heterogeneous field of "modernist culture" seems susceptible of any number of different types of division. It would be possible, for example, to perform a triage by which different movements, or rather, *tendencies within different movements,* could be seen as oriented toward, or dominated by, one of three basic axes: that of classical time, that of space, and that of movement and complexity, or force. The "time" axis, for example, would concern principally those aspects of modernist culture in which the subject is endowed with a fully transcendental radicality: mean-

6 Georg Lukács, *The Theory of the Novel,* trans. A. Bostock (Cambridge: MIT Press, 1971; orig. 1920).

ing, origins, and tradition serve as the primary elements within such a configuration, providing a ground for interpretation and exegesis, which then become the principal heuristic activities. To this category belongs much of both psychoanalysis and phenomenology, as well as the type of historicist/symbolistic modernist practice associated with the works of Joyce, Eliot, Pound, surrealism, and so on. To say that this modernism is one of *radical transcendentalism* is to describe the mode by which the subject is newly invested to form the ground, the domain, and the condition of possibility of knowledge. For time here is always a subjective time; tradition ("history") is *tradition-for-the-subject* (for this reason it may seem collapsed, spatialized, though in fact it is only reinvented at another scale). The historical significance of this development consists in having reorganized experience and reality into homogeneous and coextensive domains—reality is drawn within the subject to become but one more element of a fluid consciousness, everything is dissolved within the single element of receptive interiority.[7]

If the classical temporal axis, then, is dominated by relations bearing on the subject, the second, spatial axis indeed is oriented almost fully toward developing relations in the object. Here it is possible to group most of the modernist formalisms, as well as the tendencies, present in many forms and through a diverse range of phenomena, toward mathematical logic, and to ideality. The concept of tradition is here no longer the dominant epistemological category but is replaced by what might be called a rationalist-genetic model. Neo- (Carnap) and logical- (Ayer, Wittgenstein, Russell) positivism, structuralism, formalism (Russian and Czech), but also Cubism, the modern movement, aspects of De Stijl, constructivism, and all aspects of simultanism in poetry and elsewhere belong in whole or in part to this tendency that excludes both time and the subject from the field of the work in order to maintain, on the one hand, a certain transcendence of the object, and on the other, a certain positivistic transparency of knowledge and perception. The significant historical transformation effected here is once again the following: though this perspective dismisses the subject and its accompanying temporality and

---

7 Indeed it is arguable that Brentano's theory of cognition and Husserl's "intentionality" were in part formulated in order to de-interiorize consciousness, to discover it out there in the world of things; but the noetic framework with which they sought to reconcile subject- and object-domains is still the most perfect example of the "single element" or time-based continuum that I have here called, perhaps infelicitously, "interiority." Franz Brentano, *Sensory and Noetic Consciousness,* trans. M. Schattle and L. McAlister (London: Routledge, 1981); Edmund Husserl, *Cartesian Meditations,* trans. Dorion Cairns (The Hague: Martinus Nijhoff, 1973).

complexity, it does maintain the univocal nature of phenomena; it replaces the subject-as-ground with apodictic forms—formal logic, "rational" genetic systems—whose basis nonetheless remains transcendent-ideal.

The third axis, that of movement or force, actually breaks with the preceding classical aesthetic schema; it implodes the opposition of terms such as subject/object and space/time. Its epistemological principle is neither that of tradition nor that of a rationalist/genetic ideality but one of a radical perspectivism. This perspectivism is *not* subject-based, but is rooted in a dynamic cosmology based on multiplicity, chance, and hazard (the unforeseeable and unexpected) and a universal *immanent* individuating principle that governs these. In the words of Nietzsche—perhaps the dominant figure of this axis—"Only that which has no history can be defined." In other words, once an object or sign is embedded within the streaming, chaotic world of force, its so-called meaning must give way to a pure affectivity: the capacity to bear, transmit, or block and turn inward, a unit of Will to Power. In this domain there exist only dynamic metastabilities or meaning-events (accidents, convergences, subjugations); matter, form, and subjects ("doers") come only later, reintroduced at a second order level, not as ground but as produced *effect*.

From Nietzsche onward, what works of this nature have in common, far more than just a critique of transcendence, is the elaboration of a concrete new field endowed with an "immanent transcendental"—that is, "things," phenomena, though sundered from the metaphysical structure that grounds them in "meaning," now find their principle of being nowhere else but within themselves. Both the temporalist and spatialist axes strived for something similar to this, but because they were caught within a classical, oppositional, and especially *exclusive* framework, they could achieve this only incompletely. Space and time structures, essentially hierarchical, here give way to the flatness of a pragmatic or "evental" multiplicity (abstract becoming) where everything occurs on and among surfaces (surfaces swathe objects in relations, seize them, individuate them, orient them, but neither define them nor immobilize them indefinitely) according to the law of "exteriority" (according to which every "thing" marks the clandestine site of a willful "doing").[8] The heuristic model is neither exegetic nor deductive here, but genealogical/cartographic.[9]

8 The concept of multiplicity is developed in chapter 3, that of exteriority and surface in chapters 4 and 5, and of the "event" and "becoming" throughout.

9 Precisely, in Foucault's sense, "archaeological." See especially chapter 4, note 48.

Here then is the real meaning of perspectivism: the vertigo of the radically multiple (not subjective) *inside* viewpoint. One maps the very reality with which one is inseparably intertwined, because no external viewpoint or image is possible. In this as well lies the difference between genealogy and history: the latter describes the river, its life and its form; the former swims through it upstream mapping its currents. The one is linear, the other turbulent.[10]

Space and Time Are Not Categories

Still, so much of the theory of modernity remains deeply bound up in eighteenth-century (classical German) aesthetics. Consider the following passage from an early seminal study of modernist representation:

> In both artistic mediums [plastic arts, literature] one naturally spatial and the other naturally temporal, the evolution of aesthetic form in the twentieth century has been absolutely identical. For if the plastic arts from the Renaissance onward attempted to compete with literature by perfecting the means of narrative representation, then contemporary literature is now striving to rival the spatial apprehension of the plastic arts in a moment of time. Both contemporary art and literature have, each in its own way, attempted to overcome the time elements involved in their structures.[11]

Here the rendering fundamental of the categories of space and time (Kant), or more explicitly the opposition of space *versus* time (Lessing), determines the entire analysis. These presuppositions are at the root of nearly all theories of modernism, which almost invariably assert some new, powerful primacy of space.[12] Interestingly, without deviating an iota from these same received notions

10 The revival of interest in turbulence both in science and philosophy has played, as should now be clear, a determining role in the formulation of the problems addressed in the present study.

11 Joseph Frank, *The Widening Gyre: Crisis and Mastery in Modern Literature* (Bloomington: Indiana University Press, 1963), p. 57.

12 See, e.g., Roger Shattuck, *The Banquet Years: The Origins of the Avant Garde in France 1885 to World War I* (New York: Vintage, 1968); Sharon Spencer, *Space, Time, and Structure in the Modern Novel 1880 to 1917* (Chicago: Swallow Press, 1971); Joseph Kestner, *The Spatiality of the Novel* (Detroit, Mich.: Wayne State University Press, 1978); Umberto Eco,

the following writer posits—apparently innocently—the diametrically opposed thesis:

> The waning of affect however, might also have been characterized, in the narrower context of literary criticism, as the waning of the great high-modernist thematics of time and temporality, the elegiac mysteries of *durée* and of memory. . . . We have often been told however, that we now inhabit the synchronic rather than the diachronic, and I think it is at least empirically arguable that our daily life, our psychic experience, our cultural languages, are today dominated by categories of space rather than by categories of time, as in the preceding period of high modernism proper.[13]

This latter reflection notwithstanding, it may be said that no idea so dominated postwar thought on the modernist period as that of simultanism and juxtaposition. Regardless of whether such emphasis on an antitemporal spatiality[14] was applied to works of modernist or so-called postmodernist persuasion, one thing remained entirely consistent: the felicitous (even if illusory) harmony, unity, and fullness of phenomena was understood to have been sundered by the rapidly reconfiguring technological milieu of the modern world. From now on there would be only incompletion, discontinuity, *fragments*. Roger Shattuck's *The Banquet Years* (1955) was, and remains today, the quintessential formulation

---

L'Opera aperta (Milan: Bompiani, 1962); Steven Kern, *The Culture of Time and Space* (Cambridge, Mass.: Harvard University Press, 1983); Colin Rowe and Robert Slutzky, "Transparency: Literal and Phenomenal," in *The Mathematics of the Ideal Villa and Other Essays* (Cambridge, Mass.: MIT Press, 1982); Paul Virilio and Sylvère Lotringer, *Pure War* (New York: Foreign Agents, 1983); and Gregory Ulmer, "The Object of Post-Criticism," in *The Anti-Aesthetic,* ed. Hal Foster (Port Townsend, Wash.: Bay Press, 1983) .

13 Fredric Jameson, "Postmodernism, or The Cultural Logic of Late Capitalism," *New Left Review,* no. 146 (July–August 1984).

14 This theme would finally receive an almost paranoid refinement in Michael Fried's "Art and Objecthood," in *Minimal Art: A Critical Anthology* (New York: Dutton, 1968) and *Absorption and Theatricality: Painting and Beholder in the Age of Diderot* (Berkeley: University of California Press, 1980). A less strident development of these same themes may be found in Stanley Cavell, *The World Viewed: Reflections on the Ontology of Film* (New York: Viking, 1971) and *Must We Mean What We Say?* (New York: Cambridge University Press, 1976, orig. 1969).

of this thesis. For Shattuck the arts of the twentieth century are dominated by a type of asymmetrical assemblage of elements from which it is specifically the connective *transitions* that are missing. Formerly the arts were structured principally around expressed transition or "the clear articulation of relations between parts at the places they join." Things, events, apparently once flowed symmetrically in logical sequence and according to a univocal trajectory, while today all is said to be abruptness, interference, indeterminacy, and above all, stillness.[15] Gone with the unity and seamlessness of the arts of yesterday, however, is the monumental and closed work limited by a clear beginning, middle, and end. The modern work is proclaimed to be open.[16] With such openness comes ambiguity, polysemy, and a new boundlessness that seems capable of including anything, that is, *reflecting* anything, even the chaotic, hazardous processes of creation—yet not, notably and by design, actually *incorporating* time itself. Juxtaposition is said to be the law of such works; it replaces succession with a new type of unstable, hypersaturated moment—at once a profuse surplus of data that must instantaneously be absorbed into the field of the work and an inverse dearth of narrative "time" through or across which to effect a deferment. The result is conflict and disorder, which in turn lead to a dramatic multiplication of (ostensibly creative) random or chance effects. Yet for Shattuck all this disordering, radicality, conflict, and destabilizing supersaturation is nonetheless still reducible to a new unity, a new "intimacy" of the organic world of the "unconscious." Everything multiple, complex, and chaotic is so only apparently, he seems to argue, and is in any case ultimately resolved elsewhere, *in another dimension.*[17]

It is true that the concept of a modernist antitemporal stillness (less a fact than a skewed mode of historical understanding) did help to render intelligible the proliferation and indeterminacy of relations that were then beginning entirely to surpass and exceed the physical limits of the artistic work. The modernist work's insistence on autonomy and self-sufficiency made of it, on the contrary and more than ever before, a mere thing among the other things of the world. Indeed the "dehumanization" of the work actually bestowed upon it a

15 Shattuck, "The Art of Stillness," in *The Banquet Years.*

16 This de-hierarchization of the work into a field of multiple, receiver-determined entries is the thesis of Umberto Eco's *The Open Work* (Cambridge: Harvard University Press, 1989).

17 Shattuck, *The Banquet Years,* p. 342.

new, rather than a lesser, intimacy: the work no longer led one back (through representation) to the daily world;[18] it actually comprised (some of) the world itself.[19]

Reductionism and Complexity

Yet much of modern art stands or falls in relation to a single question: does it or does it not introduce complexity—the complexity of real things—into the domains of the work specifically and of aesthetics generally? It is here that so much of modernity seems to be at stake, because this term "complexity" invokes nothing less than all that within nature or the cultural world that is irreducible to any rigid or finite schema of intelligibility, either mathematical or phenomenological.[20] Complexity, at the first level, always implies the presence within a given system of a surplus of variables whose interactions cannot be correlated or predicted ahead of time with any degree of certainty. Modern scientific culture since the renaissance, as we have seen, has on the contrary always oriented its models in the other direction, toward the simple, the repeatable, and the universal—the criterion of intelligibility demanded that the singular in phenomena always be routed and brought back into relation with sameness, with regular known quantities or constants. But the necessity of grounding a theory of nature within the Same and the Elementary meant relegating it to a certain easily controllable though always iso-

18 Ortega y Gasset, "The Dehumanization of Art," in *The Dehumanization of Art and Other Essays on Art, Culture, and Literature* (Princeton, N.J.: Princeton University Press, 1968, orig. 1948).

19 The use of the partitive mode (e.g., /some water/, /some wood/) here and in works of this nature marks a transformation of a relation not just to the "sign" as many have argued, but to the activity of signifying itself. It signals a new indeterminacy—the whole is indeterminate, just as is the "part" (the some that indicates it)—and a new materialist and a-signifying approach both to assembling and apprehending work and world. The partitive describes a multiplicity's mode of being in relation to what is external to it, that is, to the world.

20 To be sure, even the most apparently simplifying, reductive, rationalist tendencies of modern art such as the works of Bauhaus, De Stijl, or the International Style movements in architecture were conditioned by a deep reflex toward complexity: the desire to annex or absorb influence from disparate and unorthodox domains of cultural production, i.e., technical industrial culture, politics, and modernization processes in general.

lating timelessness. Extracting individual realities from the complex continuum that nourished them and gave them shape made them manageable, even intelligible, but always in essence transformed them. Cut off from those precarious aspects of phenomena that can only be called their "becoming," that is, their aleatory and transformative adventure *in time* including their often extreme sensitivity to secondary, tertiary, global, stochastic, or merely invisible processes, and cut off as well from their capacities to affect or determine effects at the heart of these same processes—the science of nature has excluded time and rendered itself incapable of thinking change or novelty in and for itself.

This idea of modernity in itself is hardly new, for it lies inchoate at the basis of much thought beginning with the modern economic historians Max Weber, Werner Sombart and Georg Simmel,[21] the social historian Lewis Mumford, and the philosopher Martin Heidegger. What is more, this idea certainly played a constitutive role in much work on the history of science since World War II, in that of Alexandre Koyré, Ernst Cassirer, and Georges Canguilhem; though foremost by far, this theme is reflected in the work of Henri Bergson, whose *Creative Evolution* explicitly confronts the conventional scientific worldview for its inability to think about temporal phenomena in general and novelty in particular. Yet not even this, we have seen, compares in importance to the more recent phenomenon in which empirical scientific advances have legitimated and actualized the rationalistic, speculative, or intuitive claims of the earlier work. For what the various pieces of literature on stochastic processes, dissipative structures, dynamical or nonlinear systems, chaos theory, bifurcation theory, turbulence, etc. have in common is an attempt to incorporate and manipulate abstract structures whose correlations—probabilistic, global, transductive—can be apprehended only through and in time understood as an asymmetrical and irreversible flow.[22]

---

21 Marx's analyses of value in volume I of *Capital* are clearly seminal and determinant here.

22 In addition to the works cited below see F. Eugene Yates, ed., *Self-Organizing Systems* (New York: Plenum Press, 1987); John Briggs and F. David Peat, *Turbulent Mirror* (New York: Harper & Row, 1989); Arthur T. Winfree, *When Time Breaks Down: The Three-Dimensional Dynamics of Electrochemical Waves and Cardiac Arrhythmias* (Princeton, N.J.: Princeton University Press, 1987); Leon Glass and Michael C. Mackey, *From Clocks to Chaos: The Rhythms of Life* (Princeton, N.J.: Princeton University Press, 1988), and all of the published proceedings of the Santa Fe Institute in the Sciences of Complexity (Redwood City: Addison-Wesley, 1987–93). These works as well as most listed below contain extensive bibliographies on the subject, while the field continues to expand exponentially.

Time and Information

Some have claimed that a new theory of nature is emerging today[23] though it is one whose roots, whose anxiety, go back to the heart of the modernist moment, to physicist Ludwig Boltzmann's failure to put his H-theorem on a solid foundation,[24] even to Bergson's prescient but equally failed attack on Einstein's theory of time.[25] If time was excluded along with other "flow phenomena" at the origins of classical physics,[26] it reemerged with a vengeance in the nineteenth-century science of thermodynamics and theory of evolution. From that moment on, time could grow only increasingly problematic, for the infrastructure—both scientific and cultural—of our classical worldview became increasingly incapable of accounting for the phenomena that it offered up. Time, began to function increasingly as a

23 Such claims were first advanced by, among others, Ilya Prigogine and Isabelle Stengers in *La nouvelle alliance,* 2nd ed. (Paris: Gallimard, 1986, orig. 1979), and by James Gleick, *Chaos: The Making of a New Science* (New York: Viking, 1987) .

24 Boltzmann's attempt to reconcile the timeless laws of classical dynamics with the asymmetrical processes of the second law of thermodynamics is recounted in S. G. Brush, *The Kind of Motion We Call Heat* (Amsterdam: North Holland, 1976); D. Flamm, *The Boltzmann Equation,* eds. E. Cohen and W. Thirring (Vienna: Springer, 1973); George Greenstein, "The Bulldog: A Portrait of Ludwig Boltzmann," *The American Scholar,* v. 60, no.1, winter 1991; Karl Popper, *Unended Quest* (La Salle, Ill.: Open Court, 1976), pp. 156–162; Thomas Kuhn, *Black-Body Theory and the Quantum Discontinuity, 1894–1912* (New York: Oxford University Press, 1978), pp. 38–46; and I. Prigogine and I. Stengers, *Entre le temps et l'éternité* (Paris: Fayard, 1988). On the H-theorem in general, see Satosi Watanabe, "Time and the Probabilistic View of the World," *The Voices of Time,* ed. J. T. Fraser (Amherst: University of Massachusetts Press, 1980, orig. 1966).

25 Henri Bergson, *Durée et simultanéité* (Paris: PUF, 1968).

26 On the counterhistory of hydrodynamics and flow phenomena from the time of Archimedes, see Michel Serrès, *La naissance de la physique dans le texte de Lucrèce: fleuves et tubulences* (Paris: Minuit, 1977) and *Hermes IV: La Distribution* (Paris: Minuit, 1977). Prigogine cites S. Sambursky's *The Physical World of the Greeks,* trans. M. Dagut (Princeton, N.J.: Princeton University Press, 1987, orig. 1956) for the assertion that the static view of the world is rooted in the Ancient classical origins of science. Ilya Prigogine, *From Being to Becoming: Time and Complexity in the Physical Sciences* (New York, W. H. Freeman, 1980), p. x. For Hans Reichenbach it derives from Parmenides and the Eleatic School; Hans Reichenbach, *The Direction of Time* (Berkeley: University of California Press, 1956), p. 11. "Flow phenomena" in the sense that I use it here refers to anything from hydrodynamics to weather, economics, or simple iterative feedback equations.

form of pure information: it is after all that which makes differentiation and mor-phogenesis (i.e., singularities, discontinuities, events) possible, by providing a communicative middle term—a metastability—affording exchanges and absorb-ing and transmitting tensions across many and various systems of influence. It is also as an informational element that time permits phenomena at great "distances" or at radically different "temporal domains" or scales of reality to react with one an-other and to be implicated with one another.[27] Thus time is not just a novel or su-peradded variable; it is that agency which multiplies all variables by themselves: systems communicate with one another—not just different systems distributed or adjacent at a moment in time—but systems now enter into communication even with themselves, that is, with the later or earlier states of the system that may now actually interact with any given present moment.[28]

This new "complex" informational space is today often misnamed by the science that studies it as "chaos." What must interest us is this science's

27 Scaling is an important if little understood aspect of contemporary mathematics. The un-canny periodic appearance of identical elements or structures within apparently random processes has spawned so much interest since the mid-1980s that it has been hailed as a fundamental revolution in twentieth-century physical theory on the same order as relativ-ity and quantum mechanics. It is arguable that these ideas in some form have been around for some time but that the *technical* conditions enabling them to emerge as full empirical scientific discoveries, as I have already noted, have only recently made their appearance in the form of the Texas calculator, the microcomputer, and the revolution in graphic mod-eling made possible by the interactive cathode ray tube. The increasing use of "phase-space" models of dynamical phenomena—where a static or moving two-dimensional sectional image is able to express all the information about a continuously evolving multi-dimensional system, including its capacity to mutate randomly in time—is undoubtedly of inestimable importance. On this point too, fractal geometry has played a crucial role. See James Gleick, *Chaos* (pp. 152, 171); Heinz Pagels, *The Dreams of Reason: The Computer and the Rise of Sciences of Complexity* (New York: Simon and Schuster, 1988); and David Campbell et al., "Experimental Mathematics: The Role of Computation in Non-Linear Science," in *Communications of the Association for Computing Machinery*, 28 (1985), pp. 374–384.

28 In addition to positive and negative feedback, reaction-diffusion systems, auto- and cross-catalytic networks, there exist other parasitical influences such as attractor states and what is known as "sensitive dependence on initial conditions," a heightened sensitivity *at cer-tain moments* in the system to extremely minute perturbations capable of creating decisive, but entirely unpredictable qualitative fluctuations in the system's shape, activity, or organ-ization.

willingness to engage such concepts as disorder, instability, randomness, inter-activity, irreducible complexity, and especially *change* as positive (and not merely romantic) terms. For here, all systems are *open* systems; they are labile and suf-fused with temporality; they are sensitive and chaotic in the sense that they are creative and adaptive—they ceaselessly undergo change, produce novelty; they transform or transmit unactualized potentials to a new milieu, in turn giving rise to a whole new series of potentials to be actualized or not. Open systems are thus open not only to the "outside," but to wild *becoming* itself—the outside of all outsides.[29]

What then makes this possible? If time is a pure flow of information deter-mining all actuality and in turn the production of all new potentials, then time is not only that through which matter derives both its capacities and its attri-butes but is that which can be realized only in matter caught in the throes of "pass-ing out of step with itself."[30] In fact there is no "time" per se that is distinct from extension, only a perpetual, simultaneous unfolding, a differentiation, an indi-viduation *en bloc* of points-moments that are strictly inseparable from their as-sociated milieus or their *conditions of emergence.* The temporal factor here is not "time" itself (Chronos) but rather a general conception of nature as a "flow phenomenon," a dynamical, richly implicated system of evental becomings (Aion).[31] After all, if the real has a claim to make on our imaginations it is much less for any theory of what it *is* than for the fact that things *occur* within it. For when something occurs, it may be said that that which previously remained only a potential or a virtuality now emerges and becomes actual, though only in place of something else that could have arisen here at this time, but did not. This double "difference"—between what is here now but previously was not—and between what emerged and what did not, in all of its complexity and fatality and

29 The principal theme of Gilbert Simondon, *L'individu et sa génèse physico-biologique* (Paris: PUF, 1964); Prigogine and Stengers, *Entre le temps;* Michel Foucault, "Thought from Out-side," in *Foucault/Blanchot* (New York: Zone Books, 1987); and Deleuze and Guattari *A Thousand Plateaus,* trans. Brian Massumi (Minneapolis: University of Minnesota Press, 1987). Cf. also Gilles Deleuze, *Foucault* (Minneapolis: University Of Minnesota Press, 1988).

30 Simondon's felicitous if difficult expression characterizing the movement or development through which individuation occurs: "une capacité que l'etre a de se déphaser par rapport a lui-meme, *de se résoudre en se déphasant."* *L'individu,* p. 5.

31 See Gilles Deleuze's treatise on the multiple forms of Greek time in *Logic of Sense.*

in all of its own pregnant virtuality or potentiality is what I will call "the event." The event is a principle of individuation, indeed *the* principle of individuation in a nature understood as complex and dynamic—it divides, limits, but especially produces.

However, to see nature in terms of events should not be confused merely with establishing a threshold beneath which classical objects, states, or relations cease to have meaning yet beyond which they are endowed with a full pedigree and priveleged status. On the contrary, it will be seen how classical objects, states, and relations are in fact fully incompatible with a reality considered as a fluid in perpetual emergence. Indeed the units of such a theory of nature are closer to the medieval concept of the *haecceitas*—that is, singular, correlated, "evental" individualities—a concept that will be developed in chapter 5 in relation to the work of Franz Kafka.

Modernity and Ontology

There is an increasingly rich philosophical and scientific culture dedicated to the problem of time and the event. Our modernity is inseparable from this culture and undoubtedly also from its recent explosive growth. What we lack, however, is an explicit development or delineation of similar developments in the "softer" areas of our history and cultural life—in music, art, politics, literature. The present work is a rudimentary attempt to break some ground in certain of these areas, to see where analysis—and especially what type of analysis—might yield fruit, or at the very least unexpected results upon which a less blinded stab might subsequently be ventured.

From the perspective developed here, the ontology, as I am calling it, of modernity cannot be considered an entirely new one, though it is arguable that only in the twentieth century has it emerged with a specific historical force to become a dominant mode within culture. The individual studies that make up this book are indeed, in a perhaps less modest vein, an effort toward a description of this emergent ontology. Though they seem to announce less abstract objects—a visionary townplan by the futurist architect Antonio Sant'Elia, the literary works of Franz Kafka—it will soon become apparent that this is not, strictly speaking, to be the case. They seek rather to trace a number of themes that were emerging within physical theory at the turn of the twentieth century and to transfer them, however piecemeal at first, onto a single surface where their ultimate consistency can, at least in a preliminary or provisional fashion, be formulated.

In keeping with such a method I have rigorously avoided, even at the cost of a symmetrically paced exposition, the customary application of "theoretical" models to practical phenomena as well as the establishment of hierarchies of ideas where those in one domain are seen as determinant of those in another. Nor is there an equivalency being claimed between ideas developed in, say, physics and aesthetics in the early modern period. Rather, I am advancing the hypothesis that the most significant transformations in science, philosophy, and aesthetics of the time were those that most deeply expressed the charcteristics of this newly emerging ontology rather than those that were content to reflect each another's surface features. Analysis will be directed therefore toward a partial reconstruction of this ontological basis rather than at the comparative level of relations where these disciplines can be shown, however dubiously, to be linked.

3.1
La Città nuova: Terraced house with elevators from four street levels, 1914. Milano,
Paride Accetti collection.

3

Physical Theory and Modernity: Einstein, Boccioni, Sant'Elia

To movement, then, everything will be restored, and into movement everything will be resolved.

— HENRI BERGSON

The New Plasticity

We are passing through a stage in a long
progress towards interpenetration, simultaneity,
and fusion, on which humanity has been
engaged for thousands of years.
—UMBERTO BOCCIONI, DECEMBER 12, 1913

THE TWO DECADES BEGINNING IN 1876 saw the appearance of the incandescent lamp, the telephone, hydraulic generators, skyscrapers, electric trolleys, subways, and elevators, as well as cinema, X-rays, and the first automobiles. By 1903 the spectacle of the first mechanically powered airships and then airplanes had shattered the still inviolate horizontality of the phenomenological and geopolitical space of the pre–World War I era. The life-world in Europe and America was being transformed in depth—the unparalleled technical saturation of the human perceptual apparatus through innovations in transport and communications was redefining the body and its relations to the world beyond it. A new order was emerging whose configuration could be expressed either in terms of a dynamics of force and a relativism or in the privative terms of nihilism and dissolution. Whatever their ultimate convictions, the philosophies of Henri Bergson and Edmund Husserl may be seen to form one axis of this configuration: Bergson's for its insistence on the nondiscrete nature of the contents of consciousness and on the systematic dissolution of spatial form in the fluid multiplicity of *durée;* Husserl's for its attempt to work out the dynamic of (ap)perception by extending the intentional *horizon* (perceptual field) to the vector of internal time consciousness so that a perceived object (noema)—already defined as partial and contingent in space—was further relativized in a temporal complex of retained and anticipated images.

The first systematic attempt to express these new principles, however, arose in the realm of aesthetics, first and most fully in the theoretical program of Italian futurism, yet realized unequivocally only in the work of one of its members, Antonio Sant'Elia. The movement's founder, Filippo Tommaso Marinetti, published the "Foundation Manifesto" in the Paris daily *Le Figaro* in February 1909.

Certainly the most literary of any of the several dozen manifestos that would follow in the next seven years, Marinetti's text recapitulates in its organization and form the same disjunctive pattern it sought to effect in the real historical world around it. The prologue opens with a description of the Marinetti family apartment with its precious, saturating *turquerie* and claustrophobic, fin-de-siècle exoticism ("We had stayed up all night my friends and I, under the mosque-lamps whose filigree copper domes were constellated like our very souls . . ."),[1] then, with scarcely a change in tone, breaks into a heroic reverie on the new industrial culture formed by machines and "those who sweat before them." The text pauses long enough to affirm Futurists' and workers' common affinity to inhabit the night, then proceeds to the more immediate apprehension of a passing tram, its panoply of artificial lights, and finally to an unfavorable comparison of "the arthritic, ivy-bearded old palaces" of the city with the healthy "roar of famished motorcars" that speed among them. The section continues as Marinetti and his companions start out on their famous motorcar race through the streets of Milan. Both the race and the section end abruptly as Marinetti's car capsizes in a ditch, pitching him headlong into the swamp of a factory drain from which he draws at least one "nourishing" draught before emerging to declare himself baptismally delivered into the Futurist world of mechanical splendor.

The main body of the manifesto then follows, praising danger, movement, crowds, and, above all, speed as a new form of beauty, an *éloge* to mechanism and abstract energy of all kinds including war and automobilism, while denouncing museums, libraries, contemplation, history, old age, and stasis in any form, and pronouncing once and for all the abolition of space and time.[2]

In many ways this text marks a turning point in the history of avant-garde culture. Not only was it the first time a call had been made for a complete break with the past and an insistence that the techniques and subject matter of art be drawn solely from the concrete contemporary world around one, but it was the first to have conceived of this concrete world as inseparable from the industrial and sci-

---

1 *Founding and Manifesto of Futurism, Archivi del futurismo,* eds. Maria Drudi Gambillo and Teresa Fiori, 2 vols. (Rome: DeLuca, 1958/1962), vol. 1, p. 15.

2 The text not only dramatizes the passage from an outdated environment to a new, invigorated one, but furnishes in a great number of detail sources for dozens of works that would follow in its wake. To mention just a few among them, Giacomo Balla's *Velocità astratta* (1913), Luigi Russolo's *Automobile in corsa* (1913), Carlo Carra's *Quello que mi disse il tram* (1911), and Umberto Boccioni's *La strada entra nella casa* (1911).

entific technologies that arrange, and are arranged (however abstractly), within it. Correspondingly, the activities and attitudes promulgated by the manifesto were singularly devoid of reference to aesthetic or literary practice. Artistic revolution was conceived only within a more general program of transformation of the totality of human existence. "Dynamism" was the catchword for the entire movement:[3] through it was expressed the will to intervene politically, scientifically, and aesthetically in an emerging order of space-time that was already revolutionizing the social environment.

The most significant technical innovations of the era, from the skyscraper to moving pictures and the automobile, were made possible by inventions—electric motor (elevators), incandescent lamp, internal combustion engine, and so on—that themselves depended on more fundamental breakthroughs in the harnessing and exploitation of energy, most notably of the electromagnetic spectrum. Wireless telegraphy and later the wireless home radio set, the electrification of private homes, streets, and public spaces, the proliferation of telephones and automobiles together gave a new fluidity, and a new consistency, to everyday space. What once passed as unqualified or as insubstantial began to take on a new palpability, dense with wires and waves, kinetic and communicative flows. It was out of this apprehension of space as a kinetic and substantial plenum that the new plasticity emerged, simultaneously in aesthetics and in the relativity theory that was revolutionizing physics in the years between 1905 and 1916.

The Field

In his 1905 paper "On the Electrodynamics of Moving Bodies," Einstein first presented his Special Theory of Relativity. The theory's main features were, first, to preserve the Galilean principle of relativity. According to this principle, the uniform motion of any inertial system (a space-time reference frame) can be discerned only by referring to a point that lies outside the system. By the same token, motion of any kind *within* an inertial system derives its value only in relation to points also in that system. And finally it states that the laws that determine the values of any state of motion are invariant for all inertial systems. To this theory—the cornerstone of classical mechanics—was added Relativity's second important feature, the principles of Lorentz's transformation equations, which provided a simple theorem for relating and transforming time and space coordinates from one inertial system

3 Marinetti originally wavered between dynamism and futurism as names for his movement; cf. Marianne W. Martin, *Futurist Art and Theory, 1909–1915* (Oxford: Clarendon Press, 1968), p. 40.

to another. The radicality of Einstein's adaptation lay in quantifying the elastic deformation of bodies and the actual deformation (dilation) of time at high speeds. By adding a third principle whose derivation goes back to James Clerk Maxwell—the constancy of the velocity of light in empty space—Einstein was able to formulate the Special Theory of Relativity.

The theory's radicality lay in freeing time itself of its metaphysical and absolute character and reducing it to but one more dependent (i.e., variable) coordinate in the kinematical transformation equations.[4] The new four-dimensional continuum developed in this theory differed from that of classical mechanics in the following way: time and space were no longer, at least algebraically, heterogeneous; the continuous four-dimensional manifold could no longer be separated into a three-dimensional section evolving in one-dimensional time, where "simultaneous" events are contained only in the former; each inertial system, rather, would now express its own particular time determined as a mutual relation of events to the frame in which they are registered. Events occurring simultaneously can thus be said to do so only with respect to a single inertial system into which they are arbitrarily grouped and outside of which any notion of "now" becomes meaningless. By making time in this way relative and contingent,[5] space-time and the field were conceived as a new entity, irreducible to their component dimensions, objectively unresolvable with respect to their infinitely varied regions (different speeds = different times), and thickened to consistency by the world-lines[6] that career through them.

4   That is, all of the mathematics in sections 3 and 4 of part 1 of "On the Electrodynamics" dealing with transformations of (space) coordinates and times between stationary and moving systems. H. A. Lorentz, A. Einstein, H. Minkowski, and H. Weyl, *The Principle of Relativity*, trans. W. Perrett and G. B. Jeffery (New York: Dover, 1952, orig. 1923), pp. 43–50.

5   Relative to, and contingent upon, three space coordinates, one of which will undergo a change in the dimension parallel to the motion due to the Lorentz contraction, one variable (relative velocity between two reference frames), and one constant (the speed of light).

6   The term world-lines was coined by H. Minkowski in his famous article, "Space and Time" (1908), which gave the first mathematical formulation of space-time. Minkowski defined a world-point as a point in space at a point in time (a system of values x,y,z,t). Attributing the variations dx, dy, dz to conform to the value dt, this point would describe "an everlasting career" that he named a world-line. "The whole universe is seen to resolve itself into similar world-lines, and I would fain anticipate myself by saying that in my opinion physical laws might find their most perfect expression as reciprocal relations between these world-lines." Lorentz et al., *The Principle of Relativity*, p. 76.

This consistency too, was of an entirely new kind. The concept of space as it developed from antiquity was founded on Euclidean mathematics, for which space, as a continuum with its own independent reality, was never fully posited. The elements of which this system was constructed—the point, the line, and the plane—were nothing more than idealizations of solid bodies. Space itself emerged only secondarily, that is, only insofar as it could be derived from these idealized forms and the relations produced by their contact—intersections, points lying on lines or planes, and so on. Only with Descartes does space finally emerge as autonomous and preexisting: an infinite and generalized three-dimensional continuum, where points and figures are describable by their coordinates.

If geometrical descriptions in the Euclidean system were reducible to actual objects (point, line, and plane) or aggregates and derivations thereof, the Cartesian system permitted "all surfaces [to] appear, in principle on equal footing, without any arbitrary preference for linear structures."[7] Space now existed, in other words, independent of solid bodies, preceding them and containing them.

Until the introduction of dynamics, the Greek system had been adequate for all geometric needs (e.g., Brunelleschi, Desargues, Mercator), but the new Cartesian system would be absolutely indispensable for Newtonian physics, in which equations of motion and acceleration play a dominant role. This is because acceleration cannot be expressed or defined as a relation between points alone but only in relation to an abstract ground of space as a whole. Events could now be conceived of as taking place against a fixed backdrop that also served as their unaffected carrier.

Not until the nineteenth century did this concept of space and the relations between movements and bodies begin to change. First thermodynamics (problems of heat conduction in solid bodies), then the discovery of the electromagnetic interaction and the wave-theory of light provided both the first treatment of matter as a continuum (or at least as a vehicle of continuous "intensive" movements or changes) and the first evidence of states in free or empty space that are propagated in waves. In the first case matter was treated as a *system* of states, characterized by independent quantitative variables—thermal differences, volume, pressure—expressible as a *function* of space coordinates and, most important, of

7 "The Problem of Space, Ether, and the Field in Physics," in Albert Einstein, *Ideas and Opinions* (New York: Bonanza Books, 1954), p. 279.

time. In the second it was a simple transposition of these same mathematics—partial differential equations—to the propagation of magnetic and light phenomena. Passing from a field theory of masses (thermodynamics) to a field theory of empty space (electrodynamics) meant that classical mechanics had to be superseded.[8]

Maxwell's breakthrough in the theory of electromagnetic processes went far in this direction, but unable to make the final conceptual break he was obliged to posit a material vehicle or medium for this electromagnetic field: the luminiferous ether. The ether played a purely mechanical role as the material seat and carrier of all forces acting across space—though it was imperceptible and only logically derivable, based as it was on the presupposition that every state is capable of mechanical interpretation and therefore implies the presence of matter. The Michelson-Morley experiment of 1888, however, failed to yield any evidence of the material existence of such an ether. Between this event and the Special Theory of Relativity of 1905 came Lorentz's important work, which, while accounting for the Michelson-Morley results, established, according to Einstein, that ether and physical space "were only different terms for the same thing."[9] It was a momentous conceptual leap if only a short mathematical step that Einstein took to emancipate the field concept entirely from any association with a substratum. For the Special Theory of Relativity Einstein employed the Riemannian conception of space,[10] whose plastic structure is susceptible both to partaking in physical events and to being influenced by them. The Einsteinian field, and its corresponding notion of space-time, dispensed entirely with the need to posit a material substratum as a carrier for forces and events by identifying the

---

8 "Before Maxwell people conceived of physical reality—in so far as it is supposed to represent events in nature—as material points, whose changes consist exclusively of motions, which are subject to total differential equations. After Maxwell they conceived physical reality as represented by continuous fields, not mechanically explicable, which are subject to partial differential equations. This change in the conception of reality is the most profound and fruitful one that has come to physics since Newton" (Einstein, *Ideas and Opinions*, p. 269). Ernst Mach, whose theories exerted a great influence on Einstein, argued the need to abandon the metaphysics of Newtonian mechanics in his 1883 *The Science of Mechanics* (Chicago: Open Court, Eng. 1902).

9 Einstein, *Ideas and Opinions*, p. 281.

10 Einstein asserts this, however, only retrospectively. See "The Problem of Space, Ether, and the Field in Physics," *Ideas and Opinions*, p. 281.

electromagnetic field—and ultimately gravitational fields as well—with the new metrical one. This notion of "the field" expresses the complete immanence of forces and events while supplanting the old concept of space identified with the Cartesian substratum and ether theory. The field emerges as "an irreducible element of physical description, irreducible in the same sense as the concept of matter in the theory of Newton."[11]

The field describes a space of propagation, of effects. It contains no matter or material points, but rather functions, vectors, and speeds. It describes local relations of difference within fields of celerity, transmission, or of careering points—in a word, what Minkowski called the *world.* Einstein himself offered as an example of a field phenomenon nothing other than the description of the motion of a liquid:

> At every point there exists at any time a velocity, which is quantitatively described by its three "components" with respects to the axes of a coordinate system (vector). The components of a velocity at a point (field components) [fulfill the conditions of the field for they, like the temperature in a system of thermal propagation] are functions of the coordinates (x, y, z) and time (t).

This hydrodynamic model, of course, deserves no particular priority in Einstein's system for it was still only a rudimentary mechanical model describing a state of matter, whereas Einstein's physics was an attempt to think the pure event, independent of a material medium or substratum. Yet the field theory it typified was emerging in other areas of endeavor, often finding expression through similar or related models of dynamics in fluids. Its mysterious charm was none other than the partial differential function through which alone it was possible to express the principles of immanence, dynamism, and continuity.

Plastic Dynamism

In aesthetics, no less than in physics, the last years of the nineteenth century and the first of the twentieth brought about a decisive transformation in the concept of space. Beginning with Hildebrand's *Problem of Form* (1893), in which space ap-

---

11 Albert Einstein, *Relativity: The Special and General Theory* (New York: Bonanza Books, 1961), p. 150.

pears for the first time both as an autonomous aesthetic concept and, more importantly, as a continuum unbroken and indistinct from solid objects,[12] to its development in Riegl and its ultimate identification with the *Kunstwollen,* and finally to the later syntheses of Panofsky's "*Die Perspektive als 'symbolische Form,'*" space emerged with a new positivity as an object of both knowledge and direct experience. One historian situates the emergence of a modern continuum theory of space with Geoffrey Scott's influential *Architecture of Humanism* (1914), tracing it to the psychological theories of Theodor Lipps and the Beaux-Arts compositional theories of Charles Blanc and Julien Guadet.[13] This latter development, however, would not become fully integrated into architectural practice until the mid-'20s, long after Cubism (through which it was transmitted)[14] had elaborated and, to a large extent, exhausted it. A more essential evolution of these problems, and one closer to the scientific movement that emancipated physical theory from the old notion of matter and its correlative space, is the basis of the new plastic theories developed by the futurist Umberto Boccioni in his writings on plastic dynamism.[15]

Following in the wake of Marinetti's "Foundation Manifesto" there is much, undeniably, in these writings of the rehearsed denunciations that were an integral part of the futurist public relations enterprise. But more than any other of the

12 Adolf von Hildebrand, *Das Problem der Form in der bildenden Kunst* (Strassburg: J. H. E. Heitz, 1893), pp. 32–33. "Let us imagine total space (*das Raumganze*) as a body of water, into which we may sink certain vessels, and thus be able to define individual volumes of water without however destroying the idea of a continuous mass of water enveloping all."

13 Reyner Banham, *Theory and Design in the First Machine Age* (Cambridge, Mass.: MIT Press, 1981, orig. 1960), pp. 66–67.

14 Colin Rowe and Robert Slutzky, "Transparency: Literal and Phenomenal," in *The Mathematics of the Ideal Villa and Other Essays* (Cambridge, Mass.: MIT Press, 1976).

15 Umberto Boccioni, *Pittura, scultura futuriste: Dinamismo plastico* (Florence: Vallechi, 1977, orig. 1914) (abbr. *PSF* in text); *Archivi del futurismo* (abbr. *Ar* in text). English translations of some of Boccioni's writings were published in *Futurist Manifestos,* ed. Umbro Appolonio (London: Thames and Hudson, 1973) (abbr. *FM* in text). Because these translations are unreliable, all citations and page numbers given in the body of the text will refer when possible to the Italian originals. All quotes are either my own translations or are altered versions of those given in the latter work.

movement's exponents, even Marinetti—whose flair for public promotion and the right turn of phrase was less amply sustained by consistency of thought— Boccioni's were cogent and forceful ideas that came to be formed into a complex system of concepts bearing on the nature of the physical world.

In the *Technical Manifesto of Futurist Sculpture,* the first manifesto published solely under his own name, Boccioni develops in a radically unprecedented way the relationship of an object to its environment:

> . . . sculpture must make objects live by rendering apprehensible, plastic and systematic their prolongations into space, since no one can any longer believe that an object finishes where another begins and that there is not an object around us: bottle, automobile, tree, house or street, that does not cut and section us with an arabesque of curved and straight lines. (Ar. I, p. 69)

These same relations are expressed in a subsequent text, recast now in the language of (ancient) atomist physics:

> . . . areas between one object and another are not empty spaces but rather *continuing materials of differing intensities,* which we reveal with visible lines which do not correspond to any photographic truth. This is why we do not have in our paintings objects and empty spaces but only *a greater or lesser intensity and solidity of space.* (Ar. I, p. 143, italics added)

Leaving the body/nonbody opposition aside altogether, space is also characterized in terms of two interrelated and interpenetrating fields:

> *Absolute motion* is a dynamic law grounded in an object. The plastic construction of the object will here concern itself with the motion an object has within it, be it at rest or in movement. I am making this distinction between rest and movement, however, only to make myself clear, for in fact, there is no such thing as rest; there is only motion, rest being merely relative, a matter of appearance. This plastic construction obeys a law of motion which characterizes the body in question. It is the plastic potential which the object contains within itself, closely bound up with its own organic substance, and according to its general characteristics: porosity, impermeability, rigidity, elasticity, etc. or its particular characteristics: color, temperature, consistency, form (flat, concave, angular, convex, cubic, conic, spiral, elliptical, spherical, etc.). (*SPF,* p. 80)

Relative motion is a dynamic law based on the object's movement. . . . Here it is a matter of conceiving the objects in movement quite apart from the motion which they contain within themselves. That is to say we must try to find a form which will express the new absolute—*speed,* which any true modern spirit cannot ignore. (*SPF,* pp. 82–83)

Boccioni's system reveals a certain dual nature of space: on the one hand, a fixed and extended *milieu* with metrical or dimensional properties and, on the other, a fluid and consistent field of intensities (e.g., forces, speeds, temperatures, color). The resemblance to Bergson's two types of multiplicity, the numerical (discrete) and the qualitative (continuous), or, more generally, that of space and that of *durée,* deserves to be underscored here once again.[16] The basic difference, of course, between Bergson's second, dynamic multiplicity as it was formulated in the early *Essai* and Boccioni's is that for the latter there is no separate or privileged *internal* domain.[17] Specifically, it is the problematization of this separation that is the point of departure for Boccioni's work.[18] What remains to both regardless of this difference is the task of giving systematic expression to the world in the modern terms of a *continuous multiplicity.*[19]

For Boccioni such a conception of the world was sustained implicitly by means of what I shall schematize below as three interdependent hypotheses.

1. *The hypothesis of the undividedness of the object field.* According to this hypothesis, the world is at once an aggregate of separate fragments *and* a materially

16 Henri Bergson, *Essai sur les données immédiates de la conscience* (Paris: Presses Universitaires de France, 1927), chap. 2.

17 The rhetoric of Bergsonian intuitionism is, however, to a certain degree maintained. Cf. *Archivi,* vol. 1, pp. 71, 104, 108, 144.

18 "Les problèmes clefs de l'art moderne [sont] les problèmes de la représentation de l'espace, notamment le problème de la continuité dans l'espace, et ceux de la transition entre l'espace intérieur et l'espace extérieur. Grace à la spirale, l'espace n'est plus défini par un volume à trois dimensions, mais composé avec une quatrième dimension—celle du temps: la spirale permet . . . une durée réele." Noémi Blumenkranz-Onimus, "La spirale, thème lyrique dans l'art moderne," in *Cahiers d'Esthetique* (1971), p. 296. By the time of the later *Matter and Memory,* and certainly of *Creative Evolution,* the distinction of domains had retreated dramatically from Bergson's thought as well.

19 This notion of multiplicity was first developed by the mathematician Bernhard Riemann. For a more detailed elaboration of this concept see chapter 4, notes 44 and 53.

indivisible whole. The main underlying current here is an attack on perspectival space[20] and the correlative "scientific" geometry based on the optical model.[21] "Traditionally a statue cuts into, and stands out from, the atmosphere of the place where it is on view," Boccioni writes; though henceforth sculpture will use "the facts of landscape and the environment which act simultaneously on the human figure and on objects" and "extend its plastic capacities to [these objects] which till now a kind of barbaric crudeness has persuaded us to believe were divided up or intangible . . ." (*Ar.* I, p. 68). This conception yields to positive formulations such as "the interpenetration of planes" (*Ar.* I, pp. 68, 72), the notion, borrowed from Marinetti, of the (*immaginazione*) *senza fili* (both "wireless" as in radio, and "without strings"), and the "absolute and complete abolition of finite lines" (*Ar.* I, p. 70).

Closely connected with the idea of interpenetration is Boccioni's belief that the environment not only conditions and acts on objects but is contained by them, forming labile plastic zones of influence (*SPF,* pp. 81–82; *Ar.* I, p. 71). Resuscitating Marinetti's *immaginazione senza fili,* he means to insist on an *analogical*[22] (intuitive, immanent) method of reconstructing space, as well as to

20 It is important here to differentiate between those systematic attacks on perspective that were commonplace in the modernist period (Cubism) and those, such as Boccioni's and Duchamp's, which, more than a simple modification of existing pictorial theory, constitute a critique of the conception of the world as an optical phenomenon. This latter movement goes beyond questions of aesthetic dogma, casting its challenge not just to the Renaissance's rationalizing *costruzione legittima* but to the quasi-entirety of Western notions of space, back to the time of Euclid and Vitruvius. Erwin Panofsky has demonstrated the constant link between optics and geometry. For his discussion of Euclid, see *The Codex Huygens and Leonardo da Vinci's Art Theory,* Pierpont Morgan Library, Codex MA 1139, London, 1940; on Vitruvius, see *Perspective as Symbolic Form* (New York: Zone Books, 1991) and for an interesting reference to Riemann and binocular vision, see *Early Netherlandish Painting* (Cambridge, Mass.: Harvard University Press, 1964), p. 12.

21 *Archivi,* vol. I, pp. 105–106, 144; *Futurist Manifestos,* p. 94. See also Carlo Carra's *Plastic Planes as Spherical Expansions in Space, Archivi,* vol. I, pp. 145–147; *Futurist Manifestos,* pp. 91–92.

22 "Analogy is nothing more than the deep love that assembles distant, seemingly diverse and hostile things. . . . Together we will invent what I call the imagination without strings. Someday we will achieve a yet more essential art, when we dare to suppress all the first terms of our analogies and render no more than an uninterrupted sequence of second terms. . . . Syntax was a kind of abstract cipher that poets used to inform the crowd about

underscore its technological implications; the wireless radio set actualizes and, by this measure, belongs to the invisible electromagnetic plenum that surrounds and subtends it. The third formulation deals with finite lines and closed forms, elements whose plastic possibilities have been eclipsed by a new fluid order of *becoming* ("the law of the unity of universal motion" [*FM,* p. 94]). This order conceives formed matter as in flux, a momentary and metastable constellation of forces (or force-lines) that originate outside it and continue beyond it.

For all these reasons, futurist art cannot be based on visual principles. Against the fragmenting spectacle [23] of all (even modern) art, Boccioni affirms the fullness of conception (*FM,* p. 94), dynamic transformation and becoming (*Ar.* I, p. 144), and the synthesis of all body sensation (*Ar.* I, pp. 105–106). "In Futurist art," he declares, "the viewpoint has completely changed"; from now on the spectator will live in the center of the picture, embedded in the "simultaneousness of the ambient [amid] the dislocation and dismemberment of objects, the scattering and fusion of details, freed from accepted logic and independent from one another"(*Ar.* I, p. 105). Vision alone fragments the field because it gives unity and discreteness to bodies: once the integrity of the field is restored, it is "objects" themselves that appear fragmented:

> . . . the entire visible world will tumble down on top of us, merging. . . . [A] leg, an arm or an object has no importance except as an element in the overall plastic rhythm, and can be eliminated, not because we are trying to imitate a Greek or Roman fragment, but in order to conform with the general harmony the artist is trying to create. (Ar. I, p. 71)

The substance of the world is not resolvable into pure or independent materials or forms. Rather, these latter shift and fluctuate in and out of the formal

---

the color, musicality, plasticity and architecture of the universe. Syntax was a kind of interpreter or monotonous cicerone. This intermediary must be suppressed, in order that literature may enter *directly into the universe and become one body with it*" (italics added), *Technical Manifesto of Futurist Literature* (1912), in *Marinetti: Selected Writings,* ed. R. W. Flint (New York: Farrar, Strauss and Giroux, 1971), pp. 85, 89. See also *Destruction of Syntax—Imagination without Strings—Words-in-Freedom,* in *Futurist Manifestos,* pp. 95–106; and the discussion below on point of view.

23 "It is the static qualities of the old masters which are abstractions, and unnatural abstractions at that—they are an outrage, a violation and a separation, a conception far removed from the law of the unity of universal motion," *Futurist Manifestos,* p. 94.

arrangements that Boccioni calls "plastic zones"; they have become arrangements of *materials in the generic sense*—formless, random multiplicities. There is now only world-substance—an indeterminate and a-centered aggregate of different materials—no longer "ideal" form, transcendent yet made incarnate in "sublime" or noble material:

> Destroy the literary and traditional "dignity" of marble and bronze statuary. Insist that even twenty different materials can be used in a single work of art in order to achieve plastic movement. To mention only a few: iron, cement, hair, leather, cloth, mirrors, electric light, etc. (Ar. I, p. 72)

2. *The hypothesis of universal motion.* This hypothesis extends the theory of the continuity of the object field, already more of a fluid than a rigid three-dimensional continuum, onto the axis of time. As we have seen, substance is indissociably linked to motion (absolute), just as motion (relative) is linked to "speed." The world-substance (multiplicity), now animated, describes a field of vectors of differing qualities and intensities. If the formula "interpenetration of planes" adequately expressed the principle of continuity within the object-field, it is no longer adequate to express vectorial quantities in an active field of speed or celerity. Only line can express variation or difference in a field of force; line conceived *qua* line, as vector and not delimitor of form.[24] Thus the hypothesis of universal motion does not bear on the object-field and its relations.[25] It describes an entirely different cosmos whose substance, conceived within time, is speed itself, ontologically pure and without substrate (the pure "d" in dx/dt). Yet these speeds constellate, decelerate, and change quality to create object-effects wholly outside the realm of form: "the object has no form in itself; the only definable thing is the line which reveals the relationship between the object's weight (quantity) and its expansion (quality)." The object is resolved plastically into its component quantae of force, which in turn are determined by the qualities of the field—here gravity and centrifugality. Lines, or rather "force-lines" (*linee-forze*) describe the object's *nature* (character and quality of field), not its movement as such (displacement of form against a fixed ground). Force-lines are

24 See my "The Pragmatics of Turbulence," *Arts* (December 1985).

25 "A body in movement is not simply an immobile body subsequently set in motion, but a truly mobile object, which is a reality quite new and original." *Futurist Manifestos*, p. 93.

of an entirely other order; they depict a condition of interface or pure trans-mission without medium: the becoming-line of matter[26] and the becoming-immanent of both.

This is the essential meaning of *dynamism,* and it is also the reason that cine-matographic and chronophotographic division and delay have nothing to do with Futurism or its underlying physics. The ill-guided experiments of Giacomo Balla of 1912–13 are no exception to this rule.[27] Dynamism does not characterize an activity of objects in space but describes the quality of a field of immanence or becoming, where the world, in Boccioni's own words, "is conceived as an infinite prolonging of an evolutionary species" (FM, p. 95).

3. *Time and space are full and have a plastic consistency.* This third hypothesis depends logically on the previous two. As we have seen, Einstein's Special Theory of Relativity introduced the concept of relative inertial systems into physical the-ory, and in so doing replaced the absolute time and space of classical mechanics with the concept of the field. Though the laws of classical mechanics are valid within an inertial system, they do not apply to events occurring outside it. Thus local events seem to obey Newtonian principles, but they are always embed-ded in a larger fluid framework of space-time where events can be related only through the Lorentz transformation and not through a fixed or universal coordi-nate. The fundamental novelty in this theory was twofold: first, space, events, and matter ceased to function as substrata for one another and were resolved nonhierarchically as interdependent characteristics of the field; and second, the four-dimensional continuum ceased to be reducible to three space co-ordinates evolving in one-dimensional time, but became a truly unresolvable four-dimensional whole, in which the four coordinates assume their positions without privilege or qualitative distinction.

What time lost in universality when it ceased to be absolute it gained in con-creteness through its new association with space. And this is all the more para-doxical since it was the very insertion of time into the spatial continuum that first permitted physical theory (notably thermodynamics) to proceed to the theory of

26 "Every object reveals by its lines how it would resolve itself by following the tendencies of its forces," *Archivi,* vol. I, p. 106.

27 This period included an array of movement studies in which images are multiplied to con-form to the optical theory of retinal persistence. The famous *Guinzalio in moto* (1912) is one example. The idea of halting and spatializing movement rather than temporalizing and mobilizing static form further underscores futurism's fundamental difference from Cubism.

3.2

Umberto Boccioni, *Unique Forms of Continuity in Space,* 1913

the field and to abandon the limiting notion of material points. It could be said then that time replaced the physical particle, and in so doing introduced *consistency* as a characteristic of the field, where before there was only space and the mechanical need to posit material carriers.

In this sense the thermo- and electrodynamic field is always a field of consistency, a strange new entity because equally abstract and concrete; it does not exist materially yet it exists everywhere and all at once wherever there is force or matter. The field of consistency, to quote Boccioni's phrase, is "the unique form that gives continuity in space."

Force-lines can now be seen as the abstract units that articulate the object's relation to its consistent field. And as we have already seen this relation is one of immanence, or at least of a becoming-immanent. Force-lines (vectors) are to the field (space-time) what the old line was to classical mechanics. They are time- imbued and animate world-substance into plastic zones. Plasticity is a property of these world-lines.

With the field characterized in this way there is no conceivable real occurrence that would not mobilize the abstract consistency to form concrete plastic events. The field, however, does not preexist, but is always present as a virtuality, determined within and by the plastic *events* that articulate it and render it actual.[28] "We reject any a-priori reality; this is what divides us from the Cubists . . ." (Ar. I, p. 145).

By incorporating space so deeply into the body of time as to change its nature, futurist theory, like that of Einstein, Bergson, and others, undertook to resolve the problem of Being through the concept of a continuous multiplicity.[29] From this fact arises what may be the single most important contribution of Futurist theory to our modern conception of the world. The physics of space-time, one could say, gave rise to a fundamental new entity—the event—as well as the new geometry through which it could be expressed. In its own way futurist theory made of plastic dynamism a scientific hypothesis and an artistic technique, allowing this selfsame event to emerge in its full materiality as the sole substance and medium of humankinds's intervention in the world.

The modern world, then, will no longer be resolvable into separate and autonomous realms of value or meaning, that is, economic, social, and phenomenal. Futurist plasticity is above all a pragmatics that reflects all phenomena—events—through the single screen of a real material consistency. Thus the "swing of a pendulum or the moving hands of a clock, the in–and–out motion of a piston inside a cylinder, the engaging and disengaging of two cogwheels, the fury of a flywheel or the whirling of a propeller, are all plastic and pictorial elements" whose shape and effects can now be diagrammed in their continuity, in their multiple connections to the ever-differentiating outside with which they invariably form a single substance.

La Città nuova

The last-conscripted member of the prewar Futurist brigade (the group's composition, ideological predilections, and credibility would be altered radically after

---

28 Themes developed throughout chaps. 4 and 5.

29 It is a commonplace of twentieth-century physics that "Einstein did not believe in time." The statement is true, however, only in the most trivial sense. For although he did not see time as real in the sense of being irreversible, he did see it as concrete, plastic, and active (i.e., "evental"). This stems undoubtedly from his reluctance to grant time anything beyond a purely mathematical existence, albeit stripped of its metaphysical and absolute, that is, classical Newtonian, character. Einsteinian time may not have been endowed with an "arrow" but it did possess real physical agency; more so, at any rate, than the hypothetical ether that, at a theoretical level, it replaced.

3.3

Design for the new central railway station in Milan, side façade, 1912 (Period photograph).
Como, Musei Civici

the war) was the Lombardo architect Antonio Sant'Elia. Born in Como in 1888,
Sant'Elia was trained in Milan and Bologna, where he received his diploma in
1912, before returning to Milan to set up a practice and, soon after, to establish an
association with a group of architects known as the *Nuove Tendenze.* Sant'Elia's
earliest work (prior to Milan, 1912) was heavily inflected by the highly orna-
mented *stile Liberty* whose popularity was then only beginning to wane.[30] In the
two years following his move to Milan he executed a large number of drawings
and urban concept studies, largely speculative in nature, which were first grouped
together under the heading *Milano 2000,* and later, when exhibited publicly with
the *Nuove Tendenze* group in 1914, were collected under the title *La Città nuova.*
The exhibition catalog contained statements from each of the group's members,
including a preface by Sant'Elia on the tasks of modern architecture. Though
Sant'Elia was not yet an official member of the Futurist movement, this text,
called simply *Messaggio,* was undeniably futurist in tone and was adapted a few
months later, with minor alterations, as the *Manifesto of Futurist Architecture.*[31]

30 Note the first projects for the Milano stazione (there would be five in all); see figure 3.3.

31 The texts of the *Messaggio* and the statements by other members of the *Nuove Tendenze* as
well as the final text of the *Manifesto of Futurist Architecture* are in the *Archivi,* vol. 1,
pp. 122–127 (members' statements), and pp. 81–85 (Manifesto). Separate texts of the *Messaggio* and the Manifesto can also be found in *Controspazio,* vols. 4–5 (April–May 1971),
pp. 17–19. Whether Sant'Elia was or was not a true futurist, and whether he was or was not

The *Messaggio* opens dramatically, effecting the first of several fundamental transpositions of the traditionally conceived architectural object into evermore complex, abstract, yet more deeply and historically authentic configurations. Consider the opening passage with its two opposing notions of history:

> The problem of modern architecture is not a problem of rearranging its lines; not a question of finding new mouldings, new architraves, for doors and windows; nor of replacing columns, pilasters and corbels with caryatids, hornets and frogs; not a question of leaving a façade bare brick or facing it with stone or plaster; in a word, it has nothing to do with defining formalistic differences between the new buildings and old ones. But to raise the new-built structure on a sound plan, gleaning every benefit of science and technology, settling nobly every demand of our habits and our spirits, rejecting all that is heavy, grotesque and unsympathetic to us (tradition, style, aesthetics, proportion), establishing new forms, new lines, new reasons for existence, solely out of the special conditions of Modern living, and its projection as aesthetic value in our sensibilities.
>
> Such an architecture cannot be subject to any law of historical continuity. It must be as new as our state of mind is new, and the contingencies of our moment in history.
>
> The art of building has been able to evolve through time and pass from style to style while maintaining the general character of architecture unchanged, because in history there have been numerous changes of taste brought on by shifts of religious conviction or the successions of political regimes, but few occasioned by profound changes in our conditions of life, changes that discard or overhaul the old conditions, as have the discovery of natural laws, the perfection of technical methods, the rational and scientific use of materials.

Denounced from the outset is the kind of history that is sedimented and transmitted in the evolution of taste and styles, the narrative of succession, memory and encrusted representations. This history of "*differenze formali . . . sogetta a una*

---

the sole author of these texts, has given rise to many tedious debates. But that the ideas in question were those of Sant'Elia has never been put in doubt (cf. Banham, pp. 127–128; Martin, pp. 188–189), which is all that is relevant for the present context. For a bibliography on these debates, see *La Martinella di Milano* vol. 12, no. 10 (October 1958), pp. 526–539.

legge di continuità storica" is renounced in the name of a more authentic and more comprehensive historicity rooted in the "*condizioni dell'ambiente*" and the "*contigenze del nostro momento storico.*" This disqualification of the past, and the filiative relations whose tenuous claim is to link it with the present, resonates, however superficially, with Nietzsche's repudiation, made forty years earlier, of the disadvantages of history for life[32] though in a more profound sense, it resonates with the Nietzschean repudiation *in general* of history as repository and transmitter of anything like absolute truth or meanings.

Yet the sudden and quite radical assault on historical epistemology as it was waged systematically by Nietzsche and adopted by the futurists does not in itself exhaust either of these enterprises' claims to modernity. Of greater importance on this count is the particular kinds of terrain they opened up: for Nietzsche the affirmation of active affects (of which "forgetting" was an integral one) resolved historical time into both a pragmatics and an aesthetics of force (Will to Power); for the futurists history became inseparable from that transverse line which links concrete social phenomena—technology, science, art, politics—and embeds them indifferently in material life. In one case as in the other the valorization of life itself endowed it with the character of an aesthetic phenomenon; the metaphysical *telos* of history gave way to a reality that was, and indeed had to be, constructed anew at every moment, and from within.[33] For the futurists, "Man's" new privilege was to have no privilege at all vis-a-vis reality or Being: his history and time were no longer separate from the history of material nor the vicissitudes of force. Tradition was seen as not only disadvantageous for life, to use Nietzsche's phrase, but as fraudulent; it offered a metaphysics of perpetuity where really there exist only natural laws, a bourgeois academicism of representations where in fact there is only the chaotic and senseless circumstance of force, and finally the mysticism of lineal continuity—influence, transmission, origin, causality—in place of the palpable immanence of the conjunctural, the aleatory, and the simultaneous. Historical consciousness was losing its metaphysical infrastructure—a development entirely at one with the superseding of classical time in physics—only to reaffirm itself through an insistence on a profound historical consciousness of the *present,* a historical consciousness of the world and

32 Friedrich Nietzsche, *The Use and Abuse of History for Life* (Indianapolis: Bobbs-Merrill, 1949).

33 "Our houses will last less time than we do, and every generation will have to make its own." *Manifesto of Futurist Architecture.*

life *as such*, rather than through representations derived from its self-constituting grand narratives.[34]

It is no surprise that the rest of the *Messaggio* concerns itself with the specific denunciation of these forms of discredited historical representation:

> We have lost the sense of the monumental, the massive, the static, and we have enriched our sensibilities with a taste for the light and the practical. We no longer feel ourselves to be the men of the cathedrals and the ancient moot halls, but men of the Grand Hotels, railway stations, giant roads, colossal harbors, covered markets, glittering arcades, reconstruction areas and salutary slum clearances. . . . [W]e must abolish the monumental and the decorative, we must resolve the problem of modern architecture without cribbing photographs of China, Persia and Japan nor imbecilizing ourselves with Vitruvian rules. . . . We must depreciate the importance of façades, transfer questions of taste out of the field of petty moldings, fiddling capitals and insignificant porticos. . . . It is time to have done with funereal commemorative architecture; architecture must be something more vital than that, and we can best begin to attain that something by blowing sky-high all those monuments. . . .

Architectural time for Sant'Elia can no longer be that of historical styles— effete, academic, and truncated from the natural forces that were once the source of its life—nor is it the apocryphal time of monuments. Architecture is no longer a vehicle expressing the spurious contents of a singular ("grand") history-in-the-making, no longer a constellation of signs operating externally to culture through the intermediary of a code, but an entirely internal and inhering *mechanism* inseparable from the body of the world and operating on it from within.[35] Thus the classic futurist theme of elements and materials becomes crucial once again. Wood, stone, marble, and brick will be replaced by reinforced concrete, iron,

34 On narrative vs. pragmatic history, see Jean-François Lyotard, *The Postmodern Condition: A Report on Knowledge,* trans. G. Bennington and B. Massumi (Minneapolis, University of Minnesota Press, 1984). Futurist theory may be read as the first important instance of a pure pragmatics in modernist culture.

35 "I affirm that just as the ancients drew their inspiration from the elements of the natural world we too—materially and spiritually artificial—must draw our inspiration from the elements of the radically new mechanical world we have created, of which architecture must be the most perfect expression, the most complete synthesis and the most effective artistic integration." *Messaggio.*

glass, textile fibers, and anything else that helps obtain "the maximum of elasticity and lightness." The nobility of the conventional architectural mediums is undermined; instead, architecture follows sculpture toward a more promiscuous (immanent) relation to material reconceived now according to the framework elaborated by Boccioni, as a deployment of world-substance, or as an operator of whatever (relations, materials, forces, laws) is contemporary and close at hand. At the same time the tendency toward lightness and kinematic plasticity brings the traditional architectural mass to a greater approximation with force, allowing the research of forms to give way to an emphasis on configurations.[36] Architecture undergoes a revaluation in terms of a new state of knowledge and technology, and a new constellation of needs and desires (material, political, and spiritual) while simultaneously assuming its purest artistic role:

> True architecture is not an arid combination of practicality and utility, but remains art, that is, synthesis and expression.

Though Sant'Elia did not realize a single building during his mature (post-Liberty) period, he did produce a sufficient number of eloquent studies and drawings[37] that, together with the *Messaggio* and the *Manifesto,* constitute a rigorous and programmatic reconception of architectural and urbanist practice whose influence would be felt for decades and whose implications are still being realized today.

36 This theme, among many others first adumbrated by Sant'Elia, was most powerfully echoed in Laszlo Moholy-Nagy's *Von Materiel zu Architektur* (1929). "The fact that kinetic sculpture exists leads to the recognition of a space condition which is not the result of the position of static volumes, but consists of visible and invisible forces, e.g., of the phenomena of motion, and the forms that such motion creates. . . . The phrase 'material is energy' will have significance for architecture by *emphasizing relation, instead of mass.*" See *The New Vision* (New York: Wittenborn, Schultz, 1947), especially pp. 41–63. Of great importance here as well are El Lissitzky, *A. and Pangeometry* (1925), in *Russia: An Architecture for World Revolution* (Cambridge, MA: MIT Press, 1984), and Iakov Chernikhov's pedagogical notebooks (1927–33), in *Chernikhov: Fantasy and Construction* (London: A. D. Editions, 1984).

37 *Antonio Sant'Elia. Catologo della Mostra Permanente a cura de Luciano Caramel e Alberto Longati* (Como: Villa Communale dell'Olmo, 1962). The catalog lists nearly 300 drawings. Many of the drawings listed in this work and a host of others from other sources have been made available in an English edition; cf. *Sant'Elia,* Milan, Cooper Union/Mondadori, Milan.

The drawings of this period (1913–1914) will be examined in two main groups: the morphological studies in which single architectonic structures are explored—lighthouses, turbine stations, hangars, bridges, and other nonspecific structures named simply *Edifici* and *Dinamismi architectonici*—and those that more explicitly develop relations within whole regions of the city-manifold. In the first group one sees the elaboration of a formal vocabulary whose themes and implications are realized only at a second order or molar level—the city—whose concrete substance they indeed comprise yet whose units and ultimate organization they in no way reflect. The form studies will be examined first and the more complex city drawings afterward.

One is inevitably struck, when examining Sant'Elia's sketches, by the extraordinary momentum of the draftsmanship, the obsessively precise freehand style with its swift, simplified yet deliberate lines, at once restrained and expressive, volatile and refined. Few historians have failed to remark on his predilection for the extreme oblique setting of masses and the close viewpoint, which together artificially intensify perspectival effects.[38] The orthogonal lines of the depicted buildings pass almost invariably beyond the drawing's frame. This unusual technique makes the depicted forms appear as molecular fragments belonging to greater but indeterminate wholes; the impression is that of masses framed hastily and close up, further suggesting the brute immediacy of photography. Also, one notes the borrowing of a device common to nineteenth-century painting, but just beginning to discover new modes of application in the nascent art of cinema: that of allowing the contents of a frame, no matter how spare or "innocent," to become fraught with whatever occurs or exists beyond it. There is considerable method to this technique: the refusal to make available all the information about a building structure through its visual apprehension shifts the problem of its "meaning" from the expression of interior contents to an exterior syntax of combination and connection. The buildings are often remarkably asymmetrical—despite the constant use of symmetrically apposed elements at the molecular level; rather they seem to have positive and negative ends, male and female interlocking parts, open and closed elements distributed almost randomly over their surface; and most importantly, a single building complex deploys its several façades in such a way that they have no apparent relation to one another, but remain completely autonomous with respect to the "building"

38 Fewer than ten percent of all the drawings employ frontal or attenuated oblique settings. The best descriptive study of Sant'Elia's form language is Paulo Portoghesi, "Il Linguaggio di Sant'Elia," in *Controspazio* , vols. 4–5 (April–May 1971), pp. 27–30.

conceived as an integral organism. These latter are determined rather by specific functions—passage, connection, transmission, reception—defined in terms of specifically located or immediately adjacent external elements—roads, gang-ways, elevator stacks, landing strips. This general tendency of *atomization* of the building's traditionally irreducible unity is supported further by an array of secondary devices.

The simplest of the morphological studies describe elongated, ascending, elliptical masses either embedded in, or partially penetrated by, rectangular slabs, which together align in paradoxical configurations as if the result of silent, frictionless collisions. Paradoxical here is the combination of the extraordinarily sovereign and ballistic power of the collided forms, and their unexpected suppleness and permeability, their seeming lack of material resistance to one another.[39] Paradoxical semiotically as well, for the blatant interference of forms, violently splitting and passing through one another, could logically be translated internally it seems only by introducing the most vertiginous disjunctions and intermittence to their lived space. These studies always contain combinations of both tapering and rectilinear forms whose pronounced differences of inertia create effects of virtual separation and vertical momentum. This kinetic tension is further underscored by the smooth unadorned concrete surfaces on which the accelerated play of light confronts the eye less with a coherent object than with a field or glacis unencumbered by the friction of detail, texture, or articulated features. The careful combining and wedging together of forms produces a controlled interplay of right angles with oblique surfaces, battered walls with promontory-like abutments. What remains is a simple system of glyptic faces and sharply pronounced arrises whose courses, for all their breakneck precipitousness, provide the eye's only formal guides. Add to this the explicitly narrative "contraforte" theme of the canted surfaces pressing back, and often through other perpendicular ones, shoring up as if to resist great external masses or forces, and one can already intuit the presence of a more comprehensive city vision, based not on aggregation and juxtaposition of separate parts but a differentiating field of *pressures* with its corresponding mechanical language of resistance and transmission.

39 This device is already embodied in Sant'Elia's drafting style. Lines consistently overshoot the edges of the forms they describe (this had yet to become a standard affectation of architectural rendering—the indexical allusion to drafting tools), further suggesting the nodal character of "form" as if this latter were constituted only by perpetually remigrating force-lines.

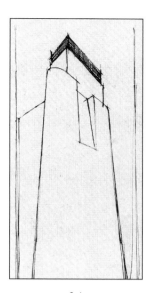

3.4
Lighthouse tower, 1913. Como, Musei Civici

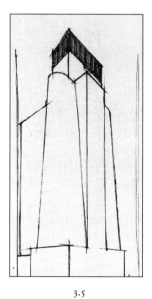

3.5
Lighthouse tower, 1913. Como, Musei Civici

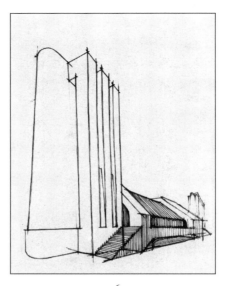

3.6
Study for a building (factory), 1913. Como, Musei Civici

At the simple morphological level, this language expresses a theory of individuated architecture as servomechanism, where individual units are mere operators or commutation devices within a much larger assembly whose greater intensity they modulate and control. The elements of this language include conduits, circuitry, rhythmized cadences and progressions including rotation, nesting, stepbacks, tapers, telescoping, and ranked columnar forms, as well as the more literal machine vocabulary of jigs, stops, and templates. Figures 3.6 and 3.7 demonstrate the rhetorical use of the conduit theme (over and above literal applications, e.g., bridges, gangways, electrical wires) acting less to buttress than to marshal and translate forces from one section to another. Figure 3.7 attains a particularily high level of abstraction by forming its own independent (short-) circuit in which the flying beams (A) support—or house—a perforated upright structure (B), themselves supported by arch (C), which in turn both transects and forms the absent base of the main structure (B).

In this *mise-en-abyme* system, where every element seems in part only fortuitously there, in part *already* there relaying forces received from other similiar elements, the earth as first principle or ground seems no longer to exist at all; rather, there is a homeostatic system of circulating currents, which, thanks to the vision-

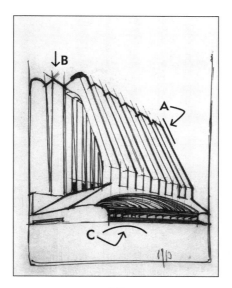

3.7
Elevation of a building with gallery, 1913. Como, Musei Civici

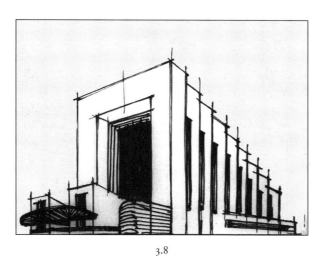

3.8
Study for a building or hangar, 1913. Como, Musei Civici

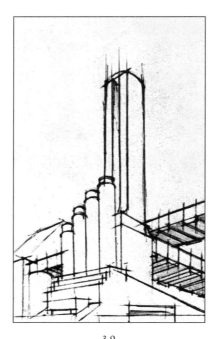

3.9

Study for a building with bridges, 1913. Como, Musei Civici

ary use of reinforced concrete, seems virtually untouched by gravity or any other *absolute* (grounded or original) cause.[40] These same drawings, as well as figure 3.11, employ repeated columnar forms, though not in the service of the traditional imperatives of proportion and spatial patterning. Here their positive/negative intervals are not static but belong to a more procedural sequence of intermittent coupling like the rabbetted digits on a mortise hinge that either espouse one another to form an unbroken surface or rotate fully beyond (fig. 3.11), opening onto other configurations or conjunctions. The themes of rotation and interpenetration belong to a more general tendency that articulates all conjunctions dynamically. Figure 3.12 provides what is perhaps the most acute example of this tendency, unashamedly miming the conventions of machine assembly with its protruding jig plate acting as guide for an ostensibly movable cylinder and the clear implications of: flexion—the jig's acute angle; torsion—the cylinder's counterpoint to its inert squared-off base; and friction—the interaction of shaft and

40 See the discussion of immanent cause below.

3.10

Study for a building (with revealed nesting), 1913. Como, Musei Civici

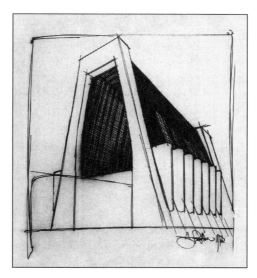

3.11

Study for a large building (hangar or covered market), 1913. Como, Musei Civici

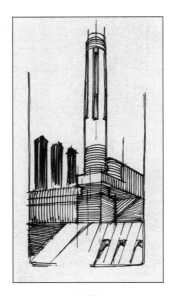

3.12

Study for an industrial building (power station), 1913. Como, Musei Civici

template. Yet it may be said that Sant'Elia's is uniquely *an architecture of conjunction,* one that does not posit forms primordially, but rather stratifying *systems* whose expansivity and acenteredness preclude classical individuated expression. Here the very notion of conjunction takes on its maximal significance: these are conjunctions not of buildings or isolated structures but of imbricating systems, both at the molecular level of interpenetrating guided, rotating, or sliding masses, and at the molar level of urban megasystems of transport, hydro-electric and informational lattices.

The combination of the system theory of the urban realm with its dynamic interpretation as a pressurized field gives rise to an assembly language based on impregnation, with system elements existing simultaneously, and at least virtually, everywhere, emerging to actualization only within nodes (conjunctions) of mutually interfering systems. Figure 3.13 literalizes this technique formally within a single structure, where three separate plans superimpose like three individual *dispositifs* or running systems on the same site—a point-grid corresponding to the chimney stacks, the square plan base of the teepee structure, and the elliptical collector that seals them all into a solid agglomerate. No one system ever predominates over the others, and though together they undoubtedly form a unit, singly

3.13
Study for a building, 1913. Como, Musei Civici

they maintain a certain autonomy and separateness owing to their extension and resonance within broader, more comprehensive networks. Interference, like the sporadic invasion of electronic images by foreign frequencies, becomes here a positive expression of polymetric spatial complexity allowing several disparate architectures (say, telecommunications towers, elevator stacks, tram systems) to articulate themselves in a single block of matter.

Thus the dominant technique for ordering the various chains within this multilayered systemic space is a special use of transparency different from the literal and phenomenal versions endemic to visual modernism. Here the transparency is functional and explicitly concrete: masses are placed seemingly only to be pierced, stratified, or disaggregated—in other words, as passive and inarticulate carriers of the movement-bearing systems that traverse and penetrate them, or else huge framelike chassis baring their lading like skeletons yielding to the newly invented X-ray gaze that the futurists so emulated. Though articulated in often grandiose and imperious sweeps, these masses, as I have noted, are in fact remarkably plastic and porous; they are easily incised and punctured, as in the window system of figure 3.14 which is literally punched out of a single inert horizontal slab—note the strong, literal implication of perpendicular momentum in the impact-absorbing triangular niches—which, once transformed by this operation, can be read as a lattice-frame.

At every level the morphological studies assume, rather than represent, an extended field of movement and circulating forces. Each element relates primarily

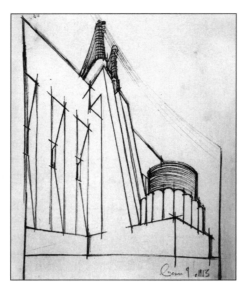

3.14
Study for a power station, 1913. Como, Musei Civici

to the "horizontal" chain of which it is a link and secondarily to the transverse or vertical system that concretizes it and weds it, however incompletely, to a discrete and grounded form. It is here, more than in any other body of futurist work, that the laws of Boccioni's physical theory found their full and unqualified application. It is as if the very nature of an art work, as understood by even the most radical avant-gardes of the time, were yet too primitive or ontologically conventional to express the conditions of a revolutionized cosmos. What clearly was needed were not new objects, but a new orientation toward a phenomenal field of events and interactions—not objects, but the abstract regimes of force that organize and deploy them. For Sant'Elia this field was the emerging modern metropolis.

Just as the morphological studies drew their principle inspiration from engineering structures—electrical turbine stations, hangars, factories, lighthouses—the large-scale studies for *La Città nuova* developed out of a series of projects to redesign the Milan Central Station. An early study, figure 3.15, still bears stylistic resonances from the Liberty period, with its denser, less precise expressionistic rendering, its primitive, organic use of materials, which gives the almost palpable sensation of weight settling toward the lower regions, and a noticeable

3.15
Station for Trains and Airplanes, 1914. Como, Musei Civici

lack of horizontal or homeostatic tension or pressure, lending the project an almost old-fashioned, earth-based rhetorical dimension. The legitimacy of such
an impression, however, comes to an abrupt end, for in many ways this scheme
already breaks substantially with previous conceptions of urban planning. The
most spectacular innovation is unquestionably the airplane landing strip built in
to the upper level of the station. Here the central thoroughfare, which traditionally ascends to and grandly frames the station's main entry, is decked over to
allow for vertical air access. The ease with which this scandalous idea is accom-
modated, though it is certainly naive from today's standpoint, is evident from
the nonchalance of the parked air vehicles on the runway, not to mention the
way the buildings that flank the Viale Vittore Pisani are allowed to frame the
runway at such close distance. This feature sets up another element crucial to
Sant'Elia's scheme, namely, its multilayered acentricity. In this exterior perspective alone, one counts seven levels of thoroughfare, not including the radio towers, elevators or funiculars, each superimposed like porous grids seeping and
flowing into one another. The project exaggerates and develops the nature of its
object—a literal commutation point—at once disaggregating its spurious but
conventional unity, and multiplying the surfaces of connection within it. It does

this by willfully embracing the city block into which it has been literally sub-merged, continuing the city's existing lines of flow (streets, tram routes, passages) through its own, pausing only to effect additional convergences by means of ramps, catwalks and steps.

It is difficult to say whether the station system is embedded in the city's fabric or it is the city that runs freely through the station. The novelty of this arrange-ment has nothing to do with the ambiguity of place produced by such dispersion nor with any mere de-centering of once integral architectural forms, but with a more fundamental overhaul that permits one to conceive of the architectural ob-ject not as a form but as an agglomeration and interaction of *functions,* each with its proper series of system elements whose architectonic value and role are defined only secondarily, and wholly in relation to these functions. Thus the Milan sta-tion becomes less a "building" than a field of convergence and linkup for many systems of flow, including air transport, trains, cars, radio signals, trams, funicu-lars, pedestrians, and necessarily all the secondary flows they host—money, goods, information. In this sense, the "station" comes to be seen as an allegorical representation of the city itself, and necessarily, in terms of the transformation of "place" into a swirling manifold of circuitry, switching points and deterritorial-ized, nongrounded flows.

In figure 3.16 we see a later, clarified version of the station project (whose title incidentally now gives priority to its airport function) where the conventional straining arches have given way to a taut linearity made possible by "new materi-als." The flanking towers of the main mass have been split into two slabs and mor-tised into a more finely divided and variegated base system, and finally the heavy monumental quality of the original is refined throughout to more slender plat-forms and laminae allowing the expression of ductwork to emerge as the domi-nant visual theme. This reworking also incorporates many of the assembly motifs from the morphological studies, principally the oscillating beats of serial elements with their implied rotation, folding and sliding. Finally, one should not fail to re-mark the unusual treatment of the plan in both these drawings, for it is identical to much of what we have seen in the morphology studies with respect to the treat-ment of façades. They are treated indifferently as pierceable slabs of matter, in-stantly transformable through perforation into space-frames revealing yet other systems (or only potential ones) beyond and beneath. In other words, the plan el-ements have a construction logic and appearance identical to the elevations, giv-ing the "node theory" of construction here a truly literal, three-dimensional validity. This total indifference to absolute (external) determinations of place and direction has the effect of further denying the earth and its "essential" forces and

3.16
Station for trains and airplanes, with cable cars and elevators on three street levels. 1914.
Como, Musei Civici

values both as the metaphysical ground of architecture and the social processes it
modulates.

> The house . . . must rise from the brink of a tumultuous abyss; the street it-
> self will no longer lie like a doormat at the level of the thresholds, but will
> plunge storeys deep into the earth, gathering up the traffic of the metropolis
> connected for necessary transfers to metal catwalks and highspeed conveyor
> belts.
>
> We must exploit our roofs and put our basements to work . . . dig out our
> streets and piazzas, raise the level of the city, reorder the earth's crust and re-
> duce it to a servant of our every need and fancy. (*Messaggio*)

The most powerful and fully developed of the *Città nuova* studies is the drawing entitled "La Città nuova: Apartment complex with external elevators, galleria, covered passage, three street levels (tramlines, autoway, metallic pedestrian
gangway), light beacons and wireless telegraph" (fig. 3.17). The elaborate subhead-
ing well emphasizes the exterior orientation and almost incidental nature of the

3.17

La Città nuova: Apartment complex with external elevators, galleria, covered passageway, with three street levels (tramlines, automobile lanes, metallic pedestrial gangway), light beacons, and wireless telegraph, 1914. Como, Musei Civici

building itself with respect to the "public works" structures. Of all the elements in the drawing, in fact, only the residential block (owing to its sheer inertia) seems to lack autonomy of purpose, becoming a passive receiver of vectors filiating in every direction and at best their mechanical or infrastructural support. What, after all, *could* remain, now that its entire organic semiotic system has been laid asunder: the once grand or at least centralizing and frontalizing entrance has given way to a promiscuous panoply of multiple perforations, the "palatial" stairwells torn from its bowels and reconstituted outside as mechanical lifts that "swarm up the façades like serpents of glass and iron," the entire enclosing structure now subordinated to a minor role as collector or distributor of primary currents. The façade itself never assumes an integral form, owing in part to the lack of organizational ornament that the manifesto so vehemently eschewed, in part to the atomizing effect of the step-back assembly, which defines each floor as a separate and apparently slidable, autonomous module, and in part to the "frame and mesh" construction that highlights the bold chassis trusses and elevator stacks, leaving the façades simply to recede as mere fenestrated infill (see especially fig. 3.18). Figure 3.19, which depicts a secondary pedestrian byway (an avenue between two backing buildings), shows

3.18

Study for the Città nuova: Apartment house with external elevators on three street levels, 1914.
Milano, Paride Accetti collection

the affected preeminence of the newly externalized, and constituted, elevator stack presented as an autonomous architectural integer in its own right, here totally disjunct from the building (to which building does it belong?) and embedded in and linked up with the exterior manifold of street levels and its pedestrian and vehicular flows. Thus streets, roads, utility stacks, and conveyor ramps are now seen as so many concrete lines, no longer simply secondary integers, connectors of architectural objects and urban blocks, but the very elemental units of which the city is composed.

The devaluation of the contained unit with its expressive façade can be seen as part of a more general devaluation of all enclosing planes in favor of superinvested surfaces. Roofs, for example, are now recoded with gardens, landing strips, beacons, and electronic transmission equipment; vertical surfaces now support bridges, balconies, gangways, often baying open to permit passage for traffic, or reconsolidating to bear the weight (and form) of a traveling arc or spanning I-beam. But perhaps the most important revaluation of all can be seen in figure 3.20, in which a neon publicity panel, explicitly built into the façade of an apartment tower, gives expression, perhaps for the very first time, to the idea that

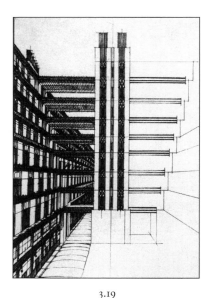

3.19

Study for the Città nuova: Secondary street for pedestrians with elevator in middle, 1914.
Milano, Paride Accetti collection

information dissemination processes (ads, signs, graffiti) constitute nothing less than a *material* intervention in the urban continuum. By adding another totally heterogeneous material to those enumerated in the manifesto (glass, iron, textile), the introduction of language—and presumably later, of images—into the urban/architectural domain would, besides having far-reaching consequences for the Russian and Dutch avant-garde of the 1920s and the later Italian work of architects such as Depero, Dazi, and others (fig. 3.21), create the conditions for the truly polymorphous, procedural—action- or information-based—architectures that began to emerge in the late 1950s and 1960s.[41]

This same study shows the typical *gradinata* or graduated setback characterizing nearly all the highrise apartment blocs, and the externalized elevator tower motif that gives salient expression to the city's third-dimensional axis, a feature

41 In this category one would certainly place the major exponents of "paper architecture," such as Archigram, Superstudio, early Coop Himmelblau, but also the work of Ant Farm, the International Situationists, and artists like Robert Smithson and Dan Graham, whose use of mirrors, video, photography, and print helped effect architecture's definitive migration into abstract space.

3.20
Apartment building with graduated setback, external elevators, and neon advertising, 1914.
Como, Musei Civici

that had certainly never found such full development in any previous town-planning scheme.[42] For this reason it would be wrong to attribute the egregious lack of plan studies in Sant'Elia's oeuvre—and the *Città nuova* project in particular—to haste, superficial reflection, or lack of technical rigor.[43] The lack of plans is at least in part a positive expression of a new form of organization of space, one

42 This is perhaps the time to mention some of the visionary schemes of planners and architects like Antoine Moilin, Henri-Jules Borie, Charles Lamb, and Hugh Ferriss. All of these proposed important schemes based on a superimposed transportation net of roads and aerial tracks and catwalks. But these schemes remained always that—superimpositions necessarily exterior to the objects they were meant to link. Sant'Elia was the first to establish movement or circulation as a first principle that does not so much act upon a substratum as meld with and mobilize the city's actual substance (including its architectural elements).

43 All of these charges have been made, either in criticism or in apology. Not atypical of the silliness of some of these claims was the publication of three desultory sketches by Sant'Elia, relating to Milan's town plan accompanied by the historian's claim, "We now show that Sant'Elia was also a practical townplanner." See "Antonio Sant'Elia," presented by Leonardo Mariani in *L'Architettura,* vol. 4, no. 9 (January 1959).

3.21

Fortunato Depero, *Futurist Campari Pavillion,* 1933

that resists reduction to two dimensions, and to the conventional planar construction method that derives three-dimensional representations by combining vertical elevations with their horizontal plans.[44] I have already called attention to the undifferentiated treatment of horizontal ("plan") and vertical plane elements in Sant'Elia's work, where they are deployed indifferently as surfaces capable of infinite investment, penetrable to a limitless depth, and revealing ever more laminae beneath and behind. Add to this the notions of the pressurized field, the preeminence of linear, vectorial units, the atomization of molar forms, the themes of circulation, sliding, frictionless impacts, and wave phemonena like interference and flow, and it soon becomes clear that one is dealing with a space characterized more by hydrodynamics and laminar flows than by statics, metrics, or the physics of solids.[45] Because such a space is characterized by a nonhierarchical organization—think of a coherent system such as a mosquito cloud, which has no center,

44 This technique is the basis of quattrocento perspective theory and originates with Alberti's *De Pictura.*

45 An interesting scientific and philosophical history of hydrodynamics in which many of the above themes are developed is Michel Serres, *La naissance de la physique dans le texte de Lucrèce.* (Paris: Minuit, 1977).

ground, or exterior cause[46]—any of its sections, whether horizontal or vertical, could express at best only its own localized configurations or events. In other words, the very idea of a plan(e) would be rendered obsolete; any information it might contain would still have no necessary repercussions on any other part of the building—and besides, which level could be privileged as matrix or master?

Paolo Portoghesi has characterized the relations of forms in Sant'Elia's work to "jets of water in a fountain," and Reyner Banham has written that Sant'Elia was "the first to give modern architecture "the habit . . . of thinking in terms of circulation, not vistas."[47] The prevalent use of parabolas, ellipses, and compressed helical forms, while undoubtedly owing something to their Liberty origin, have undergone a profound formal reorientation,[48] now suggesting an arrangement of forces in disequilibrium, crisis, and flux. Conventional town plans, organized on axes or in regular (or irregular) metrical bays have here given way to an almost stochastic distribution of elements, where material seemingly gravitates and sediments in random centers of turbulence. If the complex embedded structures are understood in this way it becomes easy to account for the centrifugal and centripetal effects suggested by the refrains of orbitting and constellated masses, the constant nesting motif, and the gradual tapering and lightening of forms as they develop toward their extremities. In what could easily have been a maquette for *La Città nuova,* Boccioni's prodigious "Sviluppo di una bottiglia nello spazio" can be read as a tour de force on the hydraulic/turbulence theme (fig. 3.22).

The most significant innovation brought about by this "new" hydrodynamic model[49] of circulation was the superseding of the most classical, reductionist

46 Pierre Rosenstiehl and Jean Petitot, "Automate asocial et systemes acentrés," *Communications* 22 (1974). The authors propose mathematical models to account for communication and propagation effects in nonhierarchically organized systems, a historically interesting early work in automata theory.

47 Paolo Portoghesi, "Il linguaggio di Sant'Elia," Reyner Banham, "Futurism and Modern Architecture," *Royal Institute of British Architects* (February 1957); and "Sant'Elia," *Architectural Review* (May 1955).

48 C. G. Argan, "Il pensiero critico di Sant'Elia," in *Dopo Sant'Elia* (Milano: Editoriale Domus, 1935).

49 The hydrodynamic model of course is not new, but goes back at least to Archimedes. As I have already stressed, modernity is not so much about the "new" as the "untimely," in the sense of Nietzsche's *unzeitgemasse* meditations. "Untimely" (and modern) is the emergence of a world-system based on relations of force rather than the qualities of form. On the untimely, see ch. 5, note 57, below.

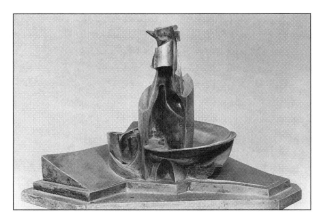

3.22

Umberto Boccioni, *Development of a Bottle in Space,* 1912

(though enduring) notion of *site* as an essential, causal, or preexisting substratum. We have already seen to what extent space for the Greeks depended on a substratum of real material bodies. For Aristotle space was never dissociated from the notion of place (*topos*), which he defined as an envelope or boundary between an enclosed and an enclosing body. "The continuity of space is transformed [in Aristotelian physics] from a geometrical and ideal determination to a kind of objective determination. The continuity of space is not, as in the idealistic theories of space, founded in 'form' and in its 'principle'; rather it follows from what space is as a substantial and objective entity, as a substratum."[50] To the Aristotelian *topos* one can oppose Lucretius's *nunc hinc, nunc illinc* (now here, now there), which describes the random appearance of the clinamen (swerve, differentiation) in the universal cascade of atoms. Here *place* lacks all determination save as a relation of pure difference within an indistinct field. The event, in other words, is there where space is suddenly differentiated from itself.[51] Thus even Le Corbusier's pylons later did no more than affirm the classical site, either by hygienically clearing it in an ultimate gesture of homage or by positing it, in relation to the architec-

50 Ernst Cassirer, *The Individual and the Cosmos in Renaissance Philosophy* (Philadelphia: University of Pennsylvania Press, 1963), pp. 181–182.

51 Lucretius, *On Nature* (Indianapolis: Bobbs-Merrill, 1965), book 2; and M. Serres, *Naissance de la physique.*

CHAPTER 3

ture, as an opposing term.[52] The site, and the hierarchical figure/ground relation it supports, has in *La Città nuova* begun to give way to a thickening, indeed to an all-encompassing univocity, where the flows that compose its space are continuous with those actually forming the bodies within it.

What physical theory in science and aesthetics had managed to express in a conceptual framework (neither Hildebrand, Rodin, nor Boccioni ever found the definitive sculptural solutions to match their ambitions in this area) Sant'Elia was the first to furnish with a concrete and sensible body. The thermo- and electrodynamic theory at the turn of the century, as we have seen, already contained a preliminary notion of the field, made possible then by the introduction of time into the spatial continuum. The hydrodynamic themes of *La Città nuova*—the vectors, the concatenating sequences, in a word, its flow—also embody time in a way fundamentally different from previous schemas, including the essentially self-contained spectacle of Baroque architecture or the excessively narrative and romantic Picturesque. Rather, time is put in the service of a certain pantheism. This is first apparent in the inclusivity of the city's networks—one can never be outside them, but always already part of a system experienceable only over time and in pieces,[53] a system in which the observer is either a mobile entity himself, or else the stationary receiver of mobile parts. Second, because the city-system is based on the circulation of force (-lines) disencumbered from fixed reference or relation to an exterior ground or site, it must derive its first principle, or principle of *differentiation,* from something inherent to it (turbulence, interference, etc.).

52 Perhaps the closest he would ever come to emancipating his work from this classical conception was in the "artificial sites" of the OBUS linear plan, nearly two decades after *La Città nuova.* On the OBUS plan see Mary McLeod, "Le Corbusier and Algiers," *Oppositions,* vol. 19/20 (winter–spring 1980). Far more radical in this direction were certain experiments in the 1920s by the Russian Constructivists—Tatlin, Lissitzky, Leonidov, Vesnin, the Stenberg brothers—as well as the Dymaxion project of Buckminster Fuller.

53 Though one will object that this is true of all cities it is not true of their individual architectural elements. It is precisely the way these latter are embedded within a temporality of generalized flow that interests us here. The objection moreover is unfounded in another way, for most cities are still today capable of traditional cartographic representation, while *La Città nuova* is not. One need only consider the difficulty New York City has had in producing an overview map of its relatively simple (maximum two levels) subway system to appreciate this problem. What would be needed for n-dimensional systems are procedural maps or protocols, which again reintroduce the question of time.

This inherent "first principle" would be an immanent cause: an infinitely re-
curring, always virtual cause, based not on the absolute time of a fixed, exterior
origin but on a mobile and relativistic time that belongs indissociably to the concrete events that give it form. Nor is the city's structure discernable from any hypothetical outside; it has no divisions or sectors that could be combined into a
second-order unity or whole. Its unity (consistency, coherence) is always present
in its local, molecular relations. For this architecture expresses at its elementary
level those global and collective urban functions that it modulates and partici-
pates in. It does not allegorize "Man's" temporality—day/night, work/rest, pub-
lic/private, childhood/school/work/family, etc.—by organizing it into overcoded
molar units. Here, "the city," in its virtuality and complexity, is the expressed content of each of its single elements—not those received ideas of what actions, and
which order of actions, constitutes a human life. The distinction betweeen global
and local is elided, preempting—for better or for worse—the molar, hierarchical,
or centralizing formations endemic to any social and political urban system.[54]
Like a three-dimensional crabgrass, the city proliferates as if through some internal mechanism—it does not expand along a boundary or front but simply produces more of itself randomly (*nunc hinc, nunc illinc*), differentiating, ramifying,
and recombining basic elements. The field it develops, like the one described by
Einsteinian physics, is radically heterogeneous if viewed globally (though it is precisely this global view that is no longer interesting or possible), yet the same laws
unfailingly hold for every local instance. *La Città nuova* is a system, then, with no
inside or outside, no center and no periphery, but with merely one virtual circulating substance—force—and its variety of actualized modes—linear, rotating,
ascending, combining, transecting.

The implications of such a new temporality were vast. The nineteenth century
had already forged an obsessive oeuvre of these and similar changes through the
works of Flaubert, Engels, Baudelaire, Dickens, and H. G. Wells, to mention
only a few. The industrial city was then rapidly multiplying and fragmenting not
only as a spatial image but as a temporal one as well; the slow or permanent
rhythms of the preindustrial towns, which once seemed to furnish a fixed reference or support for the chaotic and fluid human experience, were now themselves, owing to industrialization and accelerated technical innovation, beginning

54 This is a considerably more optimistic interpretation of *La Città nuova* than the one to be
found in Sergio Los, "Citta macchina gigante," in *La Città macchina* (Vicenza: Assessorato
Cultura, 1974). Los opposes transmissive (global) to communicational (local) systems, seeing in the former an inevitable reproduction of the "relationship of domination."

to mutate and incorporate change over shorter and shorter intervals of time, gradually atomizing and becoming ever more plastic and fluid. What once served as a global, stable ground to the temporal human figure was threatening now to become as labile as it, and in this process of drawing forth the ground to embrace the figure—a tactical innovation so well known to modernist painting—threatened to dissolve it completely.

Generations of critics have interpreted modernist culture as a specific resistance to this threat of dissolution. And this despite the fact that the unmasterable and chaotic were developed as much as possible on the side of the object, leaving "man" and his consciousness to the greatest possible extent unmolested. The works of Joyce, Proust, Kafka, and Woolf are seen as part apologia, part lament for the modern facts of fragmentation and flux, but only as part of a more resounding and reassuring affirmation of a transcendentality of the subject and internal privatized time. Today we still need to be reminded that these works, more than just mirrors reflecting a prodigiously mutable world, were important spatiotemporal entities themselves, *places* for the dedicated explorer to navigate and apprentice him or herself, no longer in the techniques of reading, but more properly in the mapping of this very world, and just as it was lapsing forever into illegibility.

What we might hope to discover today when returning to the works of this period, alongside all that was valid in the existentialist-humanist view, are principles and remains of rudimentary maps once formed, consciously or not, from some beyond point of representation. To do this, analysis would need to bypass, not only traditional notions of "meaning," but also most currently accepted notions of "structure." For even this latter "progressive" term remains victim of a perennial transparency myth: the belief that beneath the shifting profusion of appearances there lies, accessible through proper operations, the finite, essential pattern of the real. At its most sophisticated, structure was understood as the abstract but always immobile framework—perhaps even a true component—of a living signification. Yet even as interest shifted from the analysis of systems of signification to topographical configurations and mapping, what seemed a critical innovation too often fell back on the structuralist bias for spatial systems to the proper exclusion of what I have been calling the "event."

The event belongs to a complex and abstract realm of space-time; so must the cartographic techniques that sketch out its lines. Difference, a value whose so-called disappearance is today lamented by those insensible to its subtler yet increasingly insistent effects, becomes the new transcendental principle of the field: the differential equation (dx/dt) with which physics replaced the material point, the perpetual becoming of Boccioni's force-lines, and Sant'Elia's ever-differentiating field of pressures and flows. None of these configurations, however, resembles a map in the traditional sense. They are rather what I will call *procedural maps,* made up not of "global" representations, which tend to reduce entire multiplicities to static and finite schemas, but of protocols or formulas for negotiating local situations and their fluctuating conditions. To construct such a procedural map it is necessary, first, to abandon the following two principles: (1) the epistemological prejudice that gives priority to the visual, spatial logic of simultaneity—the "image" of traditional cartography; and (2) the illusory exteriority of the subject vis-à-vis the map and the reality mapped. Here again it is the insertion of the dimension of time into the field that establishes a relation of continuity between subject and object, figure and ground, observer and event. Time is no longer exclusively subjective and private nor objective and absolute, but forms the seamless plane that gathers and gives consistency to both the subject- and object-effects that are corollaries or by-products of the event. To call these by-products is not to diminish them in any way, but rather to underscore the fact that they are *derived,* locally and in immanent relation to the event that constitutes them; they are not pregiven entities arriving readymade from without.

What is at stake in the question of modernity is, of course, an ontological problem regarding the nature of Being, but equally important and equally at stake is an epistemological one dealing with the nature of knowing. Today's crisis, as discussed at the beginning of this study, may be seen as an effect of the discrepancy between the steady emergence of a new mode of Being and the failure to evolve adequate modes of knowing that would be proper to it. This situation today is often an extremely confused one. Typical, and symptomatic, is the work of one author who, while acutely eliciting a number of the most trenchant, problematic, and richly challenging artifacts of our time (the work of Nam June Paik, Michel Foucault, the analytic of schizophrenia, advanced technology, the mutations of the contemporary urban environment . . .) is led to disqualify them routinely in the name of a more overriding need for representational schemas—depth-model hermeneutics, a theory of the social field based on cultural dominants, subject-centered consciousness, and cognitive mapping—in short, the resuscitation in every possible way of the subject-object relation that by his own admission has already lapsed into oblivion.[55]

55 I refer to a series of articles and lectures of Frederic Jameson, including the final essay in which these studies culminated, called "Postmodernism, or The Cultural Logic of Late Capitalism," *New Left Review,* no. 146 (July–August 1984). The monotheistic themes propounded throughout these essays are notable and fully avowed.

It is, of course, no accident that the city has occupied a privileged position in the emergence of our modernity. It was here where the compounding of technical innovations would have its first and most profound effects on mental and social life. But the culture of cities also belongs to much more fundamental moments in our history—to the rise of the first "artificial" (technological) civilizations as they break more and more fully from the "organic" earth-based world with its illusions of a single lived-time and legible naturalistic space; and, of course, the rise of modern capitalism, whose radical reordering of the relations of production made these other revolutions both necessary and possible.

The myth of the machine was more than a metonym of this new culture, it expressed the autonomous, detached, infernal, abstract, self-regulating, euphoric *functioning* that characterized the new order. It was in itself the very recognition that this new order was about the mobilizing and productive possibilities of abstract *functions* rather than the invention and deployment of yet another register of objects and elements. The cultural space occupied by this machine obsession was always an ambiguous one. At one extreme were the excesses of mechanolatria of figures like Marinetti, whose understanding of the machine failed to develop the question of productive relations that it on so many levels implied. At the other was the Taylorism of both the Soviet revolutionary and the American capitalist variety, which conspired to draw the social field and the worker's body into the well-oiled delirium—and tyrany—of an efficiently producing machine.

La Città nuova belongs properly to neither of these groups, but rather to a third, open-ended category that left its own powerful though tacit mark on modernist culture. To this category belong those machines whose task it was to produce other machines, or more precisely the "machinic" itself, and to set this latter loose as some kind of autofunctioning demon that appropriated, combined, and connected to itself a limitless array of materials and forces, assembling perverse hybrids and mixtures of social, political, and erotic flows. Duchamp's *Large Glass,* but also the procedural *Green Box* that contains its assembly instructions, the infernal bureaucracies and apparatuses of Kafka, the exotic conjugations of Roussel's performing machines, and in both these last two cases, the strange writing machines that subtended them, are among those identified in the 1950s as bachelor machines.[56] *La Città nuova* may be understood in this light less as a literal, realizable program than as a set of instructions, governing not only the assembly of

56 Michel Carrouges, *Les machines célibataires.* (Paris: Arcanes, 1954). See also *Junggesellen-maschinen/Les machines célibataires.* (Venice: Alfieri, 1975).

isolated modules of (bachelor) machinery, but the composition, in its most pragmatic and concrete form, of a universal machinic consistency (plane of immanence). It is this consistency alone which is capable of endowing with a substantial body all those events, processes, and flows, and all those invisible or "surreptitious" alliances, communications, and even subjugations that once may have seemed, as today they still do to certain modes of thought, so unfathomable and abstract.

4.1
Michal Rovner, *Rain #4,* C-Print, 1994

4   Real Virtuality, or "the Kafkaesque"

The role of life is to insert some
indeterminacy into matter.
— HENRI BERGSON

THE WORK OF FRANZ KAFKA was among the first of European literary modernism to be situated entirely within this new field of consistency. If his work has been labeled indecipherable, it is because the kinds of relations it offers up to the reader are no longer those of the monolithic literary forms of meaning or metaphor, or "organic" (bourgeois), developmental narrative. And unlike the work of such advanced modernists as Conrad or Proust, Kafka's may be seen as remarkable, not so much for the expression as for its relative remove from the crisis and neurosis that accompanied the multiple losses of the nineteenth century.[1] This is not to say that the work is unrelated to these events, only that it is accomplished in some beyond point where the negative play of loss was already giving way to the new "positivities" or formations of the modern world: bureaucratic state power, mass phenomena, relativism (epistemological and perceptual), the recoding of social space and time by accelerated technological innovation.

Of all of these developments, however, it is the image of bureaucratic organization that is considered to loom preeminent in Kafka's work. The historical elements that determine the specificity of this relation are manifold. The rise, for example, of what one could call our specifically *modern* bureaucracy (distinct from the ancient Egyptian, Chinese, and Roman ones, or that of the Catholic Church) is based on the prolongation of the techniques of division of labor beyond the merely economic sphere—in other words, their extension into the civil and social sphere itself (a development made possible in the earliest instance by the advent of a money economy). This development can be said to bear the same relationship to modern or late capitalism as did, say, double-entry bookkeeping to capitalism's earliest stages: both increased by many degrees the administrative capacities of increasingly large-scale enterprises and permitted them to act at greater and greater distances from the social and economic flows that it was their business to monitor. Now this "distance-effect"—so profoundly and clearly a dominant motif in the Kafkan universe—is directly proportional to how generalized bureaucratic technique has become in a given society or, expressed another way, how rationalized has become the civil *separation* of produc-

---

1 Of God, of experience (urbanization, automation), of the anthropocentric cosmos (Darwin's evolution, Maxwell's entropy), etc.

ers from the means of production (here the separation of civil servants and administrators of all types from the means of public administration), a movement that always entails a *concentration* of these means in increasingly centralized organizations.

Though legitimately "bureaucratic" formations, it may be argued, were known in modern Europe since the time of Louis XIV, it is only in the twentieth century that this kind of formal and technical rationality achieved an absolute and systematic nature. Among its most acute expressions in the early twentieth century are perhaps the scientific Taylorist and Fordist methods of industrial production. Here "specialization" may be said to have been pushed to its extreme degree leading at once to the maximum alienation—that is, abstraction and separation—of the worker from the production process *and* his or her maximum subsumption into the overall capitalist mechanism itself. Undoubtedly these movements were inseparable from America's historic rise as a dominant political and economic power. This is all the more understandable when one considers that capitalism and bureaucracy, at least in certain configurations, are inseparable from the processes of political democratization. For even the basic movement toward equalizing political representation necessitates the establishment of a massive juridical and administrative apparatus if for no other end than to prevent the random exercise of privilege. That a cousin form of this bureaucratizing movement arose almost simultaneously in the revolutionary Soviet Union only to calcify soon after into its Stalinist incarnation is neither a coincidence nor a contradiction. For it is a paradoxical characteristic of bureaucratic formation that it function, in Max Weber's own words, as a "precision instrument" of technical and political rationality, "which can put itself at the disposal of quite varied interests."

The rise of National Socialism in Germany in the 1930s certainly capitalized on this preexisting virtual mechanism, as well as on the newly constituted, very specific form of "mass personality" that such an apparatus of social organization fostered. What emerged was the specific mode of atrocity made possible by the abstract regulation of individuals reduced to the status of "files." It is this coexistence of "banality" and "evil" that distinguishes the modern bureaucratic holocaust of the Nazi regime from other historical massacres.

Fascism, bureaucratic socialism, capitalist democracy; these are unquestionably the constitutive social and political ideologies that express Western political rationality in the twentieth century. Each presupposes and develops, in its own way, the specifically modern techniques of bureaucratic organization. It would already be enough to point out that Kafka's work stands at the foot of these

4.2
Orson Welles, *Le Procès* (*The Trial*)

great and ominous historical developments. But far more than this, it is in Kafka's work that one encounters for the first time in literature—no nineteenth century work, neither that of Balzac nor even of Dickens is so ontologically fraught with the abstract relations of social organization—an entire novelistic universe whose objects, spaces, and relations are apprehended and manipulated in the same distorting though diabolically fecund terms of the emerging mega-machine. One need only consider the deep structuring role in Kafka's universe of bureaucratic separation, concentration, and alienation, as well as of the "distance-effect" discussed above, to appreciate the extent to which Kafkaesque "irrationality" is always steeped in a broader, deeper, and more importunate *total* rationality.[2]

At the same time, what emerges, almost paradoxically and yet with absolute clarity from even the most cursory reading of Kafka's work, is that the sweeping panorama of the nineteenth-century novel has collapsed. Gone is the novelistic landscape, at once remarkable for its infinite capacity to contain and order phenomena from the most expansive perspective to the minutest detail, and for its capacity to lay out in three dimensions a profuse but *legible* web of social, politi-

2 On bureaucracy in relation to Marx's concept of division of labor, to democracy, to files, and to the polyvocality of bureaucratic organization, see Max Weber, *Economy and Society*, ed. Guenther Roth and Claus Wittich, 3 vols (New York: Bedminster Press, 1968), vol. 3, pp. 956–1003.

cal, and psychological relations. The world of Kafka presses rather inward; it is close, circumscribed, airless, at once saturated and vacant. It is a world without overview, without the vast and gaping perspectives that once revealed the natural relations between things. Yet it is at the same time a world fraught with immense and untraversable distances, a world where what is missing are not the connections between things—for in Kafka everything is *complicated,* in the theological sense,[3] within everything else—but the very *image* of the order they have.

The task of Kafka the writer was perhaps no different from that of "K." the land-surveyor in *The Castle* or the accused in *The Trial.* It was, on the one hand, to chart the topography of this peculiar emergent world, to discover the laws of how things combine, and on the other, to trace by trial and error the mysterious principle of its functioning. But at the same time no sketch or figure is anywhere offered up, unless it be one of those deliberately scrambled and inscrutable images like the officer's blueprints for the inscription apparatus in the *Penal Colony.*[4] For in Kafka, the task is no longer to trace the *visible* form of the world by recourse to an external schema or representational mode, but to somehow espouse its very substance, to become *of* the world by becoming one with it.

It is in Kafka then that one may begin to speak not only of a new narrative order of space-time, but of a new topographical mode of writing.[5] Problems of transmissibility and nontransmissibility, affiliation and separation, and of the

3 "Complication," from the medieval pairing *complicare/explicare,* is one of the earliest proto-concepts of immanence. It derives from the Platonic concept of participation and becomes "theological" only later when developed and adapted by Plotinus (emanative cause, *Enneads*), Proclus, Boethius *(complectiri, The Consolation of Philosophy),* the Ecole de Chartres, and finally Cusanus *(complicatio, De Docta Ignorantia).* See also note 20 below.

4 Figures of indifferentiability abound in Kafka's work. *The Castle* alone offers dozens of examples: K. considers his two assistants as a single person (this is later echoed and underscored in the pair of officials Sordini and Sortini); the town's telephones supply a cacophony of voices in the place of distinct, differentiable messages; signatures accompanying written messages are invariably illegible; Bürgel's monologue degenerates into a formless outpouring of gibberish; the landlady's photograph of Klamm is so unreadable that it becomes an object of delirious speculation and conjecture; K. finds vocation and life so profoundly interlaced in the town that "sometimes one might think they had exchanged places"; and finally, of course, the Castle's relationship to the town is, from the very outset, never anything other than an indifferentiable and absolute coextensivity. Franz Kafka, *The Castle* (New York: Schocken Books, 1978).

5 See footnotes 17 and 38 below.

complex relations of physical parts to (metaphysical) wholes now replace the traditional literary meditation of interiority: meaning, psychology, truth.[6] The subject—either as protagonist or narrator—is no longer continuous, stable, or identical with itself, but is caught in a perpetual, complex, and nearly imperceptible process of variation and transformation. An objection will quite likely be raised here, for clearly one could argue that no character, neither in life nor in literature, could withstand a close and rigorous scrutiny that sought to reveal the flux and discontinuity beneath its self-identical persistence in being. But this is not the question. Take at random Fielding's Tom Jones, Stendhal's Lucien de Rubempré, or even Dostoevsky's Ivan Karamazov. The question to be asked is: Are these characters—however dialogically constituted they may be, and however unsure of their metaphysical grounding—constituted as subjects, that is, as formal and organic essence? And does this essence function as a constant, despite the fact that it is perpetually introduced into equations where it is challenged and put into dynamic relation with variables of the most chaotic order? The answer invariably is yes, though in the case of Ivan Karamazov one wonders (along with Lukács and Bakhtin) whether one is not already witnessing the emergence of an entirely new relation. These questions indeed all reduce to one: What is the relation of these characters to their respective worlds, that is, *with what type of individuation are we dealing*?

On the one hand, we have the individuation of essences (realization) and the development of forms (representation): it is here that subjectivity is produced as the defining characteristic of an "individual" ("character" or "subject" in the classic and recent senses, respectively), creating of this individual a first term in relation to which all else differs: the world, other individuals, and so on. Formal or

6 Theodor Adorno: " 'For the last time psychology' . . . Immersion in the inner space of individuation, which culminates in such self-contemplation, stumbles upon the principle of individuation, the postulation of the self by the self, officially sanctioned by philosophy, the mythic defiance. [In Kafka] the subject seeks to make amends by abandoning this defiance." In a comparison of Kafka with Freud: "To come closest to understanding the relation between the explorer of the unconscious and the parabolist of impenetrability, one must remember that Freud conceived of an archetypal scene such as the murder of the primal father, a prehistorical narrative such as that of Moses, or the young child's observation of its parents having sexual relations, *not as products of the imagination but in large measure as real events*. In such eccentricities Kafka follows Freud with the devotion of a Till Eulenspiegel to the limits of absurdity" (my italics). Adorno goes on to compare Kafka's work with the detective novel genre, where the "world of things" takes precedence over "the abstract subject." *Prisms* (Cambridge, Mass.: MIT Press, 1981), pp. 270, 251, 265.

Ideal essence is posited here as the *principium individuationis,* or in other words, the *principle* of individuation is understood as preceding every actual instance of individuation as its substratum, that is, as if it were an already existing possibility that needed only to be realized.

But, one is impelled to ask, can the principle of individuation be found, as I attempted to do in previous chapters, on the side of the *event* rather than on the side of forms and essences? After all, how do we account for the fact that in this essentially static mirror-world of reflected Ideas and Forms there is nonetheless a constant production of innovation and change? It may be possible, then, to oppose to this kind of individuation another type whose principle is developed in relation to the *new,* that is, in relation to its conditions of *emergence* (as opposed to "formation"). These "conditions" are once again inseparable from a temporal order; they always imply an ever renewable *present* that is complex and multiple, a continuous proliferation of divergent or singular instants/points. In fact, every new mixture of a "now" and a "this" suffices to constitute such a singularity. The world could then be seen to unfold as a perpetual production of individualities continually *actualizing* themselves in blocs or ensembles of moments/relations rather than *realizing* themselves in stable or eternal forms.

But in what could this singularity or individuality exist if not in subjective essence? It would exist precisely in the ever-shifting pattern of mixtures or composites: both internal ones—the body as site marked and traversed by forces that converge upon it in continuous variation; and external ones—the capacity of any individuated substance to combine and recombine with other bodies or elements (ensembles), both influencing their actions and undergoing influence by them. The "subject," then (like the "object" discussed in chapter 1), is but a synthetic unit falling at the midpoint or interface of two more fundamental systems of articulation: the first composed of the fluctuating microscopic relations and mixtures of which the subject is made up, the second of the macro-blocs of relations or ensembles into which it enters. The image produced at the interface of these two systems—that which replaces, yet is all too often mistaken for, subjective essence—may in its turn have its own individuality characterized with a certain rigor. For each mixture at this level introduces into the bloc a certain number of defining *capacities* that determine both what the "subject" is capable of bringing to pass outside itself and what it is capable of receiving (undergoing) in terms of effects.[7] It is in this sense that *the ground is brought forward to embrace the form,* and the subject dissolves back into the very immanence from which the central

7 See the discussion below of Umwelt theory and the work of Jakob Johann von Uexküll.

problems of the culture of modernity arises. It is this immanence that character-izes the world of Kafka's fiction.[8]

Metamorphosis, in a profound sense, is in Kafka's case *opposed* to develop-ment. The principle of "character" no longer belongs to a naturalistic (geometric) universe governed by "rational" and pseudo-organic development, where these latter are determined both by a protagonist's displacement through space and time, but also his or her linear spiritual and biological evolution and growth. Character abandons the usual linear processes of accumulation and embeds itself in a different field of movement that can only be called the realm of the *intensive.* Intensive may be roughly understood in its simple opposition to *extensive,* fol-lowing Bergson's distinction between qualitative (intensive) multiplicities and quantitative (spatial, extensive) ones.

Bergson defines the qualitative or intensive multiplicities as those that cannot be divided without changing in *nature.* This is because extensive, quantitative multiplicities are actual and discontinuous and, unlike intensive ones, which are virtual and continuous, can divide without changing in nature precisely because they change *only in degree.* Duration, according to Bergson, is the milieu in which continuous multiplicities are distributed. These multiplicities are fundamentally intensive and are characterized by the process of continuous actualization. Be-cause the becoming actual of the virtual proceeds by differentiation rather than representation-reflection, it alone is capable of accounting for the production of the singular and the new. Bergson called this creative movement "élan vital": the principle of individuation conceived as a mobile "immanent cause." This defini-tion of intensity, again, does not refer to a merely interior state but to the entire continuum of the world.[9]

Among Kafka's central motifs, then, is the problem of passage from one state to another. But what exactly is a state? For Kafka, "states" are never simply in-terior or autonomous moments but always have to do with larger—often im-material—ensembles in which individual elements are caught up. It is these ensembles that Kafka's work attempts to map, and it is the passage from one

8 The principle of individuation known as *"haecceitas,"* first used by Duns Scotus and his school in the thirteenth century, is sometimes used today to describe these instant/points or "singularities" as I have called them here. Cf. Gilbert Simondon, *L'individu et sa genèse physico-biologique* (Paris: PUF, 1964); Gilles Deleuze and Claire Parnet, *Dialogues* (Paris: Flammarion, 1977), pp. 110–115.

9 Henri Bergson, *Essai sur les données immédiates de la conscience,* and *L'Evolution créatrice* (Paris: PUF, 1941).

such ensemble to another, *a purely intensive and not extensive movement,* that constitutes the principle dynamism of his work.[10]

Kafkan narrative structure is itself a consequence of these same attributes. Events do not obey the logic of succession; they do not concatenate evenly, follow or flow through one another as effects might be said to unfold from causes. Things (i.e., narrative objects: characters, places, events) no longer necessarily find their links, nor their sense, in the flow of abstract time.[11] Characters, for example, bear little orientation to a past or a future, and certainly none at all to a "real," that is, supranarrative historical time. What is more, his works are almost singularly devoid of Events in the traditional sense.[12] For anything in the

10 Much of the present analysis might at first seem already to apply in the most commonplace way to other literature, e.g., Romantic poetry, even in wholesale fashion to the entirety of the modern literary tradition (Eliot, Joyce, Proust, Woolf, etc.) though only if one fails to recognize the following distinctions. First, the notion of intensity is used here to characterize a real, physical milieu, a universe in the concrete sense, not simply consciousness or an internal or psychological state. And unlike Romantic poetry, the *Umwelt* that corresponds to the protagonist's perceptual apparatus is not suspended "out there" in isolation from a self or as a field of natural but distant signs accessible through the body's senses; nor is it introjected and infused with private meaning. It is a dense network of concrete ensembles of which the protagonist is an integral part, yet which is not available, as such, to perception. Much of literary modernism certainly was tending in this direction; Kafka perhaps only its most pure example.

11 What I refer to here as "abstract" time is a linear, homogeneous, or numerical time, as opposed to pure and plastic "duration" in the Bergsonian sense: the *real* time in which everything exists as virtuality, as intensive, in becoming. Abstract time is measurable, spatialized time, a time that can be divided *without* changing in kind or nature. It is what Bergson called an "impure composite." It is the (spatialized) time of the clock, the fixed, external ground *against* which events occur, not the actualizing flow within which they arise.

12 An Event with uppercase "E" may be defined as an objectively significant (signifying, despotic: see chap. 5), historically measurable occurrence that extends its effects simultaneously into a quasi-totality of phenomena, thereby gathering reality around itself like a center and commanding a certain measure of space. (Such "Events" are analogous to what constitutes, in philosopher Jean-François Lyotard's terms, the grand narratives of a still metaphysically determined enlightenment modernism.) It may be said, on the other hand, that it is precisely the development and especially the problematic treatment of *random* occurrences and peripheral or minor happenings (as well as "petits récits") that characterizes much of modern literature from Robert Musil to Maurice Blanchot. These effects, which are in fact the extension of the historical progress of the "mixture of styles" as far as possible

Kafkan universe that could legitimately be called an "Event" has either already happened, preceding the narrative as its dubious and distant cause, or else is trapped in a vertiginous and endless pregnance, perennially on the verge of occurring. Indeed Events never actually occur *in narrative time,* properly speaking, as in a before or an after. They exist rather in some atemporal, *virtual* space, already incorporated into phenomena, already contracted in, and unfolding from, the real.

The essential tensions of Kafka's universe follow from the Bergsonian distinctions between virtual-actual and possible-real developed at the outset of this study. Consider how the "beyond"—regardless of whether understood as an "inside" to which one painstakingly seeks admittance, or an "outside" that serves *ex machina* as a divine guarantor of origins and ultimate meanings—is always in Kafka placed at a distant, even infinite, remove. No message emitted from its depths— and these depths are nothing if not riven with messages emitted with implacable constancy—will ever arrive. All of Kafka's work may be said to be lodged within the wait for a message from a realm beyond, not for what it might contain but rather because the very accomplishment of such a transmission would imply the existence of an unbroken tissue, however convoluted, linking recipient and Law (origin) in a seamless emanation and across a single and traversable divine substance. But no such transmissions are ever successfully completed, which leads to the more fundamental set of questions: What links the here and now to what exists both before and after, as well as beyond and below it? Is this world here, these events, anything more than a series of accidents freely adrift on a shifting sea of indetermination? What filament or anchor links them to the terra firma of the Law, eternal, infinite and absolute? Being itself suddenly appears hopelessly cut off from its substratum and now risks a type of mortal shipwreck, or worse, risks losing itself utterly at sea without hope even of negative deliverance. In Kafka, the ship of Being has been made rudderless and subject only to the peripeties of winds, currents, and tides:

---

beyond the domain of a naive, positivist realism, were supported by a new and emerging form of "literacy" fostered by the ontology of the cinema (see note 26 below), the collapse of the external universal viewpoint, and the rampant psychologism that dominated the novel for decades and which, by offering it refuge, ultimately preserved this form in its quasi-integrality. Significantly, this third factor does not apply to Kafka's work. On grand narratives and *petits récits,* see Jean-François Lyotard, *The Postmodern Condition: A Report on Knowledge,* trans. G. Bennington and B. Massumi (Minneapolis: University of Minnesota Press, 1984).

I am here more than that I do not know, further than that I cannot go. My ship has no rudder and it is driven by the wind that blows in the undermost regions of death.[13]

On the other hand, what one discovers, in the default of this transcendence and founding link to a beyond, is always a massive and complex *mechanism*[14] comprising an infinity of little parts, miniscule events and fragments—all intrinsically empty and meaningless—*yet all functioning together* without forming an apprehensible whole. Each part of the mechanism is linked to the others not through its meaning but *through its functional interconnection,* through the mutual partaking of a complex event or complex of events, which in themselves *have no relation to a substratum.* Reality reveals itself, however partially, and never more than partially, in the immediate, the fragmentary, the close-up, the minute, never

13 "The Hunter Gracchus," *Franz Kafka: The Complete Stories,* ed. Nahum N. Glatzer (New York: Schocken Books, 1946), p. 230. In this story the mythical fourth-century hunter falls from a precipice while chasing a chamois. The fall is fatal; yet for reasons unknown he is unable to die from this world. The bark or death ship meant to carry him to the eternal beyond loses its way: "a wrong turn of the wheel, a moment's absence of mind on the pilot's part, the distraction of my lovely native country, I cannot tell what it was; I only know this, that I remained on earth and that ever since my ship has sailed earthly waters. So I, who asked for nothing better than to live among my mountains, travel after my death through all the lands of the earth," p. 228.

   This story simultaneously traces the two themes of the impossibility of transcendence (passing to a beyond) and the theme of life as a dying into the world, a rudderless, meaningless wandering without real beginning or end.

   These themes later found acute elaboration in the work of Samuel Beckett, beginning with his trilogy of novels onward. Futhermore, the idea of rudderlessness elicits the extremely rich and complex motif regarding the role of dysfunctional or partial objects in such "death in life" narratives—Beckett's partial objects and aids to locomotion: crutches, broken bicycles, bum legs, walking sticks, etc., and of course the strange, equally sparse, but different range of objects in Kafka—Odradek, the Penal Colony apparatus, the flying bucket, books, brooms, buttons, tops, teeth, human bridges, stairs that grow, doors that multiply, balls, photos and articles of clothing in *The Trial,* Leni's webbed fingers, Georg's box and the uncle's desk in *Amerika,* and so on.

14 The ship, the hotel, the desk, and later the Nature Theatre in *Amerika,* the judicial apparatus in *The Trial* which is at least as complicated as the world itself (and then some), the civic bureaucracy of *The Castle,* the imperial system of rule in "The Great Wall of China," and so on.

through the monolithic Event whose origin and meaning arrives externally constituted and given in a beyond or in another dimension (that of the possible). The event now becomes coextensive (immanent) to the real, though it is as if in so doing it had to be divided into a million small pieces to be woven all the more indistinguishably into the fabric of Being itself.[15]

Kafka's world, as I said, is on first impression a still one, without the habitual grand lines of progress, development, or climax.[16] Its narrative seems rather to develop in terms of fine hairline movements and frozen images, and this latter undoubtedly explains the importance of photographs and snapshots in his work as well as in his life.[17] Yet it would be a mistake to treat too simply or literally the notion of "images," for their ultimate use is not always primarily visual or represen-

15 The "learned ignorance" of the philosopher character in the story "The Top" expresses perfectly both the heuristic model of knowledge in the "complicated" Kafkan universe as well as the pantheist theme:

> [H]e believed that the understanding of any detail . . . was sufficient for the understanding of all things. For this reason he did not busy himself with great problems, it seemed to him uneconomical. Once the smallest detail was understood, then everything was understood, which was why he busied himself only with the spinning of the top. (Franz Kafka, *Complete Stories,* p. 444.)

See also notes 20 and 42.

16 Many commentators have stopped here, preferring to describe—though often admirably—what they mistakenly take to be the lineaments of an apparent Kafkan stasis. The interesting exception—the only one I know of—is Austin Warren's observation that Kafka's world is no different from that of "a Mack Sennett comedy—one of chase and pursuit, *of intense movement,* horizontal and vertical," in "Franz Kafka," *Kafka: A Collection of Critical Essays,* ed. Ronald Gray (Englewood Cliffs, N.J.: Prentice-Hall, 1962), p. 124. My italics.

17 Kafka placed a great value on photographs, both as a technique for collapsing and expanding distances, and for breaking down grand and vertiginously sweeping movements (love/marriage) into fine, manageable ones. The photograph, like the gesture, freezes movement, though by no means does it immobilize it completely. Its true purpose is to condense movement in order to transpose it from one ensemble or series to another—in other words, to permit the excision of specific elements so that they may be placed in relation to an entirely different series of objects or affects. This *"ralenti"* effect bears more than a merely incidental similarity to the cinematic montage, in which, in addition to the unique mode of progression through successive still images, any object may be put in relation to any other

tational.[18] These images compose nothing less than a concrete plane of the real, a constellation of elements and fragments projected onto a surface, that is, an *ensemble,* or site of a potential transformation of states. Every image (those by means of which the narrative proceeds as well as those literal, photographic ones that are embedded as objects within it) implies a world, at once autonomous and connected in perpendicular fashion to every other. Every world conjoins and intersects with every other one. We may agree with Erich Heller who has written that Kafka's works "take place in infinity,"[19] though one is obliged to add that it is an infinity

merely by placing it, however arbitrarily, into the same sequence. Lev Kuleshov's famous filmic montage experiments in Russia in the late 1910s and early '20s only slightly predate Kafka's. Kafka gave over an enormous amount of time to the analysis of photographs. See, e.g., the correspondence accompanying his first exchange of photographs with Felice, *Letters to Felice,* ed. Erich Heller and Jürgen Born (New York: Schocken Books, 1973), pp. 29, 62, 65, 67, 75, 82–83, 84, 88, 90, 91–92. For a rather acute example of a literal montage effect in Kafka's narrative use of photographs, see the lengthy but precisely framed parenthetical excursus in "Blumfeld, an Elderly Bachelor," *Complete Stories,* pp. 178–179.

18 In their seminal work on Kafka, Gilles Deleuze and Félix Guattari argued that photographs can function only as representations and therefore as zones of blockage of affect, of destructive regression to interiority and subjectivity (reterritorialization). See Gilles Deleuze and Félix Guattari, *Kafka, pour une littérature mineure* (Paris: Minuit, 1975). The matter, however, is considerably more complex, as we will see presently. Many of the arguments in the present study rely heavily on the methodological writings of Michel Foucault, as well as on the work of Gilles Deleuze including his work with Félix Guattari (i.e., *A Thousand Plateaus*). The *Kafka* study cited above in many ways represents a somehow weaker effort—schematic, reductive and often awkwardly and regressively structuralist in approach—and one in which Deleuze's influence appears to be at a minimum. Yet the work nonetheless inaugurates—and in this, no other study comes even close—the possibility and the necessity of an ethical, or even ethological reading of Kafka's works unhindered by the baggage of literary critical-hermeneutic tradition. While relying heavily on the ground broken and cleared by this study, and in an attempt to extend their analyses, I have often made use of arguments taken from Deleuze and Guattari's other works to refute some of the Procrustean propositions they offer in *Kafka.* With respect to the present example, I have thus found it more useful to develop their own concepts of postsignifying and passional regimes, and of *faciality* to explain Kafka's use of photographs in particular and images in general. See especially the discussion below in ch. 5 of the "double turning away."

19 Erich Heller, *The Disinherited Mind* (New York: Harcourt, Brace, Jovanovich, 1975), p. 200.

of a very special kind; not an infinity of extension, but one of an unlimited *complication* in the sense developed by theological philosophy.[20] Every moment and every point in this universe constitutes a crossroads, the need for a decision, and the vertigo of an accelerated escape—real, not fantastic—into an alternate

20 The term *complicatio* was developed by renaissance neo-Platonists, particularly in the work of Nicholas Cusanus. *Complicatio* describes the enfoldedness of the many, including all opposites, in the One, or the (mystical) ascent from the many and the particular *to* the One (the infinite). Its complementary term, *explicatio,* describes the inverse process, an *unfolding* of the many from the One, or the descent from Unity (God) to particularity (the world). Like the ancient neo-Platonist concept of *emanation,* the *complicatio/explicatio* relation attempts to reconcile the Platonic doctrine of transcendence or separation of realms (existence on one side and ideality or "meaning" on the other) with the Aristotelian concept of development, which posits a continuous though graduated path between opposites. The fundamental difference, however, is that whereas the earlier schemes sought to maintain the transcendence of the One and the centeredness of the cosmos, the later one seems to argue for the immanence of the many in the One, a move one of whose tasks was *to bring the infinite into the realm of the sensible.* For if the "center is everywhere and the circumference is nowhere," this is because all of Being, though it is certainly the explication of the Absolute, is also present as mirrored, or complicated, in each individual part. Being may thus be actualized in either or both directions at once—in the direction of abstraction and unity as well as in the direction of the concrete and the multiple.

Transcendence and the doctrine of the graduated universe were weakened by God's "immanation" in the Many (all things). The principle of the *coincidentia oppositorum* simultaneously enriched the minutae of existence but also flattened Being by giving it a kind of overall equality (God existed more or less equally everywhere, as do all opposite terms), which ultimately gave way to a new field of virtuality or immanence. This system laid to waste Aristotle's geocentrism and prepared the ground for the pantheistic cosmologies of Bruno and Spinoza. It is also, undoubtedly, the philosophical origin of the idea of an expressive universe.

These and other Cusan notions seem indispensible to a proper understanding of the Kafkan universe. For it is here that the "modern" (renaissance) problem of a hierarchical vs. univocal Being is given a fully political dimension. I have related the emergence of a particular kind of immanence in Kafka's work to that of his contemporary, Henri Bergson. The *complicatio/explicatio* doublet appears in Bergson as contraction/detension (virtual/actual).

See Ernst Cassirer, *The Individual and Cosmos in Renaissance Philosophy;* Giordano Bruno, *Cause, Principle, and Unity,* tr. with intro. by Jack Lindsay (Westport, Conn.: Greenwood Press, 1962, 1976); Erwin Panofsky, *Perspective as Symbolic Form;* Frances Yates, *Giordano Bruno and the Hermetic Tradition* (Chicago: University of Chicago Press, 1964); Alexander Koyré, *From the Closed World to the Infinite Universe* (Baltimore: Johns Hopkins, 1957); Gilles Deleuze, *Expressionism in Philosophy: Spinoza* (New York: Zone Books, 1990); Henri Bergson, *Matter and Memory* (New York: Zone Books, 1988).

world.[21] Writing becomes less a question of representing a world than of explicating or unfolding the many potential worlds complicated within every point or instant and of tracing the routes and connective pathways between. Not the horizontal line of development, superhighway of the grand Event, but the diagonal line of connection and changes of state, webwork of microscopic fissures and openings. Reality here develops as a multiplicity of hypotheses continually etching themselves into the concrete, a reality founded not in Truth or given a priori, but re-created at each point anew through minute, specific gestures, actions, or speculations.[22] This world is more like that of Nicholas Cusanus or Giordano Bruno: infinite, centerless, and *complicated.*

The qualities of such a world are nowhere so deeply inscribed as in Kafka's descriptive techniques. We have already noted the absence of "rational" (continuous, homogeneous, etc.) space-time relations in this narrative universe. This may now be seen as linked to the absence of traditional novelistic overview, that is, the lack of a fixed vantage point or focus *external* to the world depicted. The viewpoint in Kafka tends, as I noted above, toward the microscopic, the extremely proximate, and the apparently insignificant or contextless detail. Wholes neither exist nor are constituted within the realm of perception. This microscopy also plays its role in diminishing "temporal perspective";[23] for there are no true yesterdays or tomorrows, no temporal depths or backgrounds from which events emerge, only an intensified and autonomous present. Everything is presented as if pushed up to an ever murky foreground so that characters seem to be born each day (if not each scene) anew. If particular descriptive elements or relations remain constant from one "frame" to the next, this is owing only to chance or else the narrator's explicit decision that they do so.

---

21 "Because I could not help it, because my senses were reeling, [I] called a brief and unmistakable 'Hallo!' breaking into human speech, and with this outburst broke into the human community. . . ." "A Report to an Academy," *The Complete Stories,* p. 257. There is probably no better example than this of the theory of individuation based on fluctuating mixtures (human and simian) and changes of state.

22 Exemplary among critics who have seen Kafka's works as experiments or hypotheses pushed to logical (or illogical) outcomes are Hannah Arendt, "The Jew as Pariah: A Modern Tradition," *The Reconstructionist,* April 3, 1959, pp. 8–14; Gunther Anders, *Franz Kafka,* p. 52; and Deleuze and Guattari, *Kafka.*

23 This notion is borrowed from Erich Auerbach's *Mimesis: The Representation of Reality in Western Literature,* trans. Willard Trask (Princeton, N.J.: Princeton University Press, 1953). See especially p. 7.

The vertigo, for example, that is an inherent effect of the story "Description of a Struggle" is due precisely to this continual shifting and inconstancy of usually stable elements. What is important here is that the main protagonist himself does not experience the vertigo, which, in a sense, is why we do. We experience the labile, shifting, always incomplete and dislocated world through the protagonist's only nominally unified "I," *a world that is manifestly not a problem for him,* and one that he manages to navigate with the same seamless, ramifying trajectory represented by the {I, II i, II ii, II iii a, . . .} nomenclature that divides and connects the story's parts. For this story is generated by means of a forced convergence of three distinct diegetic conventions: narrative, description (*Beschreibung*), and the promenade. Here "description" of course overcomes the other two, but only because the pseudo-parallelism of narrative and promenade—for these are neither analogies of one another nor are they coextensive—is first exposed as such so that their asymmetry may then be deployed to such spectacular effect: not to perpetuate a linearity (narrative) but rather *to propagate singularities.* Such a potent narrative technique is achieved merely by exploiting the technical and ontological possibilites of the ever-renewable and always virtual chance encounter.[24] What results is an unmooring of narrative flow and the release of new, less-organized movements such as "precipitation" and "drift."[25] This disorganizing tendency caused by the friction of the asymmetric narrative/promenade convergence finds

24 This very element, although conceived in a more superficial sense, would later be exploited and fetishized by the French surrealists Guillaume Appolinaire and André Breton. It is also worth recalling here the brilliant, eccentric hypothesis of Walter Benjamin, which derives the incessant breaks in the continuity of modern existence from the shock effects that the worker experiences at his machine, and that the citizen experiences in the metropolitan crowd. Such atemporality both favors chance and hazardous occurrences— thus the cults of the boulevards and especially of gambling—and annihilates the time of labor and economic accumulation and imbues events with a special indeterminacy and volatility—even at the cost of their enduring meaning. Walter Benjamin, *Charles Baudelaire: A Lyric Poet in the Era of High Capitalism,* trans. Harry Zohn (London: Verso, 1976), pp. 134–145.

25 Both of these of movements, which properly might be characterizable only as modal intensities such as occur in a musical continuum, have yet to be formalized in a literary critical context. It is worth noting that the German tradition provides what are perhaps the purest forms of these qualities. It might be said that precipitation belongs to the Kleistian narrative just as drift would find its fullest expression only in the modern day post-Kafkan film "narratives" of Wim Wenders. In one of Wenders's later works for example, *Wings of Desire,* the desultory pattern of human encounters is rendered as a musical convergence of

4.3
Fritz Lang, *M.*

a correlate in the motif of the continual crumbling—literally dislocating—and redressing of the body as it occurs throughout the story. This bizarre process, however, serves perfectly to underscore this work's essential tension: the (ironic) development of a narrative "form" that is in its nature radically opposed to and ultimately undermined by the propagation of pure points-moments, individuations, singularities, *haecceitas*.

The extraordinary *proximity* of the subject to the world and its contents is a prime quality of the Kafkaesque and may be likened to the then emerging cinematic techniques of description. Walter Benjamin compared these new camera-based techniques to a "surgical" penetration of the body. He opposed this to the typical, more removed position, the "natural distance" from reality that characterizes the theatrical or painterly gaze. By retaining the natural distance from

errant voices momentarily passing into individuated presences only soon to pass back into the indistinct ground of choral babbling. The angels drift through this field, producing narratives, or narrative fragments, through their capacity to isolate momentarily a single voice from the densely tangled background murmur. They do this merely by randomly linking up to other drifting mortal bodies, individualities existing now truly only as pairs (conjunctions), or as pairing-events (anchored to a *haecceitas*), that is, in "struggle." Within German expressionist cinema itself the two terms of the pair might be typologically represented by Wiene's *Dr. Caligari* (precipitation) and Lang's *M* (drift, replete with musical theme).

phenomena, theater permits the simultaneous apprehension of organized wholes and the organic relations that exist between parts. The painter or theatergoer obtains a total, or at least totalizing, picture of reality, but only because she does not penetrate into it, that is, she forgoes her own potential position within it. The cameraperson however, like the surgeon, penetrates deeply into the body of reality at this or that specific place, to isolate and render precisely a single, previously invisible detail. These separate details are then recombined, though not built up into the totalizing space of "natural" perception (for the very dream of such a total space had been definitively abolished by cinema); rather, they are arbitrarily assembled in a synthetic narrative continuum according to entirely new laws: montage.[26]

Clearly, the cinema owed its capacity simultaneously to augment and fragment reality to its penetrative function and its multiplication of perspectives. It was in cinema that it first became possible to montage vast panoramas in a sequence with tiny, otherwise imperceptible details, so that these latter, by staking the same claim to reality and having the same capacity to fill a frame, were given an ontological status equal to (if not greater than) that of the composed and totalized world that offers itself up to "natural" perception. Second, not only was there an infinity of individual details capable of standing in as the full ontological substitute of traditional "world-shots," but there was an infinity of different angles, an infinity of different distances, mise-en-scènes, perspectives, possible combinations with other objects, and positions in the chain of montage.

In brief, what is brought literally into the realm of everyday human perception, though here in a discontinuous mode, is the same phenomenon whose development so strongly marked the seventeenth century—then in a continuous mode and not at all in the realm of everyday perception—with the invention of the microscope and the telescope. These two technologies merely concretized a problem that had already come to dominate Renaissance thought and aesthetics: the reconciliation of "the two infinites"—the infinitely large and the infinitely small. It was only in the diegesis of cinematic montage, one might say, that this problem was ultimately resolved *for the senses*. Needless to say, cinema is the art par excellence of illusion, and this is owing to the fact that it proceeds by means

26 Walter Benjamin, "The Work of Art in the Age of Mechanical Reproduction," in *Illuminations* (New York: Schocken Books, 1969), pp. 228–238. Eisenstein's reflections on the importance of Kabuki theater for cinema, and particularly his concept of a "monism of ensembles," are equally important here. Sergei Eisenstein, "The Unexpected," *Film Form* (New York: Harcourt, 1977), pp. 20–22.

of exclusion; it claims, through its perpetual fullness, to construct perfect and integral worlds, but does so, relatively speaking, with an extreme economy of details.

Even in these strictly technical developments it is possible to recognize the particular physico-cosmological conditions upon which Kafka's "theological" solutions were brought to bear. Modernity in general and cinematic ontology in particular re-posed the classic philosophical theme regarding the relations of the One (the good infinity) and the Many (the bad infinity). For how many separate details are needed to compose the world in its integrality? And since details can be shown to proliferate inexhaustibly (as noted, even a single detail offers to the camera an infinity of aspects), this direction of inquiry cannot be other than futile. Kafka's own strategy thus often tends toward a negative or apophatic theology, toward the mystical/mathematical procedure by which one arrives at a state of Wholeness (the good infinity) through *elimination* of enriching though fragmenting and infinitizing detail.

Further, it is worth considering in what way precisely the penetration of the camera eye into the continuum of objects actually transforms these objects into "expressive," even animistic entities, or at the very least, into *monadic* "singularities," each expressing the world from its own specific and unique perspective. The camera eye is in no simple way a mere extension of a subjective point of view; it is a windowed object that transforms other objects into windows too. For the camera, Being is distributed (more or less) equally everywhere and is reflected, and complicated, in every detail.

The pervasive and oppressive closeness to things that one finds in Kafka, though it depends on much that was first worked out in cinematic ontology, is here fully assimilated to a technique whose effective purpose is to deprive the world of anything that might resemble a larger or more comprehensive meaning. Kafka's genius was to situate his work within this new field—in a way to occupy it like a terrain—and to conduct a series of operations from, in, and on it. One might well say of Kafka's narratives that in organizing themselves in this way, they constitute not a strategic space, but rather a tactical one:

> J'appelle "stratégie" le calcul des rapports de force qui devient possible à partir du moment où un sujet de vouloir et de pouvoir (un propriétaire, une entreprise, une cité, une institution scientifique) est isolable d'un "environnement." Elle postule un lieu susceptible d'être circonscrit comme un *propre* et donc de servir de base à une géstation de ses relations avec une exteriorité distincte (des concurrents, des advérsaires, une clientèle, des "cibles" ou "objets" de

recherche). La rationalité politique, économique ou scientifique s'est construite sur ce modèle stratégique.

J'appèlle au contraire "tactique" un calcul qui ne peut pas compter sur un propre, ni donc sur une frontière qui distingue l'autre comme une totalité visible. La tactique n'a pour lieu que celui de l'autre. Elle s'y insinue, fragmentairement, sans le saisir en son entier, sans pouvoir le tenir à distance. Elle ne dispose pas de base où capitaliser ses avantages, préparer ses expansions et assurer une indépendance par rapport aux circonstances. Le "propre" est une victoire du lieu sur le temps. Au contraire, du fait de son non-lieu, la tactique dépend du temps, vigilante à y "saisir au vol" des possibilités de profit. Ce qu'elle gagne, elle ne le garde pas. Il lui faut constamment jouer avec les evenements pour en faire des "occasions." Sans cesse le faible doit tirer parti de forces qui lui sont étrangères.[27]

The principal difference between strategy and tactics, then, has to do with the space in which they are developed. Or rather, the "space" by definition remains the same—being wholly attributed to, even *constructed by* the strategic regime—what differs are the modes of negotiating that space, of holding it, or holding oneself in it. Strategy proceeds by projecting, fixing, and consolidating; it circumscribes in order to oppose (this to that, the Same to the Other). Strategy belongs to the discrete totalizing order of space; it comprises distinct things and "proper" places. It is oriented toward the domination and mastery of global phenomena: a territory or domain. Tactical regimes, on the other hand, do not exist on the same level, nor are they oriented toward the same types of phenomena. Tactics does not have a "proper" *place;* it belongs to a nonspace, which is that of a shifting, transitory, and volatile materiality, a materiality of flux and movement—in a word, the materiality of the event.[28]

27 Michel de Certeau, *L'invention du quotidien; 1. Arts de faire* (Paris:10/18, n.d.), pp. 20–21. See also pp. 82–92. For an elaboration and approximate translation of this passage, see Michel de Certeau, *The Practice of Everyday Life,* trans. Steven Rendall (Berkeley: University of California Press, 1984).

28 The theory of a nonempirical materiality, which is not merely that of meanings or relations, is a cornerstone of post-Nietzschean genealogical method. The phrase "un matérialisme de l'incorporel" is Michel Foucault's (*L'Ordre du discours,* p. 60); the theory of events and incorporeals in general is elaborated by Foucault in *The Archaeology of Knowledge* (New York: Harper and Row, 1976), by Deleuze in *Logique du sens,* by Foucault on Deleuze in "Theatrum Philosophicum," and by Deleuze on Foucault in his *Foucault* (Paris: Minuit, 1988), chaps. 1 and 2.

Tactics relies upon and embraces emergences, irruptions, changes—the continually individuating flow of stochastic durations. It is herein that tactics intervenes not in space but in time, and in this sense it may be said always to produce its adversarial effects within the domain of power, yet without actually opposing or confronting it as such. There are two reasons for this. First, tactics does not have a form separate from a content (such as the pair State/Army), a performance separate from a competence; tactics is both given and actualized only in its own movements. Furthermore, tactics proceeds not by global oppositions but by local interventions, for it is effectively immanent not only to itself but also to the general medium of strategic (institutional) power in whose interstices it plays. Tactics does not give itself distinct objects (oppositions) or totalized schemas; it relies on its very "homelessness," its indistinction, and its "weakness" as a screen for a perpetual mobilization. It embraces the ceaseless individuation of forces and in turn recognizes only the proliferation—and instability—of singular moments.

This, then, introduces the second reason: tactics is never autonomous but always contingent. It depends on the very conditions—power—that it both lacks and seeks to subvert. It mines it blindly, provisionally, and always at intimate proximity from within. Tactics proceeds, one might say, by redistributing the macroeffects of power into a micrological "space" that strategy itself, precisely *because it is strong* (and bound to territory/ *un propre*) cannot enter. Consider the advice Bürgel gives to K. in *The Castle:*

> When one is new here, the obstacles appear quite insurmountable . . . but take note, now and again opportunities do indeed arise, which scarcely conform to the general scheme of things, opportunities in which, through a glance or a sign of trust, more can be achieved than through the exhaustive efforts of a lifetime.[29]

Tactics is based on mobility and the capacity to redeploy relations of the fixed. It thus favors the "weak" by reconfiguring the theater of contact and establishing a new scale of thresholds and effects. This finally is why tactics cannot be oriented to a triumph—after all over what?—but only to perpetuating and extending its own movement and effects. First of all tactics, being the political modality of the disenfranchised, cannot "store" its triumphs (spatialization), but only renew them, make them proliferate (in time). This implies an entirely different ethic from that of the strategic. Because its mode is to atomize and break down

---

29 See *The Castle,* p. 337. The translation given here is that of Christan Gooden in "Positive Existential Alternative," *The Kafka Debate,* p. 106.

monolithic formations, because it is oriented less to a victory than to "a next move," one might say of it that it is primarily *analytic.*

Kafka's is indeed an art, or an "analytics," of the weak operating within, and against the strong.[30] Strategic (strong, totalizing) forces are everywhere and make their appearance in the figures of the Law, the Father, the social conspiracies of Matrimony, Work, Family, all carving out and projecting a certain *milieu (un propre)* to which access is effectively—though never literally—blocked. Yet if there is anything in Kafka as acute as the obsessive desire for access to the Law[31] *(le propre),* it is the intolerable fear and horror of subjection that such access would entail. For here, both transcendence (to a beyond and to the interior of the Law) and subjection (the strategic formation of subjectivity—husband, son, citizen, subject[32]) go hand in hand. Kafka's tactical war is two-tiered: It entails the piecemeal, even if provisional, construction of a universe freely navigable and unobstructed by transcendent, totalizing forces, as well as the liberation of personal, corporal forces from the constraining forms of social subjection.[33] These two aspects constitute, respectively, the cosmological (theological) and the political side of Kafka's work.[34]

30 Adorno: "Kafka seeks salvation in the incorporation of the powers of the adversary." *Prisms,* p. 270.

31 See "Before the Law," but also "In the Penal Colony," "The Great Wall of China," "The Judgment," *The Trial,* and *The Castle.*

32 Adorno's felicitous if tendentious formulation of this idea: "Kafka's figures are instructed to leave their soul at the door at the moment of the social struggle in which the one chance of the bourgeois individual lies in negating his own composition and that of the class situation which has condemned him to be what he is." Adorno, *Prisms,* p. 270.

33 I follow here the double notion of subjection developed by Foucault: "There are two meanings of the word *subject:* subject to someone else by control and dependence, and tied to his own identity by a conscience or self-knowledge. Both meanings suggest a form of power which subjugates and makes subject to." Michel Foucault, "Why Study Power: The Question of the Subject," in H. L. Dreyfus and P. Rabinow, *Michel Foucault: Beyond Structuralism and Hermeneutics* (Chicago: University of Chicago Press, 1982), p. 212.

34 Exemplary here is "The Report to an Academy." The deliberate self-transformation from ape to human is portrayed by the protagonist as a mere (tactical) search for a "way out," not a hubristic and human-all-too-human quest for freedom: "There was no attraction for me in imitating human beings; I imitated them because I needed a way out, and for no other reason." See also Kafka's discussion of Flaubert in Gustav Janouch, *Conversations with Kafka* (New York: New Directions, 1968), and Canetti's reflections on Kafka's systematic will to disappearance in *Kafka's Other Trial* (New York: Schocken, 1974).

Both of these levels of research help explain the peculiarly unrounded, even random quality of a typical Kafka novel or story when taken as a unit or whole. The economy of these works does not resemble the slow buildup-crisis-denouement pattern of traditional fiction.[35] Nor, however, does it reproduce the merely fractured economy of much modernist fiction, alternately atomized, compressed or evenly distributed across the entire surface of the narrative. These latter works tend to displace the problem of a "unity" either to the realm of consciousness as in the interior monologue (Woolf), or to a prior or ultimate state from which the work has either fallen (Eliot) or is in the process of restoring (Joyce). In Kafka, one might say, the "unity" is elided, perhaps abolished; for such unity is the very "*propre*" itself, whose existence, all too complicit with the Law (the beyond), must be disavowed a priori. This is not done by means of fragmentation per se, as this too often implies the existence of an even more encompassing unity at another level. It is achieved by means of an assembly or combinatorial process exactly like the one Kafka himself describes in *The Great Wall of China:*

> [The] principle of piecemeal construction . . . was done in this way: gangs . . . were formed who had to accomplish a length, say, of five hundred yards of wall, while a similar gang built another stretch of the same length to meet the first. But after the junction had been made the construction of the wall was not carried on from the point, let us say, where this thousand yards ended; instead the two groups of workers were transferred to begin building again in quite different neighborhoods. Naturally in this way many great gaps were left, which were only filled in gradually and bit by bit. . . . In fact it is said that there are gaps which have never been filled in at all, an assertion, however, that is probably merely one of the many legends to which the building of the wall gave rise, and which cannot be verified, at least by any single man with his own eyes and judgment, on account of the extent of the structure. . . .

Here then is a construction process devoid of overview, at least from the vantage point of the laborers. Yet the question that this story poses is none other than the question of wholeness, totality, and closure. In what space and in what time

35 Notwithstanding Kafka's claims regarding his novel *Amerika* of trying to write a Dickens-style work, one cannot deny the extreme nomadic and arbitrary nature of the various and loosely concatenated segments that make up this unfinished, and almost by nature unfinishable, work.

does the unity of the wall exist—in its idea, in its origin or decree, in its ever-deferred state of completion? The wall is presently of course but a series of disconnected linear segments, yet the existence of an Emperor (a cover term here for Law, Center, Inside, community, *propre*), if only one possessed some evidence of his existence, would assure Unity, if only even a future or possible one, at every level. But the absent Emperor is also the center, or center-function, of the Story, at once the spurious source of its unity and the principle of its integrality and closure. Like the message in the parable[36] that has no hope of ever reaching the "periphery"—that typically murky, indeterminate region where both the story and the Wall are assembled—narrative becomes a lawless, marauding object unfixed from any center, beginning or end. Like the nomads of the north against whom the Wall is being built (the *propre* of the Tower of Babel is opposed here more than just allegorically to the tactical *non-lieu* of the steppe), information, that is, *knowledge,* is constantly grounded in a form of circulation directly opposed to the centralized, emanative model of transmission. For nearly all knowledge in Kafka arrives indirectly in the form of rumor.

To understand the appropriateness of this theme let us first consider what one might call the rumor's threefold structure. The rumor (1) propagates by means of immediate and localized interactions (one to one contact between units, segments or cells); (2) functions not to saturate or consolidate a territory (space), but in a certain sense rather to invade it by producing its effects slowly and gradually over time; and (3) is indeterminate, especially with regard to its source: it seems never to have a fixable origin. All of these factors help explain not only the continual use of the rumor refrain in Kafka and the relativizing and almost exclusive reliance on free indirect speech, but also the structure of his entire narrative machine: its sequential, centerless, proliferative yet a-developmental nature.[37]

Because Kafkan narrative is able to tolerate both discontinuity (of space, time, and character) and heterogeneity, without imposing on these the epistemological status of "contradictions" or "problems" of representation, each individual scenario takes on rather the full ontological status of a "possible world," and the bizarre laws that determine the passage from one of these worlds to the other may best be understood as a process of practical experimentation. The works in gen-

---

36 *An Imperial Message.* This parable was published separately but is also contained in *The Great Wall of China.*

37 See chap. 5, note 132.

eral, like the Great Wall itself, must not be judged from an exterior (mythic) viewpoint and as totalized structures, but rather from within, from the relative blindness of an immanent viewpoint:[38] "The nomads, rendered apprehensive by the building operations, kept changing their encampments with incredible rapidity,

38   A distinction must be made between two types of science, or scientific procedures: one consists in 'reproducing,' the other in 'following.' The first has to do with reproduction, iteration and reiteration; the other, having to do with itineration, is the sum of the itinerant, ambulant sciences. . . . Reproducing implies the permanence of a fixed point of view that is external to what is reproduced: watching the flow from the bank. But following is something different from the ideal of reproduction. Not better, just different. One is obliged to follow when one is in search of the 'singularities' of a matter, or rather of a material, and not out to discover a form; when one escapes the force of gravity to enter a field of celerity; when one ceases to contemplate the course of a laminar flow in a determinate direction, to be carried away by a vortical flow; when one is involved with the continuous variation of variables, instead of extracting constants from them, etc. And it involves a completely different sense of the Earth [the world]: with the [first] legal model, one is constantly reterritorializing around a point of view, on a domain, according to a set of constant relations; but with the ambulant model, the process of deterritorialization constitutes and extends the territory itself. (Deleuze and Guattari, *A Thousand Plateaus*, pp. 460–461.)

What I'm calling the "immanent model" is of course the ambulant, "following" one. Compare Bergson:

Take, for example, the movement of an object in space. I perceive it differently according to the point of view from which I look at it, whether from that of mobility or of immobility. I express it differently, furthermore as I relate it to the system of axes or reference points, that is to say, according to the symbols by which I translate it. And I call it *relative* for this double reason: in either case, I place myself outside the object itself. When I speak of an absolute movement, it means that I attribute to the mobile an inner being and, as it were, states of soul; it also means that I am in harmony with these states and enter into them by an effort of imagination. Therefore according to whether the object is mobile or immobile, whether it adopts one movement or another, I shall not have the same feeling about it. And what I feel will depend neither on the point of view I adopt toward the object, since I am in the object itself, nor on the symbols by which I translate it, since I have renounced all translation in order to possess the original. In short, the movement will not be grasped from without and, as it were, from where I am, but from within, inside it, in what it is in itself. (*Introduction to Metaphysics* [New York: Philosophical Library, 1961], pp. 2–3.)

like locusts, and so perhaps had a better general view of the progress of the wall than we, the builders."[39]

It is in this sense that "story" may finally be seen to assume a literal and concrete function as map or diagram of the real. The work is a "working out," a working out of the real, in the real. One may look at a Kafka story as a set of random hypotheses, but on the condition that one take everything literally. Kafka's literary oeuvre is not founded within signification (metaphor) any more than within expression *(Existenz)* or reference (realism). It is founded rather in the illocutionary realm of the speech act (pragmatics):

If . . .
"As Gregor Samsa awoke one morning from unsettling dreams he found himself changed in his bed into a monstrous vermin,"
Then . . .[40]

Narrative is less a medium here for the telling of events than a procedure for developing the practical consequences of events and their radiation and imbrication in material reality.[41] What this means, however, is that *every* gesture, utterance, or accident, no matter how small or insignificant, is raised to the stature

39 Franz Kafka, "The Great Wall of China," *Complete Stories* (New York: Schocken Books, 1946), pp. 235–236.

40 Though this is functionally the case of all of Kafka's work, it is literally the case for his story "Up in the Gallery," *Complete Stories,* p. 401.

41 Theodor Adorno, Gunther Anders, Walter Sokel, and Malcolm Pasley are among the many critics who have argued that Kafka's works generally and *The Metamorphosis* particularly are the literal extension of a figure of speech. For Adorno it is the phrase "These travelling salesmen are like bedbugs"; for Anders it is a literalization of Samsa's desire to live as *ein Luftmensch* though he will be considered a *dreckiger Käfer* by the respectable world. Adorno goes even further to suggest that the story is a trial run of a type of dehumanization. For Sokel the tendency toward the enactment of metaphor, cliché, or idiom determines to some extent all of Kafka's work. It is Pasley, however, who has provided what are certainly the most rigorously argued examples as well as the most extravagantly categorical claims in this vein: "Kafka's images . . . almost always spring from literature, or at least from words. They grow mainly out of metaphor or hyperbole, and they remain in some degree attached to their origin." Malcolm Pasley, "Semi-Private Games," *The Kafka Debate: New Perspectives for our Time,* ed. Angel Flores (New York: Gordian,1977), p. 189. See also his "The Burrow," *The Kafka Debate,* and "Two Kafka Enigmas: 'Elf Sohne' and 'Die

of an "event," that is, given functional ontological status. Everything is always, and everywhere, at stake. This is, in fact, but another formulation of the peculiar sort of pantheism that I had already begun to identify in Kafka when I characterized his universe as an infinite *complicatio* of crossroads and hypotheses.[42] If there are no grand, dominant meanings or privileged events, this is because significance, and by extension, Being itself, is no longer ordered in graduated or hierarchical fashion. Being (and significance) is distributed equally everywhere, at every level, and is equally present even in the smallest details. This is the only true sense in which one can speak of the radicality of modernist "flatness," indeed an important aspect of Kafka's legacy to modern literature. For if Being is univocal it has no peaks, troughs, deserts, or oases, and it may best be reflected on a flat surface.

"Flat," of course, does not mean a diminished or impoverished dimensionality. Quite the contrary, for what we have here belongs more than anywhere else to the world of fractal geometry, a world whose singularity lies in its ability to maintain a prodigious but *constant* level of complexity at every scale. A fractal object is *complicated* because it contains the principle and rule of its being at every point; it contains an infinity of stages or cycles, and, instead of occupying new unitary

---

Sorge des Hausvaters,'" *Modern Language Review* 59 (1964), 40–46, as well as Adorno, *Prisms,* Gunther Anders, *Franz Kafka,* chap. 2, and Walter Sokel, *Franz Kafka* (New York: Columbia, 1966). That this process actually takes place in the work seems undeniable and undoubtedly significant, though none of these critics has attempted to show why it should be significant. One need only consider the work of Kafka's related contemporary Raymond Roussel to appreciate the massive impact that such incipient textual practices had on modernist redefinitions of the relation of world and text.

42 I have already referred to Cusan and Brunian cosmologies. But in what sense pantheism? Pantheism is a doctrine or theory of Being opposed to theism on two fundamental levels. First, theism belongs to a metaphysical tradition of transcendence integral to which is the doctrine of two worlds: a finite, temporal, and imperfect world, under which (or beyond which) lies the perfect eternal and true world that serves as its ultimate ground. In pantheist cosmologies, there is but one world, and God, to the extent that one exists, is indistinguishable from nature or the created world. There is no external or transcendent schema; in pantheism God (or Cause) is said to be immanent so that Being need not refer beyond or outside itself for its cause or ground. Immanence has been called a "pure ontology," for it implies a complete equality of Being unfolding on a single plane. Thus the second characteristic of pantheism: it implies a field of pure virtuality whose principal (God) and potential cause are given equally everywhere. See Karl Jaspers, *Spinoza,* trans. Ralph Manheim (New York: Harcourt, 1966), ch. 3.

dimensions, it inhabits the infinitely variable space *between* dimensions (fractions of dimensions, thus "fractal dimensions").[43] Flat spaces with *n* dimensions have for a long time been commonplaces in topology; there is no reason they should not be so as well in literature, metaphysics, or politics.[44]

One of the accompanying effects of flat Being, as I said, is the intensification and the increased importance given to individual details. Yet it is not simply that the scenographic lights have suddenly been made brighter, as if illumination were now extended to the very depths of narrative space to reveal an even more subtle, rich, and refined play of motives and details. In fact, one does not see more in such a system; one sees less. The perspectival effects, the telescoping into depths, the instant apprehension of rational (visual) spatial relations between elements, the "fraughtness" of what is present with invisible (because absent, or merely distant) influences and forces, in a word, *backgrounding,* is in fact sacrificed to an unsettling new proximity, one expressed often as a certain blindness, as the inability to grasp or form a total picture.

Franz Kafka land-surveyor, like character K. of *The Castle,* maps without producing images, maps with his body proper by merging it as completely as possible with the body of the world.[45] From this new, pragmatic perspective, what is sought is not an image or reflection of the world as it might appear, but an unfolding, an *explicatio* of the world implied and *complicated* in every one of its elements and gestures. The coherence of a world formed and totalized by an external agency (the Law, the *propre*), is replaced by a new, internal, and concrete multi-

---

43 See Benoit Mandelbrot, "How Long is the Coastline of Britain," in *Fractals: Form, Chance, and Dimension* (San Francisco: W. H. Freeman and Company, 1977).

44 The concept of the *n*-dimensional manifold was first described in Bernhard Riemann's 1854 paper, "On the Hypotheses Which Lie at the Foundations of Geometry," in *A Source Book in Mathematics,* ed. David Eugene Smith (New York: Dover, 1959). T. E. Hulme's concept of "intensive manifolds" is meant to elaborate a similar concept in Bergsonian philosophy just as Deleuze and Guattari's concept of the "plan d'immanence $(n-1)$" is an extension of a similar concept to the realm of politics and metaphysics. See T. E. Hulme, "The Philosophy of Intensive Manifolds," in *Speculations: Essays on Humanism and the Philosophy of Art* (New York: Routledge, 1965), and Deleuze and Guattari, *A Thousand Plateaus.* On the eighteenth- and nineteenth-century origins of the term, see also note 53 below.

45 As the pundits in Tibet covertly penetrated and mapped a cloisoned geographical space with their own bodies; see Peter Hopkirk, *Trespassers on the Roof of the World* (Los Angeles, J. P. Tarcher,1982). Cited in Manuel Delanda, "Policing the Spectrum," *ZONE 1/2 The Contemporary City,* ed. Michel Feher and Sanford Kwinter (New York: Zone Books, 1986).

plicity that contains not only the residue and trace of this mythic, totalized world but also the random, irreducible profusion of vectors and windows that each opens onto alternate worlds.

To navigate such a universe is plainly to renounce all constancy of Being:

> As someone said to me—I can't remember who it was—it is really remarkable that when you wake up in the morning you nearly always find everything in exactly the same place as the evening before. For when asleep and dreaming you are, apparently at least, in an essentially different state from that of wakefulness; and therefore, as that man truly said, it requires enormous presence of mind or rather quickness of wit, when opening your eyes to seize hold as it were of everything in the room at exactly the same place where you had let it go on the previous evening. That was why, he said, the moment of waking up was the riskiest moment of the day.[46]

And this is not only a metaphysical but also a political imperative:

> There was no attraction for me in imitating human beings; I imitated them because I needed a way out, and for no other reason.[47]

This does not mean, however, that one is to replace the terms "order" and "stability" with an ethics of disorder, fragmentation, irrationality, and so on. One must at all costs go beyond the platitudes of modernist millenarian rhetoric. In Kafka we find not a mere epistemological opportunism—the pillaging of the ruins of the humanist era—but something approaching the positivity and fullness of a "praxis"; the deployment of velleities, gestures, hypotheses and the elaboration (explication) of these in something eminently concrete: what one could call, borrowing from Foucault, their "espace correlatif."[48] This method explains why nowhere

---

46 *The Trial,* trans. Willa and Edwin Muir (New York: Schocken Books, 1968), deleted passage, pp. 257–258.

47 "A Report to an Academy," *Complete Stories,* p. 257.

48 Foucault's detailed elaboration of the mechanics of language (discourse) as a system of material effects operating within an equally material medium of institutions, practices, and objects relies more heavily than generally acknowledged on the Anglo-American pragmatic theory of language. The "illocutionary" act (from the earlier "performative") had the virtue not only of restoring to the study of language its character as an "event" but served to embed it concretely within an unlimited complex of dependent, extralinguistic relations and acts.

in Kafka's works are the trials, unions, and metamorphoses ever depicted as interior events. These "events" always embrace, and are structured by, an outside:[49] the ensembles that events may be said to inhabit and deploy. Their logic is much closer to the Lucretian notion of *clinamen,* or swerve.

The clinamen (principle of immanent and causeless cause) is a minimal deviation from a given trajectory or course. It is produced randomly (any place and any moment in the universe is capable of "supporting" it), and the "world" is nothing more and nothing less than the direct physical set of consequences that derive from it. The *clinamen* interacts with a *milieu;* the real is nothing more than the product of this interaction but is not reducible to either member of the interaction. The principle of Kafka's fictional universe can be recognized here quite clearly. A change or distortion is introduced into the world. This change is usually circumscribed at first,[50] and may be either corporeal (*The Metamorphosis*) or not ("The Burrow," "The Hunger Artist," *The Trial*). What follows is a rigorous plotting of all the subsequent and consequential transformations, again both corporeal and noncorporeal, that ensue. We have already identified one type of subtle, noncorporeal transformation, the change of state.[51]

Foucault developed these insights, and especially the illocutionary act's capacity to form an effective hinge between discursive and nondiscursive continua, throughout the work of his middle period (*Archaeology of Knowledge* through *Discipline and Punish*). The concept of "collateral space" belongs to his attempt to flesh out a rich but abstract field of adjacency, which would supplant the traditional or merely empirical space-time of "transcendental" historiography, with the material-evental continuum of an "archaeology." All here depends on the definition of the "statement" (énoncé) which, as he shows, is defined not by any singularity as a new or intermediary linguistic unit—its linguistic *level* is demonstrably unfixable and shifting—but by its peculiarly dense domain of interaction and mutual implication, by the plane across which it interacts with other statements and other phenomena, by its complex field of play. There can, at any rate, be no statement without a material, worldly support, and no "collateral space" or material support without statements that actualize it. Michel Foucault, *The Archaeology of Knowledge,* pp. 80–106, 40–50, 118–122.

49 The outside is not only the domain of pure materiality, desire and force, but also that of the Law. See Michel Foucault, "Thought from Outside," *Foucault/Blanchot* (New York: Zone Books, 1987), pp. 7–58.

50 See the discussion on infinitesimal deviation and slippage in "Death and the Double Turning Away," in chap. 5 below.

51 The "change of state" is inseparable from the problem of individuation in Kafka's work and is a central theme of the next chapter. As an example of how changes of state are everything,

It is sufficient here to note that in the Kafkan universe, states, or essences, are determined in relation to an exterior domain,[52] to the milieus that they simultaneously produce and affect. They derive from the configurations (of ensembles), assignations (of elements to positions within these ensembles), and tensions (problems, paradoxes) that follow in the wake of these deviations/events.

What one finds at the heart of the static, finite, and airless Kafkan universe, then, is a remarkably labile, shifting, ever-mobile domain. But this dynamo, which seems ceaselessly to generate deviations (difference), transformations, and changes of state, is not a principle of motion or space-time as we saw it to be in Einstein, Boccioni, and Sant'Elia, but belongs even more absolutely to the realm of qualities, that is, to an *intensive* manifold. The term manifold or "multiplicity"[53] is the term that best describes the *milieu* of Kafka's fiction. It is in every way analogous to the world-substance of the futurist-Minkowskian universe of extension developed in the previous chapter. The primary role of events is not as a vehicle of signification, but much more simply, and literally, to shape or carve out paths and ensembles within such a manifold, initiating elaborate series of consequences from even minute shifts and transformations. All the so-called

---

consider Kafka's discussion in *The Castle* of Klamm's "two bodies," the one civil, the other official, as well as the distinctions between real and illusory contact, and, in *The Trial,* of the constitutive distinction between ostensible and real acquittal.

52 Exteriority is characterized by a field of dispersion, or a material multiplicity; it reverses the centered space of an initiating subjectivity upon which traditional hermeneutical systems are based. For these latter merely reconstruct "in the opposite direction, the work of expression: it goes back from statements preserved through time and dispersed in space towards that interior secret that preceded them, and (in every sense of the term) is betrayed by them. . . . [I]t is always the historico-transcendental theme that is reinvested." Michel Foucault, *The Archaeology of Knowledge*, p. 121.

53 The original term is probably the Kantian *Mannigfaltigkeit*, which refers to the sum of elements present to the senses *before they are ordered and synthesized in the understanding*. This does not refer to sense data, only to the preformed, presignificant particulars of the world as such. The same term belonged to nineteenth-century geometry and was used by Riemann to refer to a topological space capable of being extended in n dimensions. The French, it seems, translated the mathematical term first as *variété* and then *multiplicité*, though the Kantian term is typically referred to as *le divers*. Nonetheless, Bergson's *multiplicités* may have been equally derived from these two sources.

movements are tactical, and they are all aimed at carving out a terrain, or passing from one level terrain to another.[54] Hence the cartographic element of Kafka's enterprise.[55]

Kafka's work is inseparable from the historical formation of the concept of manifold, or milieu, and it is to this conjuncture, so important an aspect of modernist physical theory, to which we must now turn. As I have already shown in the

54 Kafka was indeed a central figure among modern writers for whom writing itself was no less than a perilous encounter with *real* forces, a risked submergence into a field of language that contained real obstacles, real powers and dangers to be either mastered or not. The awesome consistency of this new field of language is unquestionably the legacy of the foundational modern triumvirate of Marx, Nietzsche, and Freud. Yet Kafkan discourse, as I am presenting it here, is oriented principally toward that of Nietszche, for only in Nietzsche, it may be said, does the relation of language and force (Nietzsche's world-substance) become that of an absolute identity and no longer that of container to contained.

55 Gilles Deleuze has made the same claims for the work of Michel Foucault, whose works arguably bear important similarities, in style and method as well as in content, to those of Kafka. Here *Discipline and Punish* would serve as the richest and most obvious example of any such comparison. Isolating Foucault's use of the concept of the "diagram" as a principle that simultaneously both supplies a continuous link between discursive and non-discursive (institutional) formations and permits a topographical mapping of their dual articulations, Deleuze develops the idea of a cartographic *versus* a signifying method:

> Pourquoi pas le capitalisme ailleurs ou à un autre moment, puisque les formations précédentes ou extérieures en contiennent déjà tant de séquences? Il est difficile de renoncer à ces questions de raison, et de penser le diagramme animé de pures mutations. *Pourtant un diagramme ne fonctionne jamais pour représenter un monde objectivé;* au contraire il organise un nouveau type de réalité. Le diagramme n'est pas une science, il est toujours affaire de politique. Il n'est pas un sujet de l'histoire, ni qui surplombe l'histoire. Il fait de l'histoire en défaisant les réalités et les significations précédentes, constituant autant de points d'émergence ou de créationnisme, de conjonctions inattendues, de continuums improbables. On ne renonce à rien quand on abandonne les raisons. Une nouvelle pensée, positive et positiviste, *le diagrammatisme, la cartographie.* ("Ecrivain non: un nouveau cartographe," in *Critique,* no. 343, vol. 31, Paris (Dec. 1975), p. 1223.)

And Foucault himself:

> A la logique de l'inconscient, doit se substituer une logique de la stratégie; au privilège accordé à présent au signifiant et à ses chaines, il faut substituer les tactiques avec leurs dispositifs. (Interview, *Le Monde,* Feb. 21, 1975.)

second chapter of this study, certain aspects of Lucretian physics already played an important role in the Einsteinian concept of the "field." The chemist Ilya Prigogine, in his work on the history of thermodynamics, also placed great emphasis on stochastic space and indeterminacy in quantum dynamics, especially the reliance on statistical functions (probabilities) as defining criteria of "objects" in quantum field theory.[56] These developments in the first three decades of the twentieth century were, however, by no means limited to physics. In biology, nineteenth-century Darwinism had already contaminated the once static classification systems of morphology and physiology through the unprecedented and quite radical introduction of the factor of time (developmental mechanics). In *Matter and Memory* and *Creative Evolution* Bergson addressed with great success in biology what he managed to do with only limited results in physics. He established the essential inseparability of the trajectories of living matter and the "dead" world into which it is projected, by submerging them both in a single flow of a continually creative and ever-generating *duration*.[57]

The German theoretical biologist, Jakob Johann von Uexküll, formulated one of the more concise and explicit philosophical attacks on premodern biology (as he saw it, that of empirical description relieved only by undisciplined speculation) and in so doing introduced, by way of an alternative model, the important concept of the *Umwelt*.[58] An Umwelt, according to von Uexküll, comprises of two functionally distinct spheres or worlds: the world-as-sensed and the world of action. Both of these worlds are made up of cues or *indications,* which are such only in relation to a biological apparatus—receptors or effectors—capable of

56 Ilya Prigogine and Isabelle Stengers, *La Nouvelle Alliance,* 2nd ed. (Paris: Gallimard, 1987); I. Prigogine, *From Being to Becoming: Time and Complexity in the Physical Sciences,* San Francisco, W. H. Freeman, 1980. The crucial work in this field remains Thomas Kuhn's *Black-Body Theory and the Quantum Discontinuity, 1894–1912* (New York: Oxford University Press, 1978).

57 Bergson, *L'Evolution Créatrice.*

58 The present discussion is limited to the work of von Uexküll despite the fact that the term "theoretical biology" refers more broadly to a much more unified—and historically significant—set of developments in biology and philosophy during the 1930s in Austria, England, and the United States, developments based in embryological and morphological studies, rather than in ethology. All of these studies, including those of von Uexküll's resumed here, led to the development of postwar cybernetics and its multiple offshoots.

recognizing them, that is, being triggered by them. The specific organs at play are here only of secondary importance. What counts are the functions, or *function-circles,* that organs, and parts of organs, as well as external indications (parts of the surroundings) constitute as a sort of feedback circuit or transmissional chain. The sum of these conductive function-circles composes the Umwelt of a given organism. The organism, according to von Uexküll, does not, properly speaking, exist outside of this manifold function-nexus. Von Uexküll thus distinguishes between the animal conceived as an "object" (which it isn't) and as a "framework" (which it is). For the framework refers to the animal's capacities to organize and dispose functions (select indications), or, more simply, its capacities to impart and receive affects to and from its surroundings. (In very advanced animals the body is capable of imparting and receiving signs from itself, thus embedding it simultaneously in both the world-as-sensed as well as in the world of action.) The Umwelt, then, is a part informational, part affective space; it contains no preexisting biological unities, only fragments built up into chains and gathered and made whole under a function ("function-rules").

Once again we have here a radical new distribution, what may be called *a biology of events.* For in this distribution it is the event that is central and determinant: it alone selects what is necessary in the subject (organism) and the object (surroundings, including other organisms) to complete a communication (function) cycle (this latter not unrelated to the illocutionary act). "Function acts like a magnet which attracts toward it now some qualities and now others." For von Uexküll there was no such thing as evolution in the Darwinian sense, for the biological continuum, considered from the point of view of function (-circles), never contains anything but already perfect organisms (perfectly fulfilling their function-rules or organism-events) regardless of the level of complexity. An organ(ism) must not be related to a different—higher or lower, more or less "evolved"—organ(ism), but always and only to its function-circle, and the elements with which it is there brought into relation. "We may assume that where there is a foot, there is also a path; where there is a mouth, there is also food; where there is a weapon, there is also an enemy."

Though von Uexküll's work rose explicitly out of, and remained embedded within, a strictly neo-Kantian framework—the Umwelt was technically a phenomenal world corresponding to an a priori schema, filled in only with data acquired through the senses—it does not betray the integrity of his thought to insist here on the system and field qualities of his epistemology at the expense of the classical subject-object doublet that is supposed to be the ground of its Kantian inspiration. If von Uexküll's work generally is disparaged today by biologists for its naive antievolutionism, this has been at least partly compensated for by the prestige it has gained in the fields of systems theory and semiotics, for example, in the work of René Thom.[59] Indeed von Uexküll's oeuvre fell nothing short of achieving a fully developed mechanics of the biosphere in which the most basic irreducible elements ("moment signs" and "local signs") agglomerate into increasingly complex chains that in turn gravitate into coherently performing unities: the functions. Functions do not correspond to organs or material forms, but describe a milieu of pure exteriority, a site of selection and interconnection of informational codes and energies.

In a sense it was by pushing Kantian doctrine so far that von Uexküll eventually found himself on the other side of it. For the Kantian division of experience into a "material" and a "formal" component, in which "material" refers to sense-qualities on the side of the object (the manifold or *Mannigfaltigkeit*), and "form" refers to the a priori organization introduced from the side of the subject (mind), von Uexküll explodes: the subject becomes increasingly material (a multiplicity) and the object increasingly schematized. Though the two terms of each pair were already wedded in Kant (it was impossible to have one without the other without reducing reality either to a hollow abstraction or else to a senseless kaleidoscopic scattering) it was von Uexküll's achievement to have topologized the field of their encounter. He endowed this field with a precise system of rules that would bear on a new concrete "body" or plane of exteriority. Herein lies both von Uexküll's biological "modernity" as well as his potential (and more than chronological) kinship with the new novelistic space and organization of "character" as it had begun to emerge in modern writing in general and in Kafka in particular.[60]

Finally, what is perhaps the most essential feature of the Kafkaesque has to do with how the narrative embraces its underlying dynamo, the dynamo that precludes the formation and appearance of grand Events by generating

59 René Thom, *Structural Stability and Morphogenesis: An Outline of a General Theory of Models* (Reading, MA: Addison-Wesley, 1975). *Esquisse d'une semiophysique* (Paris: Intereditions, 1988).

60 Jakob Johann von Uexküll, *Theoretical Biology* (New York: Harcourt Brace, 1925), *Streifzüge durch die Umwelten von Tieren und Menschen* (1934), and *Bedeutungslehre* (1940), (Frankfurt: Fischer, 1970).

"microevents" everywhere as a perpetual flow of deviations or *difference*.[61] I have already suggested the way in which all events and all details seem to have the same status in Kafka; there is no hierarchy of Being, no particular foreground and background, no particular second-order significations that would sift data into piles or wholes graded according to importance; in short, *there is nothing behind phenomena.* Certainly this is an integral aspect of any immanentist (pantheistic) worldview. It also endows "flatness" with a richness that would not normally be its due. For this flatness is the result of a contraction *(complicatio)* rather than a reduction, and this new contracted space obeys a set of principles different from that of the space of visual perception. Contiguity, for example, no longer presupposes proximity.[62] Things no longer combine into ensembles strictly according to naturalist criteria such as cause/effect or in the rhythm of two events following one after another. This is owing partly to the "aggravated" present of Kafka's fiction, a characteristic whose tendency is to render every instant autonomous and isolated from every other.[63] Any instant and any element potentially can connect or segue into any other, or else may suddenly discover an untraversable distance wedged between itself and what at first seemed closest at hand.

61 There are always, for example, more files, more offices in *The Castle;* Titorelli always has more nearly identical versions of the same paintings in *The Trial;* and there are always more chambers and passages to be built in "The Burrow"; and so on. In the first case the files and corridors prevent K. from ever attaining access to or even an integral image of the castle. In Titorelli's attic one is treated to a vertiginous image of the "Summit" of Being; squalor, license, and the infinite proliferation of counterfeit images, whose function, however, was never to represent but rather to render indefinite (through multiplication), and to postpone (through perpetual substitution) the arrival of the finite and whole (the law, the sentence). Finally, in "The Burrow," the threat, whatever it may be, also never arrives, thanks to another kind of proliferation whose strategy seems perfectly adequate to Titorelli's third form of acquittal, "indefinite postponement." On this last point, see Franz Kafka, *The Trial,* pp. 152–163.

62 Deleuze and Guattari, in *Kafka,* actually oppose these two terms. The most acute treatment of this theme, however, can be found in Kafka's own story, "A Common Confusion," *Complete Stories,* p. 429.

63 This effect is so generalized that it is difficult to provide a single sufficient example. Consider, though, how in the corridors outside the assembly hall of *The Trial,* or the antechambers/bar of *The Castle* the narrator slips unproblematically from utter detachment and indifference to sexual frenzy and back again with less than the blink of an eye.

Thus the constant, sudden and inexplicable shifts of tone and scene, the changes of place and character—these are all endemic to the labile Kafkan universe. One might say that the principle of this universe, like the Heraclitean one, is "everything flows (becomes)," for one must by now at least recognize that in Kafka everything is in flight. Every element, every instant seeks its tangent, so that a story can be measured practically in quantifiable terms: for here, meaning has begun to give way to gradient.[64]

64 Again the land-surveyor or cartographic motif: This is why talk about "measuring" (in nonclassical, nonoptical environments) is always necessarily in relation to "gradients," not autonomous spatial quantities. A gradient, such as a temperature gradient, always implies a *differential* between two points or states and a *rate* of exchange, with a particular direction, etc. It measures a change in *value* of one quantity in relation to other variables—in a word, changes within an intensive field, not extensive space. It describes movements that though definitive and essential, are not visible. Again, Clerk Maxwell and Einstein actively supersede Newton.

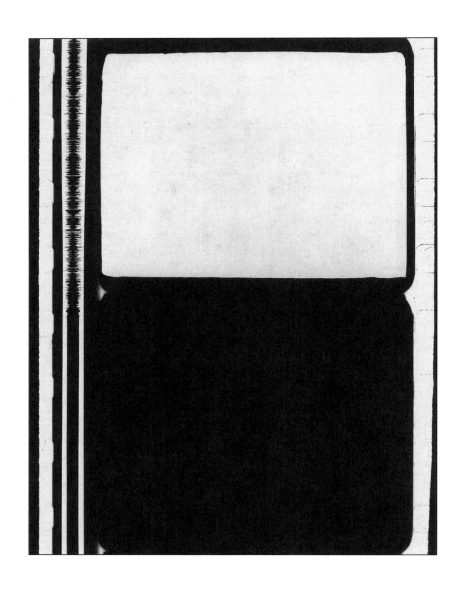

5.1
Peter Kubelka, *Portrait of Arnulf Rainer,* 1960 (film still)

Kafkan Immanence

The universe is not made,
but is being made continually.
It is growing, perhaps
indefinitely, by the addition
of new worlds.
—— HENRI BERGSON

NOTHING CHARACTERIZES THE SURFACE of a Kafka story better than its continuous marquetry of story fragments, each embedded beside the other as if it were the most natural thing in the world that such abrupt and disjunctive blocks of narrative should meld seamlessly across a single plane. Concrete, empirical propositions are systematically offered up only to be withdrawn or radically modified in the following step, by recasting them on a psychological, speculative, or other plane. Or just as commonly it is the reverse: events are introduced in the most diffuse, conjectural fashion only to be granted incontrovertible reality with the next breath:

> It was summer, a hot day. With my sister I was passing the gate of a great house on our way home. I cannot tell now whether she knocked on the gate out of mischief or out of absence of mind, *or merely threatened it with her fist and did not knock at all.* A hundred paces further on along the road, which here turned to the left, began the village. We did not know it very well, but no sooner had we passed the first house when people appeared and made friendly or warning signs to us; they were themselves apparently terrified, bowed down with terror. They pointed toward the manor house that we had passed and reminded us of the knock on the gate. The proprietor of the manor would charge us with it.[1] (my italics)

What principle allows one to move from the weightless series of "or"s of the third sentence, already threatening to proliferate in a delirium of unharnessed speculation, to the metaphysical absolutism of guilt and its entire correlative universe into which the protagonist is inexorably installed with the last two sentences? There are in fact two questions here, one on the level of form: How to account for the nonchalant, unprepared passage from the mundane ("It was summer, a hot day . . .") to the incomprehensible but profoundly organized world of the grotesque ("they were bowed down with terror," "The proprietor would charge us with it," plus the inexplicable complicity of these two statements); and one on the level of content: How could news of the knock have been transmitted to the village so immediately and so thoroughly, by what means or mechanism?

---

1 "The Knock at the Manor Gate," *Complete Stories,* p. 418.

Or are these two questions perhaps resolvable into one: What conditions need apply for an entire world suddenly to spring up *tout fait,* inaugurated with little more than a single gesture—as if it had been preparing silently and always to meet only this gesture when, and if, its time had come—drawing it fully formed from a state of pure incipience or virtuality? How, we may ask, does a gesture organize a world, and how does such a world, by agency of a gesture, arise out of another world?

Yet a Kafka story as we have seen is less a picture of a world than a progression of world fragments, aspects, images, sections. And as a literature of the fragment Kafka's is undoubtedly more unsettling, more radical, even if less spectacular, than those of other early modernists such as Eliot, Joyce, or Djuna Barnes, whose principle of "consistency" or "holding together" is, at least arguably, one of "spatial form." In these latter works the individual fragments find their unity, harmony, and place within an overall architectonic that can be perceived only, but all the more surely, after the entire work has been read, set apart from its inherent processes of unfolding and projected as an integral, richly woven but still structure.[2] In Kafka the fragment does not belong to a whole from which all temporal order has been sundered yet whose wholeness nonetheless persists at the level of its spatial relations. His fragments more properly resemble uncompleted movements or fragments of time; they are fleeing tones, qualities, and moods; that is, these fragments are oriented much more to punctual and intensive states than to uniquely extensive or spatial structures.

But much more importantly, the essence of what we have been describing as "the Kafkaesque" is found not in the mere fact of a disjunctive narrative, but precisely the contrary, in the bizarre and uncanny properties of the fabric that so completely weaves and weds its elements together. The space of Kafka's literature is not architectonic (cf. Joyce's Dublin, Eliot's encyclopaedia); it has no boundaries, fixed positions or places, or even a definable ground—it is made up entirely of relations, movements, passages. Kafka's work does not present an image of a total or even partial world but rather concerns itself with carving pathways, trajectories, vectors, and transverse movements that touch, penetrate, and filiate through an always indeterminate number of worlds. It is, then, necessarily a literature of shifts and tangents (in the deep as well as figurative sense), flights from level to level, world to world, tone to tone; its principle,

2 Joseph Frank, "Spatial Form in Modern Literature," *The Widening Gyre,* pp. 3–62. This is but the purest, most developed, and most intransigent of the spatialist readings of modern literature.

understandably, is one of opening, connection, and linkage. These openings and linkage points are continually provided by objects—which contract gestures—and gestures themselves. Behind every object a gesture, and within every gesture a virtual world.[3]

The Break with "Time"

> When the sage says: "Go over," he does not mean that we should cross to some actual place, which we could do anyhow if the labor were worth it; he means some fabulous yonder, something unknown to us, something that he cannot designate more precisely either. . . .[4]

"When Gregor Samsa woke up one morning from unsettling dreams, he found himself changed in his bed into a monstrous vermin."[5] So begins *The Metamorphosis,* the first of the several "animal stories" that Kafka wrote between 1912 and 1924.[6] It is the first major story written after the so-called breakthrough of Sep-

---

3 The meaning and significance of the gesture is undoubtedly among both the most delicate and insistent of problems in Kafka. Only for Walter Benjamin, however, did the gesture take on its full ontological and *heuristic* importance. The gesture, he shows, belongs truly only to the animal world, sharing with this world what he describes as its "utmost mysteriousness" and "utmost simplicity." Kafka, he says, proceeds methodologically by "divesting the gesture of its human supports and then has a subject for reflection without end." The gesture functions as both a bridge and a break—in any case a crossover point, the place where one world erupts, or injects its raw data, into another. These are the tear points, the breaks in Being that produce, however infinitesimally, radical, unstable moments of freedom. Benjamin, *Illuminations,* pp. 121–122. These themes are developed below in "Corporality/Communication and the Two Modes of Traffic" and "Pure Form."

4 "On Parables," *Complete Stories,* p. 457.

5 All references to *The Metamorphosis* will be to the Stanley Corngold translation published by Bantam Books, New York, 1972, except where the original German is used.

6 I use the term "animal stories" here only in quotation marks and with a measure of caution. This category is at best a vague and at worst a false one, since the specific phenomena, affects, and effects it is intended to cover appear almost universally throughout the works, even where animal characters are not explicitly animals, and even in those in which they are, their modes of appearance are quite varied: they are sometimes main protagonists ("The Burrow," "Josephine," *The Metamorphosis*), sometimes secondary or incidental characters ("Jackals and Arabs" for the former, the various horses, snakes, martens, etc. for

tember 22, 1912, the night in which Kafka composed the entire story "The Judgment," the result of a single, protracted convulsion that delivered not only this story, one of the few for which Kafka would maintain a degree of satisfaction and enthusiasm, but also the mature, simplified, and personal style that characterized all of the work that would follow.[7] No better example of the power and versatility of this discovery, this technique, can be found than in the opening of "The Metamorphosis." The abruptness of the overture, its humorous but terrifying revelation, is marked not only by a sudden transformation or passage of a body from the human to the insect world, but also the passage of this same body from a state of sleep to one of wakefulness. The sleep state, perhaps in its analogical relation to the human world from which the *Verwandlung* has simultaneously delivered this body, is characterized as one of "unsettling dreams."[8] What are we to understand by this? Is the state into which Gregor has suddenly found himself transformed little more than a reflection or realization of an image previously formed and prepared in sleep? Certainly the *Verwandlung* belongs to a much more unstable and chaotic process than this, for we have already learned that "the moment of waking up is the riskiest moment of the day."[9] After all, doesn't this moment of waking already imply an abrupt passage or transformation from the

---

the latter), and sometimes the central, but absent theme ("The Village Schoolteacher," "Blumfeld . . . ," "Cares of a Family Man"). In any case, the animal theme derives its intelligibility always in relation to that of the human, or human world *into* which it erupts, and which, in a certain sense as well, it molests. As I will argue below, "animality" constitutes perhaps the central ontological theme in Kafka's universe, characterizing as it does the irreducible, undivided, ineffable "other" world that is contracted in and interpenetrated with our own.

7 Klaus Wagenbach, *Franz Kafka: Eine Biographie seiner Jugend, 1883–1912* (Bern: Francke, 1958), p. 9.

8 For Kafka, sleep was always associated with volatility and with the possibility of death—thus his almost chronic insomnia and, one ventures to speculate, his morbid fear of sex (la petite mort). See Gustav Janouch, *Conversations with Kafka* (New York: New Directions, 1971), p. 143, and Ernst Pawel, *The Nightmare of Reason: A Life of Franz Kafka* (New York: Farrar, Strauss, 1984), pp. 426–427, 82, 83.

9 *The Trial,* section quoted above. The precariousness and volatility of things and the inconstancy of being is a universal theme in Kafka. To give this phenomenon a positive formulation is the principal task of this study. Several examples are supplied throughout the ensuing arguments.

world of sleeping or dreaming, that is, a passage from a world characterized by a flow of images embedded in a duration from which the spatially extended world is excluded, to a world comprising distinct and stable things that in fact only magically (though we are accustomed to say "scientifically") persist in being?

This is an example of those peculiarly important moments in Kafka, the moments when all virtuality is forced up close to the surface, when everything suddenly is at stake, when something is most likely to "happen" or to go wrong.[10] Thus, in an almost symmetrical fashion, the first sentences of *The Trial* describe K. visited while still in bed one morning by strangers whose absurd dress and nonsensical and indeterminate pronouncements, though these neither explain anything nor introduce anything new, somehow effect a fundamental change that radiates outward and contaminates everything, makes everything at once equally indeterminate, unclear, fluid, and above all, connected.[11] These bifurcation points are all the more paradoxical because the world of objects itself need not change in the slightest, only the meanings of the objects and the relations between them.[12]

10 For example, in the story "The Married Couple," the salesman/protagonist reflects: "in the present unstable state of affairs often a mere nothing, a mood, will turn the scale, and in the same way, a mere nothing, a word can put things right again." This state of affairs is harrowingly demonstrated in the story that ensues. Hovering at the brink of sleep, the father/husband N. suddenly passes into the realm of death only to be miraculously resummoned to life a few minutes later by his wife who attends, with infinite faith and innocence, to his reawakening (return). The interface between sleep and wakefulness developed as a chaotic hinge between alternate worlds is developed as well in "Description of a Struggle." See also note 38 below. "The Married Couple," *Complete Stories,* pp. 451–456.

11 Waking, but also drunkenness, inattention, etc. See the following analyses of "Blumfeld," "Knock on the Manor Gate," "Description of a Struggle," "The Hunter Gracchus," "The Little Woman," and "The Married Couple."

12 What we have to do with here is not, of course, "meaning" in its classical sense, but rather an "expressive" capacity that belongs materially to objects like a skin (i.e., neither signification, reference, nor intention), and which groups them together within some larger global element or tissue—either a becoming or a transcendent and globalizing code. What an object "expresses" is different than what it means, signifies, or intends—what it expresses are supra-objective qualities that derive either from the events (becomings) that affect or alter them, or else the "order" in which they hold a place. All of Kafka resides in the conflict between these two modes of "expression."

Such "break-with-time" overtures are hardly rare in Kafka's fiction. They determine, for example, such effects as the maddening inscrutability of the motives of action as when the protagonists of *The Castle,* "Before the Law," and so on arrive embedded in their predicaments with seemingly no capacity whatever, nor even a need, to relate events to a personal past, that is, to a *life,* which, by virtue of its traditionally sovereign extension through a linear past and future, ought indeed to transcend or encompass the events at hand. In Kafka, however, the opposite is always the case: events are primary and constitutive, the bearers of their own sovereign law and their own temporality. The proper tendency of this temporality is to encompass, indeed in a certain sense to demolish, the unity of the "life."[13] Out of this inescapable fact the peculiar Kafkan landscape arises, with its oppressively contracted horizons and perceived (though illusory) static nature.

Similar effects have been noted with respect to more classical literatures and in relation to different affects, notably love, and especially jealousy. In post-Kafkan literature these effects become almost common conventions with "paranoia" furnishing the historically most significant trope. Proust's *A la Recherche du temps perdu* could serve as a model study of the former, with Pynchon's *Crying of Lot 49* and *Gravity's Rainbow,* the work of Robbe-Grillet, and F. Scott Fitzgerald's "The Crack Up" as prime examples of the latter. It goes without saying that the transfer of the locus of such powers from subjectivity to a transpersonal characteristic of the field is a defining characteristic of this latter type of literature and indeed of modernity as well.

13 As Gunther Anders has argued in his *Franz Kafka,* the work of Rilke and especially Kafka mark a crucial reversal of classical (Kantian, Schillerian) aesthetics. For here, *renunciation,* once the province of a beholder (man) in relation to an object beheld, has now become associated, through a kind of reverse projection or animism, with the external world itself. It is now rather the abstract figure of power that "looks" and that alone is in a position to renounce, and man who is now merely the "seen." The phenomenological marriage of terror with beauty transforms the world into a transfixing gorgon's mask. Thus, it may be said, *the flow of influence now travels from the outside in,* no longer from the inside out. This reversal of subject/object relations explains much of the vertiginous but diffuse anxiety that characterizes both Kafka's works and the reader's or critic's reception of them. What we have here is a peculiar, but deeply modern, antihumanism in which forces are increasingly seen as determinant but also as transpersonal and indeterminate. In other words, narrative increasingly dissociates itself from "character" to adhere ever more intimately to events. (Musil here is perhaps the most important example.) Worth noting as well is Anders's inadvertent "facializing" treatment of the world, which bears important resonance with my later discussion of the theme of the "double turning away" (see below, section on "Animality"). Gunther Anders, *Franz Kafka,* pp. 55–70.

Thus the break with time is often also inseparable from a negation of worldliness and a collapsing of space. "The Hunger Artist" and "First Sorrow" as well as *The Metamorphosis* are clear examples in which the cage, the trapeze, and the filial chambers become emblems of a radical exclusion separating the protagonist from that modality of time in which his past is lodged, and with it the very essence of what he *is*, and wishes no longer to be.[14]

Thus the moment of waking reproduces—though in a much more complex way, since it belongs wholly to the individuating continuum of instants and need not undergo a translation into space—these same border or limit conditions. As the narrative begins it becomes clear that nothing can explain what is happening, just as nothing could have predicted it. One world continues indifferently, un-moved and unchanged, while another spills into it, filling all the cracks and chinks between objects with the swirling indefiniteness of a wanton becoming. Though the dream-time of sleep has come quietly to an end, somehow the pure virtual-ity that animates it has burst its barrier and invaded the real, depositing there precisely what had always been anathema to it: the so-called untimely, or the irreducible, absolute, and incontrovertibly *new*. We are assured now that this grotesque immixing (and this is developed in the narrative as a befouling and as a pollution in every possible sense) is in every manner real: "this was no dream." The very phrase "in his bed" further underscores this: a simple, objective obser-vation, yet made from a vantage point external to any hallucination or merely psy-chological delusion. Again, nothing in the objective landscape has apparently changed; bed, apartment, family, job, and so on remain entirely and maddeningly regular and intact.

The dynamism of this transformation is complex, and it is established from the opening sentence with the use of the deliberately imprecise, double negative of *ungeheures Ungeziefer* (translated "monstrous vermin").[15] Gregor's passage to the animal world is not a transformation from one steady state to another, but from

14 Roman Karst has argued, in relation to these and other works, that on the contrary, the cancelling of the past gives way to a fully immobile and endless present that cannot pass. See "Franz Kafka: Word-Space-Time," *Mosaic* 3, no. 4 (summer 1970), pp.1–13.

15 See Stanley Corngold's discussion of these terms in the notes to his translation of *The Meta-morphosis,* pp. 66–67. Corngold cites the arguments of three German critics—Kurt Wein-berg, Walter Pong, and Heinz Politzer—regarding the negative linguistic and semantic characteristics of the double "un-." Wilhelm Emrich also calls attention to the earth-negating "un-" of *"unirdischen Pferden"* in "The Country Doctor" (*Franz Kafka: A Critical Study of his Writings,* trans. S. Zeben Buehne [New York: Frederick Ungar, 1968], p. 159).

formal fixity itself to something by nature unfixable and therefore unimageable and in continuous (potential) variation. Kafkan narration typically employs such techniques as diffuse and continually deferred descriptions, extreme parsimony of details, and the embedding of knowledge in a webwork of tentative statements, confused facts, and spiraling entanglements, all to draw narrative away from pure representation and into a miasmatic domain of uncertainty and illegibility. Vagueness, then, is less an effect than a precondition of Kafka's narratives. Their ground is composed of murmurs, rumors, and always questionable and indeterminate evidence. Only what is immediately *at hand* has any real plasticity. For here as elsewhere, the important thing is neither what is potentially to be seen nor even what *is*—for the bug is many things, and critics have not tired in pointing to its inconsistencies and speculating on its "reality" and "true nature"[16]—rather, what is fundamental to the story is the dynamo of *trans*formation, the movement of becoming something *other*, the (intensive) *dis*placement across the interface that separates realms. In short, what is at stake is not what the bug is, but the vehicular processes that have seized and transformed a body and are enabling, or causing, its effective migration of realms. Witness Kafka's adamant refusal to allow any concrete illustration of the vermin for the book's dustjacket:

> It struck me the [the illustrator] might want to draw the insect itself. Not that, please not that! The insect itself cannot be depicted. It cannot even be shown from a distance. . . . If I were to offer suggestions for an illustration, I would choose . . . [a] room that lies in darkness.[17]

Thus the "un-" prefix, by its sheer abjection, violence, and compound negation, expresses this mysterious force of displacement and migration, the deforming or the blunting of the boundaries of Form and the reorientation of a static world of solids toward the fluid and visually imprecise one of shaping forces.

Later, the second section of the story opens by recapitulating in almost identical fashion the events that introduced the first: "It was already dusk when Gregor awoke from his deep, comalike sleep." It is still only the first day of his ordeal yet Gregor's situation has already begun seriously to deteriorate. He has incurred a wound, and what's more, his sleep, no longer merely troubled by

16 See, for example, William Empson's essay, "A Family Monster," *The Nation* 162, Dec. 7, 1946, pp. 652–653.

17 Kafka's letter to his editor Kurt Wolff on Oct. 25, 1915, in *Letters to Friends, Family, and Editors* (New York: Schocken Books, 1977), pp. 114–115.

dreams, is now characterized as comalike, thus offering a premonitory sign not only of death, but more generally of the apophatic, subtractive, evacuating, and "negative" method of this story. A salient feature of this part of the narrative is the steady progression of Gregor's anomie especially with respect to time— Gregor's second awakening takes place in the late afternoon. In the story's first section the protagonist's obsession is never with the transformation itself but rather only with lateness: lateness for work, lateness for the train, lateness to rise; the narrative is punctuated by reports of clocktime shouted out to Gregor by family members through the closed doors of his room; his reflections regarding his hateful job fix primarily on the constraints of schedules—early rising, train connections, meals taken at wrong hours, and relationships continually cut off before they can begin; the invasion into his life of organization and numerical time has him so overwrought that even his nights are now given over to "studying timetables"; and finally, it is the presence of a single iconic object, the alarm clock, against which, it may said, the metamorphosis, in the first instance is directed.[18]

Yet it is not just one object but rather two that dominate the first section: besides the alarm clock, the strange portrait of the lady in furs receives an inexplicably weighted significance (a significance we will see developed subsequently and throughout the story). There can, however, be no mistake; these two objects, and the respective worlds they express, are in systematic opposition to one another. The portrait, the frame, and the fretsaw with which the latter is fashioned, belong to a temporal order distinct from that of the alarm clock. Gregor's mother articulates this while defending her son against an implicit charge of laziness:

> That boy has nothing on his mind but the business. It's almost begun to rile me that he never goes out nights. . . . He sits there with us at the table, quietly reading the paper or studying timetables. It's already a distraction for him when he's working with his fretsaw. For instance, in the span of two or three evenings he [once] carved a little frame. You'll be amazed how pretty it is. . . .
> (p. 10)

We shall see in the following section how the alarm clock's absence in the story's second part is only an apparent one, for its function actually comes to suffuse all other domestic objects, particularly Gregor's furniture.

18 The opposition is expressed in phrases as simple as " . . . Then I'm going to make the break [from work]. But for the time being I'd better get up, since my train leaves at five."

Gregor's late awakening and the explicit but never explained absence of the alarm clock in the second section are signs not only of the encroaching temporal miasma, but equally of the steady regression of the exterior world,[19] and of all external determinations that go along with it—in other words, that of measure, and the rationalized institutional relations of the commercial and social world from which Gregor is gladly, and we now see successfully, emancipated. But clearly it is not enough to reduce the dimension of the temporal conflict of *The Metamorphosis* to such a simple one as that between a spatialized numerical-rational time and a qualitative-intensive one of pure actualization (creation). For the alarm clock is associated not only with schedules, appointments, and management, but most importantly with accumulation, that of money and especially debts. The office manager's visit to the Samsa apartment so early in the morning (and so early in the drama)—he had to have intuited Gregor's lateness before it occurred in order to have arrived as promptly as he did—underscores the utter pervasiveness of the specter of the family debts (whose responsibility Gregor had fully taken on) that adheres to everything in the story like a miasma that cannot be blown away. There are several factors at play here. First, there is, undeniably, the mode of time associated with *accumulation;* this again is represented by the clock and the debts (and later by the discovery of a stock of family savings). At the other pole, one finds an elaborately developed entire cosmos constellated around the opposing object of the bed—an obvious emblem of a different modality of time, that of a pure *dissipation,* a relation established by the single self-reproach: "'Just don't stay in bed being useless,' Gregor said to himself."[20] Second, there is the temporality of a certain kind of transitivity—an irreversible time associated with patrilineal filiation and according to which the transmission of debts *(Schulden)* from one generation to another both affirms and concretizes a hierarchical bond and serves as an instance of a *double* accumulation. *The*

19 In the first section, Gregor, upon awakening, can still see outside the window though his vision is limited by heavy fog. At the start of the second section his perceptual contact with the outside is limited to the passive reception of a shadow-play on the ceiling. Later in the section the window takes on a purely symbolic and nostalgic role, as the waning of Gregor's vision allows him to discern in the world outside his window only a "desert where the gray sky and the gray earth were indistinguishably fused." After Gregor's death the windows are immediately opened and the Samsa family gather in front of one of these, holding each other and gazing outward. On the systematic role of windows in Kafka see John M. Grandin, "Defenestrations," in *The Kafka Debate,* pp. 216–222.

20 *The Metamorphosis,* p. 7.

Metamorphosis and "metamorphosis" per se constitute a complex response to, and a systematic attempt to break with, these different aspects of a single monolithic time.

As the horizon of Gregor's world continues steadily to contract around him, the exteriority of the *socius,* still prominent even if negatively in the first section, soon gives way in the second to an exteriority of the body.

Corporality/Communication and the Two Modes of Traffic

The remainder of the first paragraph of *The Metamorphosis*—beyond the introductory sentence that supplies the story's premise—is devoted to a neutral and exact examination of Gregor Samsa's new body, devoid of both horror and psychology. Rather, it tends to the wistful consideration of practical questions: "His many legs [were] pitifully thin compared with the size of the rest of him." Attention is then turned to the room in which the strange transformation has taken place, but this now, compared with the treatment of his body, is only cursorily described—the narration veers this way only to note the presence of fabric samples, fixing Gregor for the reader as a traveling salesman with sufficient reason not to be where he presently is, a table on which the fabric samples lie, a strange portrait hanging above it—and furthermore assumes a clearly secondary importance compared with the latter portrait to whose comparatively lavish description the remainder of the paragraph is devoted. The portrait consists of a cutting from a "glossy magazine"—presumably a photograph—depicting a woman done up entirely in furs: hat, boa, and muff. The woman is suspended in the midst of a strange gesture, "sitting upright and raising up against the viewer a heavy fur muff in which her whole forearm had disappeared."

This completes the curious beginning of *The Metamorphosis:* two paragraphs, one describing the body of a man become insect, the second describing an image behind glass of a woman swathed in animal skins, caught in a strange act of address while simultaneously retreating more deeply still into her own animal mantle. What connection exists between these two bodies seized in the throes of a "going over," their bodily surfaces bearing the chitin and fur of an incomprehensible animal being? Though it would be difficult to declare anything definitive at the outset—without considering, for example, how this particular pairing returns again later to play out the central and most intense moments of each of the succeeding sections of the story—a number of observations may already be made. To begin with, the body clearly is the site within and upon which *metamorphosis* is played out. But this body concerns much more than simply the anatomical bodies that correspond to characters; it is also a collective or social body, a body constantly mutating, multiplying, and redeploying its surfaces. In a very deep sense, then, it concerns the traffic of bodies: their movements, interactions, and above all *their capacity to affect other bodies* (or partial bodies) as if across a common tissue or membrane. Within such a system of bodies—and this is true for all aspects of Kafka's work—everything comes to be linked in a system of mutual, even symbiotic, implication, that is, in a network of relations of exchange; but these relations are purely material and vital and generally have neither interior nor content. This network explains the strange role of gestures in Kafka's work; they are at once a supremely important element of expression though at the same time always apparently at odds with what *ostensibly* is taking place in the narrative.[21] The traffic in words and forms belongs to the realm of discontinuous and divided Being—the spaces between them cannot be traversed, messages of this nature cannot and do not arrive.[22] Indeed, entities of this nature have an interior, that is, a meaning, but this meaning is not transmissible.

21 On the subject of gestures, see, besides Benjamin (cited in note 3): Walter Sokel, *Franz Kafka, Tragik und Ironie: zur Struktur seine Kunst* (Munich: Langen, 1964), pp. 227 ff.; Karl J. Kuepper, "Gesture and Posture as Elemental Symbolism in Kafka's The Trial," *Mosaic*, 3, no. 4, summer 1970, pp. 143–152; Gesine Frey, *Der Raum und die Figuren in Franz Kafkas Roman "Der Prozess"* (Marburg: Elwert, 1965); Heinz Hillmann, *Franz Kafka, Dichtungstheorie und Dichtungsgestalt* (Bonn: Bouvier, 1964), pp. 130–136; Deleuze and Guattari, *Kafka;* and Gustav Janouch, *Conversations with Kafka,* p. 14.

22 Direct examples of this phenomenon in Kafka's work are far too obvious to require listing them here. But the preceding comments offer a somewhat convincing explanation for why it is, both in Kafka's oeuvre generally and in the short piece "On Parables" specifically, that it can be claimed that "in parable . . . one always loses." For in parable, that is, in all traffic in words, one can never get beyond sterile tautology "that the incomprehensible is incomprehensible, and we know that already." For in the story in question, parable—linguistic or narrative presentation of Truth—is understood in opposition to "reality," that is, to "the cares we have to struggle with every day." The aporia explicitly entertained in the story, every bit as much as the question of whether narrative/language can form a bridge to the real, to undivided truth, is the inverse: Can we cross over into parable, transcend the empirical and everyday? The unequivocal answer is no. But then again, this lesson (ours) too is given only in language/narrative (parable). See *Complete Stories,* p. 457. It is worth noting again that the site of Kafkan narration is conceived as a hinge or interface *between* two (potentially communicating) nested worlds.

But there remains another modality or organization of reality that might be described as a kind of glacis of pure continuity and exteriority, which is populated by, indeed itself constitutes, a kind of full body. This latter may be characterized as a domain of sheer immediacy, that is, of real and perpetual contact, though this contact is always "meaningless" as such, or "empty." In fact, it is possible to say that a body is "fullest" precisely when it is most empty, that is, when it forms a continuous, even if folded, surface and not an interior, signifying space. Moreover, it is continuous in two senses: first, because it bears a capacity for continuous variation (continuity in time) and second, because it is continuous with—and immanent to—all other bodies (continuity in space).

The first and most prominent way in which this continuity comes to be inscribed in the text is in the traffic of and many discussions concerning nourishment in general and food in particular. The second section is particularly fraught with such discussions of nourishment, both that of Gregor and of his family; for food is the medium and plane on which the social bond (here of the family) is so often articulated in Kafka.[23] It is also arguably the story's central leitmotif; for Gregor's final revelation, which after all may be taken for the story's climax, arrives in no other form than the discovery of music as a new and "unknown nourishment."

Food is both that which sustains the body, giving it weight, gravity, and stature, and, in its more sublimated, rarified forms (of which music is one, but also philosophy—the inquiry into first causes, mysterious origins), that which weaves the very web that links all bodies together.[24] Food in fact becomes a

---

23 "The Hunger Artist" and "Investigations of a Dog" are the most obvious examples. On the ambivalence toward food as connective substance and as world, see Kafka's reflections on his own thinness and vegetarianism in *Letters to Felice,* trans. James Stern and Elizabeth Duckworth (New York: Schocken, 1973) (see note 25), and Gustav Janouch, *Conversations with Kafka,* and especially the commentaries by Elias Cannetti, *Kafka's Other Trial; The Letters to Felice* (New York: Schocken Books, 1974), pp. 22–29; also Ernst Pawel, *The Nightmare of Reason.*

24 The correlation between music and food will be established presently. On this form of nourishment and the connection with nonindividuated, social fabric, "Josephine the Singer" and "Investigations of a Dog" are perhaps the two most explicit examples, though the whistling sounds that emanate from *The Castle's* telephone networks, the paper-rustling sounds of the adjuvant's own body movements, the droning in "The Burrow," the clicking sounds of the balls in "Blumfeld, an Elderly Bachelor," as well as the persistent rumor motif throughout the works are all unquestionably related to the same ambivalence toward continuity and communication.

kind of language in Kafka,[25] where language in its pre- and nonindividuating forms—mute corporality, gesture, music, rumor, and finally, food[26]—is a principle of inhering, connection, and radical immanence; while in its individuated forms—messages, letters, pronouncements, sentences, science, etc.[27] and

25 If food became a kind of language, language undoubtedly also became a kind of food, the more rarified form of nourishment—writing—coming more and more to replace the more earthly one of meat. Again Kafka's anticarnivorous habits articulated another social relation: "For months on end . . . my father had to hide his face behind the newspaper while I ate my supper." Kafka's vegetarianism did not have to be self-conscious or aggressive for it to have constituted nevertheless an "outsideness," or a divergent line vis-à-vis his family lineage. Kafka's father, himself the son of a butcher, had little tolerance for Kafka's meatless diet. *Letters to Felice,* p. 30 and passim. On another occasion Kafka turns his vegetarianism into a weapon against Felice: "One night at dinner with your sister, I ate almost nothing but meat. Had you been there, I would probably have ordered a dish of almonds."

What else, one must ask, is the art of hunger in "The Hunger Artist"? The refusal of a certain kind of food not only constitutes a rejection of a certain complex of social relations, but the providing of access to another. Food is both the pivot point to sustain a "going over" or a change of state (often toward enlightenment) and the material stand-in for language in Negative Theology's "negative path" *(via negativa)* to the Absolute. The apophatic "not" of the mystics ("He is not soul or intelligence, not imagination or conjecture, not reason or understanding, not word, not intellection, not said, not thought . . .") becomes anorexia and abstinence. Language's inability to express the infinite is a preoccupation common to Kafka and to the Christian mystics. See Pseudo-Dionysius, *Areopatica* in Elmer O'Brien, *Varieties of Mystic Experience: An Anthology and Interpretation* (New York: Holt, Rinehart, 1964), pp. 86–88.

On the apophatic theme in relation to Kafka, see also sections from the *Diaries* quoted in Jean Wahl, "Kierkegaard and Kafka," *The Kafka Problem,* ed. Angel Flores (New York: New Directions, 1946). Wahl's argument is to show that Kafka's tendency *to affirm through negation* actually opposes Kierkegaard's "transcendental mysticism with an immanent mysticism." Wahl goes even further to thereby discover in Kafka a certain (anti-Christian) "Nietzscheism." See especially pp. 271–272, 268. A related argument is put forward by Maurice Blanchot in his *Espace littéraire* (Paris: Gallimard, 1955), pp. 75–79, as well as by Malcolm Pasley regarding a putative reverse transcendence through the construction of a "negative edifice" in "The Burrow." See his essay "The Burrow" in *The Kafka Debate,* p. 419.

26 These latter are nearly always linked, as we will see, with the animal universe (i.e., Leni, Josephine, etc.).

27 Though any inventory here would be endless, a few of the most salient examples are "An Imperial Message," *Letters to Felice, The Castle,* "The Penal Colony," and "A Common Occurrence."

especially fasting[28]—it is little more than a principle of distance, division, and exclusion, a bad infinity. Thus the theme of communication, bound up as it is with that of food, dominates the second section. The communications in question are those between Gregor and his family, communications in which his sister stands in, not at all as the incest object that she is conventionally seen to be, but rather as go-between and custodian of the code, or rather, in collaboration with food itself, as the corporal vehicle of communication.

Gregor's sister straddles both worlds, her comings and goings from Gregor's room, her daily reports to the family, her special and almost too insightful understanding of Gregor's situation—here given full play in the void left by Gregor's own loss of (individuated, human-all-too-human) language. This is further underscored by her role as the sole entitled bearer of nourishment, for she of course is everywhere identifiable with it, from the initial maternal offering of a bowl of fresh milk and soaked bread[29] to the final ecstasy in which Gregor's hunger is both sublimated and satisfied by the music his sister produces with her violin, an excitement so intense that it must be extended in a fantasy of incorporating her entirely and consummated with an extraordinary, vampirous kiss to her soon-to-be

28 Fasting is a special case ("The Hunger Artist," "Investigations of a Dog," etc.). Though not really a language as such, it is nonetheless an explicit negation of food and worldly corporality, an extension of the apophatic method to a silent incantation. (Thus, in the story "The Silence of the Sirens," silence is described as a "still more fatal weapon" than even the Sirens' treacherous song.) It also renders corporal individuation even more acute, closing the body off from its milieu, while literally hardening its boundaries. This is, of course, in every possible way but one, in opposition to music, whose role is to gather, merge, and consolidate. What they have in common is the capacity to elevate and deliver, though in one case (music, nonindividuation) it is to a state of preindividuated immanence, in the other (fasting) to a (false) transcendence (ostensible acquittal); Kafka: "one must throw away life to conquer it," Gustav Janouch, *Gespräche mit Kafka* (Frankfurt: Fischer, 1968), p. 250. The appearance at the end of "A Hunger Artist" of the lithe panther, and at the end of *The Metamorphosis* of Gregor's sister's "stretching young body"—two images of a healthy unselfconscious animality—is the reaffirmation of what I have called a "mute corporality" in the face of the false transcendence proposed by Gregor's and the Hunger Artist's apophatic withering away and consequent "enlightenment."

29 Let us skirt the obvious Freudian cliché merely to underscore the food/body conflation. Note as well the inedibility of this offering as an unambiguous if trivial gesture signifying a refusal of maternity and Oedipal worldliness in the same sense that the hunger artist himself renounces not food itself but only the wrong type of nourishment. "The Hunger Artist," *Complete Stories,* pp. 268–277.

uncollared neck (p. 49).[30] Indeed Gregor's sister is indistinguishable from relations of food: it is she who prepares meals, not only for Gregor but also the family, now that the cook, unable to tolerate the recent developments in the household, has resigned; it is also she who feeds Gregor, yet within the same activity also communicates with him both by deploying his food and interpreting it like so many mute alimentary codes:

> His sister noticed at once, to her astonishment, that the bowl was still full, only a little milk was spilled around it; she picked it up immediately—not with her hands of course, but with a rag—and carried it out. Gregor was extremely curious to know what she would bring him instead, and he racked his brains on the subject. But he would never have been able to guess what his sister, in the goodness of her heart, actually did. To find out his likes and dislikes

30 The motif of necks rightfully has received an immense amount of attention in Kafka studies. Most have focused on the symbolism of the downward bowed or upward cocked postures, and occasionally with the covered/uncovered duality. What both these characteristics bring equally into evidence, however, is a peculiar but typically Kafkan *plasticity;* the neck here becomes a zone in perpetual kinetic and elastic variation, and this seems to express some inherent (either potential or realized as in the case of certain "animal" characters) freedom of the body as a proliferation of mute but purely affective (uncoded) or intensive states. Indeed the peculiar lability, slipperiness, and flexibility of this body part induces it almost to separate off from the rest of the body (except, of course, when other body parts are equally seized by incomprehensible gestures and elastic deformations, at which time they too approximate a certain plastic "neckness") giving it an almost self-animated, autonomous, and for this reason, highly eroticized quality.
The elasticity and slipperiness also lends the neck a certain quality of nakedness and genitality, which is in no way diminished by being covered up. Here it is only the encounter with a garment (foil) that is crucial—whether this be a loose, open one or a tight-fitting one does not matter—for it is here that the body in Kafka seems always to be caught slipping, decomposing, or falling while at the same time opening up obscenely into a kind of hyperanimation, continuity, and nakedness. Kafka's short description of Titorelli as he appears to K. on first meeting bears each of these themes out clearly: "'Oh those brats!' said the painter, trying unsuccessfully to button his nightshirt at the neck. He was barefooted and besides the nightshirt had on only a pair of wide-legged yellow linen trousers girt by a belt with a long end flapping to and fro. . . ." Thus the relation to nakedness—here of a decidedly genital nature—links necks in no uncertain way to the peculiarily erotic, even obscene animal and object world (Odradek and the philosopher's top are clear denizens of this elastic, neck/genital, animal realm, just as is Titorelli, who is at once filthy and fecund in the rodent sense of the term), whose characteristics are developed further below.

she brought him a wide assortment of things, all spread out on an old news-paper: old, half-rotten vegetables; bones left over from the evening meal, caked with congealed white sauce; some raisins and almonds; a piece of cheese, which two days before Gregor had declared inedible; a plain slice of bread, a slice of bread and butter, and one with butter and salt. In addition to all this she put down some water in the bowl apparently permanently earmarked for Gregor's use. And out of a sense of delicacy, since she knew that Gregor would not eat in front of her, she left hurriedly and even turned the key, just so that Gregor should know that he might make himself as comfortable as he wanted. (p. 24)

Gregor's relations with his family are increasingly reduced to the alimentary axis: the acceptance or rejection of their food. Since Gregor has not managed to produce even the semblance of human speech since the first pages of the story they wrongly imagine that he is also incapable of understanding their speech. For this ostensible reason, and this is undoubtedly as much a purpose as a side effect of the metamorphosis, communications, at least linguistic ones, cease to be direct,[31] that is, they either pass over into other nonlinguistic—gestural, alimentary—mediums or simply become indirect—rumor, hearsay, inference. The family's time and ac-tivities now, as if perceived through the focus of a one-track animal consciousness, are entirely oriented, even defined, in relation to meals: "there were family consul-tations at every mealtime about how they should cope; this was also the topic of discussion between meals. . . ." All news of Gregor as well is transmitted through perfunctory accounts of his eating habits, verbal exchanges from which he himself in turn is able to infer the state of his family's morale, yet in doing so must endure hearing himself addressed only in the third person,

It was only later . . . that Gregor sometimes caught a remark which was meant to be friendly or could be interpreted as such. "Oh, he liked what he had to-day," she would say when Gregor had tucked away a good helping, and in the opposite case, which gradually occurred more and more frequently, she used to say, almost sadly, "He's left everything again." (p. 25)

Gregor's hunger, which from the first page is described as ravenous, is soon ori-ented less and less to food, and more to news or communications:

31 Two important exceptions are when Gregor is made to endure direct insults from his fa-ther and from the charwoman, though in both cases Gregor is treated not as an interlocu-tor but merely as an object.

But if Gregor could not get any news directly, he overheard a great deal from the neighboring rooms, and as soon as he heard voices, he would immediately run to the door concerned and press his whole body against it.

Sequestered in his room, and seemingly at an infinite remove from the world, Gregor finds all his sensual data—light, vibration, sound, duration—become, through interpretation, sources of knowledge. Every surface is now a sensible one—walls, doors, food—and as speech recedes in importance as a vehicle of information, it is the surface itself of Gregor's body that grows in subtlety, sensitivity, and articulateness. Pressing himself against the door—the image is one of two membranes communicating across an interface—he employs his entire body as if engaged in a total act of sensuous reception. Elsewhere one notes the many references to body heat—usually accompanying extreme negative agitation, as when overheard family discussions of money elicit the flush of guilt and shame—and coolness (the leather couch, the glass frame of a picture), which either calms and provides solace, or accompanies the passage from a negative intensity to a positive one (the abstract union with the furclad woman). Here the hardness of Gregor's carapace is but a figure of tragic irony, as when he wonders to himself, noticing his new if only temporary powers of robustness and quick healing, "Have I become less sensitive?"; or later, when wounded by an apple that easily penetrates his shell and embeds itself in his back, he endures the "unbelievable pain" that forces him to stretch out his body "in a complete confusion of all his senses."

In addition to the communication and interaction through food, Gregor continues to communicate some residual human affect through the uses he makes of his body, especially through the means employed to keep it hidden. He expresses at least some degree of self-consciousness, humility, compassion, shame, and even apology, by keeping himself pressed under the couch while his sister is present in the room and, when this is no longer sufficient, under a sheet that hides him entirely. Nor are the track marks that he leaves around his room signs lost on his sister, who immediately deduces from them that Gregor is in need of more free space and less furniture. Later the father will prove less astute at reading this language, failing to interpret Gregor's gesture of pressing himself against the door of his room as one of submission, good will, and remorse at having broken out of his confinement. Gregor's wound, however, will be the basis of an intersubjective relation of guilt that temporarily reunites him to the family sphere in the beginning of part 3, a connection effected both literally and symbolically through the gesture of leaving open the door to Gregor's room. And last but not least, the psychological debilitation of his final days is accurately deciphered by his sister at the story's end, upon examination of Gregor's emaciated and dessicated corpse.[32]

The many passages about money—the family finances, the debts, and the obsessive calculations—are also meditations on food (nourishment), or more exactly on social (familial) relations.[33] Gregor's success and subsequent pride at sustaining the family after its financial disaster has lapsed now into failure and shame. What food and money have in common is the ability to contract and store quantities of force; they constitute a source and a reserve of vigor. Thus the father is early on characterized as ineffectual, slothful, and parasitic, a result, though, and not the cause of having been ruined financially. He is bereft of business, but also, correlatively, of youth and vigor. His seemingly hopeless physical bankruptcy is further inscribed in the form of his debts, which, as has already been noted, are transitive, like an inherited guilt, the very reason Gregor must continue to work and defer his yearning for freedom.[34] The demands made on Gregor's body for the most part serve the void left unfilled by the father's.[35]

Yet with Gregor's metamorphosis—the sudden creation of a massive debt vis-à-vis himself—the balance swings in the opposite direction. The father's authority returns, as does his health, vigor, and to a certain degree his wealth (his financial situation is suddenly revealed to have been far more favorable than previously understood), and, in symbiotic fashion, fills the familial "force-" gap, evacuated this time by the debilitated and hungry Gregor.[36] Perhaps most impor-

32 The demoralization of the Samsa family is expressed as well by the loss of appetite and the phrase, often overheard at mealtimes, "Thanks, I've had enough" (p. 26).

33 Here again the complex link between the sister's body, music, and the lessons Gregor was meaning to offer her by way of money also becomes an exchange for the "unknown nourishment."

34 The profound kinship between debts and guilt *(Schulden, Schuld)* is here self-evident. It was of course Nietzsche's central theme in book 2 of *The Genealogy of Morals.*

35 The body as derelict continent from which all selfhood has been drained and the body as a site of perpetual recoding by social, transindividual forces are but two sides of the same perpetual theme in Kafka. The body offers itself at best as a "deputy self" for traffic in the individuated world *or* as the site and source of a pure, inalienable gestural expressivity (animality). See "Wedding Preparations in the Country," pp. 55–56.

36 Once again this reciprocal economic (in fact thermodynamic) relation is underscored after Gregor's expiration at the story's end in the final image of his sister's newfound

tant of all, though, is the manner in which these developments constitute a reversal of certain relations of exchange. Most significantly is the reversal of the patrilineal debt (guilt), which is passed back *against the flow of patrilineal time* to the father who must now assume the added burden of a son constituted as a pure economic and social liability. Later we will see how this process of "waste" constitutes the positive (at the level of relations) if doomed (at the level of subsistence of the organism) act of *The Metamorphosis.*

Gregor's earlier vigor as a "breadwinner" and his regular donation of money to the family established a bond of warmth and exchange among them that, however, soon withered.[37] Only the bond between him and his sister remained strong, and this is inscribed, as every social bond must be, in a concrete exchange. Here it is the money for the music lessons that Gregor had hoped to provide for his sister, and this unrealized gesture grows into an extended reflection on Gregor's part, which, because it also explicitly notes the parental opposition and therefore the antifamilial nature of such a scheme, opens up definitively the axis or bond-line of the story's greatest affective intensity. The exchange of money, food, music, and gestures consolidates the individual levels, or rather, concrete continuums, of force, vigor, sonority, and corporality, respectively, across which power and desire are continually articulated. Every object embedded in this system necessarily bears a complex relation to all others. The sister's body enters deeply into this relation, for now linked to Gregor in an almost vital way on all levels, part deputy, part appendage, but also part host, for her body is also the vessel of the "unknown nourishment."

We move now to the scene in part 2 in which Gregor's mother and sister begin, after serious deliberation and debate over the therapeutic benefits of such an act, to evacuate his room of all its contents. Furniture, too, will now play a role like that of nourishment. In this form, however, it is a kind of food or nourishment that connects Gregor less to his family and to human society, per se, than to the past, to the temporal and historical human world. During her first visit to her afflicted son's room, a transgression attempted only on the sly during the father's momentary absence from the house and with the daughter's express permission, Gregor's mother hesitates and protests:

---

physical and sexual vigor: "they watched their daughter getting livelier and livelier. . . . [S]he had blossomed into a good-looking, shapely girl. . . . [A]t the end of their ride their daughter got up first and stretched her young body."

37 *The Metamorphosis,* p. 37.

doesn't it look as if by removing his furniture we were showing him that we have given up all hope of his getting better and are leaving him to his own devices without any consideration? I think the best thing would be to try to keep the room exactly the way it was before, so that when Gregor comes back to us again, he'll find everything unchanged *[unverändert]* and can forget all the more easily what's happened in the meantime. (p. 33)

The sudden, unexpected presence of the mother gives Gregor a temporary shock, touches him, and catching him off guard, redraws him into the familial (oedipal) and social world from which his terrible transformation had provided a means of escape.

Had he really wanted to have his warm room, comfortably fitted with furniture that had always been in the family, changed into a cave, in which, of course, he would be able to crawl around unhampered in all directions but at the cost of simultaneously, rapidly, and totally forgetting his human past? Even now he had been on the verge of forgetting, and only his mother's voice, which he had not heard for so long, had shaken him up. (p. 33)

Kafka states specifically that it is the mother's *voice* more than anything else, compounded by the recent lack of any direct personal address, that shakes him out of his state of forgetfullness.[38] Language characteristically is the element par excellence of the beyond (memory), that is, of a certain rootedness in Being.

38 In "Description of a Struggle," the overhearing of the mother's voice by a child still submerged in the precarious drift of partial wakefulness is (mistakenly) taken as evidence of an inaccessible realm of stable being, within which "even a little liqueur glass [manages to] stand on the table steady as a statue." The personality in question here, that of "the supplicant," is characterized by pure turbulence and dispersion; he suffers from a "seasickness on land," and all the elements of his world continually "sink away like fallen snow." He is described as if inhabiting a kind of aphasia:

Don't you feel it's this very feverishness that is preventing you from being properly satisfied with the real names of things, and that now, in your frantic haste, you're just pelting them with any old names? You can't do it fast enough. But hardly have you run away from them when you've forgotten the names you gave them. The poplar in the fields, which you've called the "Tower of Babel" because you didn't want to know it was a poplar, sways again without a name, so you have to call it "Noah in his cups."

He interrupted me: "I'm glad I haven't understood a word you've been saying."

Clearly, forgetting is always a forgetting of the past. If the ontological stability of character is a function of what Thomas Pynchon once called its "temporal bandwidth," that is, the degree to which a character's being is extended and oriented to its past and future,[39] then forgetting is the prime characteristic of its lability and an indispensible element of transformation, actualization, or becoming. In relation to the present case, we see that Gregor's potential increase of mobility (freedom) is linked directly to an inverse but corresponding loss of the past, that is, the removal of furniture.[40] The story's major theme is here articulated ever more deeply. For the actual metamorphosis that serves as its ostensible basis, or more specifically Gregor's animality, is, as has been noted, continually developed in opposition to a certain mode of time; the time of accumulation, rational measure, and surplus (alarm clock, office manager, debts). It develops another form of time proper to a different system of exchange, a mode of time that may be said to characterize Kafkan animality. Here is developed what one could only call the time of a pure expenditure or pure waste in the Bataillean sense.[41] From this perspective, Gregor's body, through the sacralizing passage of metamorphosis, is extracted from one system, that of *productive* economic exchange, and inserted into another, in which it is transformed into a purely sumptuary object, a kind of *potlatch* or sacrifice (literally, a making sacred) offered in a deliberate spectacle of destruction and waste.

The Metamorphosis recounts the insertion of a disruptive violence into a certain economic traffic of objects, power, and desire (here represented by the system of the family, though this is but a model and microunit of a greater, more ominous entity). But it is at the same time inseparable from a certain sacralizing

39 *Gravity's Rainbow* is profoundly indebted to Kafka, not the least for its development and refinement of a radical either/or: "either everything is connected [in a realm available to perception] or else nothing is." These alternatives, however, boil down perhaps to the same thing: the world involves an impossible ethical decision between a hyperfocused paranoia and a pure scattering. Slothrop is a direct descendant of the supplicant. See Thomas Pynchon, *Gravity's Rainbow* (New York: Viking, 1973), p. 434.

40 In *The Trial*, mobility is clearly associated with indefinite postponement, that is, with K.'s only chance of triumphing over his charges and his ordeal. He considers the following advice from Block: "let me remind you of the old maxim: people under suspicion are better moving than at rest, since at rest they may be sitting in the balance without knowing it, being weighed together with their sins," p. 191.

41 Georges Bataille, *The Accursed Share, Vol. 1*, trans. Robert Hurley (New York: Zone Books, 1988). See discussion below in "Animality," this chapter.

process whereby corporality and animality may be seen as two aspects of a single movement of becoming that, in shattering one order—that of numerical time, discrete forms, and subjective essence—make possible the composition of, and access to, another—that of continuity, virtuality, catastrophe, and the instant.[42] The connection between the religious and the economic dimensions of animality will be treated later. It is sufficient here to note the importance played by Gregor's body as the site of convergence and strife of different systems and forces, and its dual capacity—owing to its profound implication and immanence within these systems and forces—to receive affects from bodies around it and to affect in its turn, through its own transformations and peripeties, those same bodies.

This is why the humiliation that ensues from Gregor's transformation into a bug is felt more strongly by the family than by Gregor himself. The dramatic staging of an *unproductive* expenditure, that is, an activity whose entire meaning derives from the possibility of personal loss, and as great a one as possible, also links it in no uncertain terms to those necessary activities in any culture not oriented to production and conservation: luxury, war, sex, play, art.[43] The conflict of the two economies was central to Kafka's life: on one hand, the need to work, to earn a salary, and to belong to the responsible world of men, and on the other, the desire to write, and to belong to the world of *Luftmenschen,* but a short semantic step from *Ungeziefer* and *Untiere* (vermin and beasts).[44] Moreover, Kafka's relationship with Felice focused this conflict as one between the eminently productive unit of the family, and the sacrificial, sumptuary life of solitude and literature.

At another level, closer to the details of the story, one is compelled to interpret Gregor's reaction in the scene with his mother only as a temporary faltering of resolve and as a punctual regression, wholly at odds as it is with the general move-

---

42 Catastrophic is used here in the purely descriptive sense of open, metastable, sensitive, fluctuating systems, as developed separately by Bataille and René Thom. See René Thom, *Structural Stability and Morphogenesis* (Reading: Addison-Wesley, 1975).

43 It is no coincidence that the bed and the alarm clock are presented as opposing, rather than complementary, objects in part 1 of *The Metamorphosis*. (Interestingly enough, both these objects vanish entirely, and inexplicably, after the opposition is established.) The role of the bed and the question of uselessness has already been established.

44 See Maurice Blanchot, "L'Exigence de l'oeuvre" in *L'Espace littéraire;* Pawels, *The Nightmare of Reason;* Cannetti, *Kafka's Other Trial;* Heller, *Franz Kafka* (New York: Viking, 1974), chap. 2; Emrich, *Franz Kafka*, pp. 136–151; Brod, *Franz Kafka: A Biography;* and on the Luftmensch trope, Anders, *Franz Kafka,* chap. 2.

ment of the story. For no matter how *The Metamorphosis* may be interpreted, it must also be seen in its aspect as an escape from the hierarchical/political violence of the Oedipal family (the Law). Its positivity lies in constructing a field in which relations and forces (communications) are deployed horizontally (planometrically), which, in the case at hand, means along the brother/sister plane.[45] At moments the narrator seems to develop the intense relationship between Gregor and his sister as a fantasy belonging entirely to her, a childish "romantic enthusiasm" that would exacerbate Gregor's situation for no other reason than to guarantee an even greater exclusivity of relations with him.[46] Her effective power and authority over the situation is further established by allowing her to be the first to pronounce Gregor's death sentence. However, one need only recall the spectacular fantasy to which Gregor is given over at the story's end, in which he imagines himself shut up forever in a room with his sister (his own version of exclusivity) with nothing but the music of her violin to sustain them, to convince oneself whose fantasy this really is. Moreover, in this piece, following as it does on the tail of Kafka's breakthrough story "The Judgment," one immediately notes the structural transformation: in the first story, two horizontal relations (*engagement:* Georg/fiancee; *friendship:* Georg/correspondent in Russia) are interrupted by an order originating from above (the father), and the story consequently ends in the protagonist's death.[47] In the present story, the horizontal relation (brother/sister) supplants the hierarchical, vertical one, and never so strongly as in the daughter's peremptory pronouncement of Gregor's death sentence that finally and

45 The locked doors of Gregor's room, though feebly masked as a "traveling salesman's habit," explicitly effect the preliminary "break"—here a spatial, architectural one—with the organization of the Oedipal household, one which the metamorphosis extends to a more essential realm. On the onanistic theme in relation to this elaborate bachelor apparatus of locks, photos, glass panes, fur, exudations, etc., see the section below, "An Isomorphism: The Bachelor Machine," and note 120.

46 *The Metamorphosis,* pp. 31–34.

47 This same structure, in which a message, swathed simultaneously in death and enlightenment, is passed from above to below, will make its most stark and unmitigated appearance as a piece of political technology in "The Penal Colony." The "Letter to His Father" partly duplicates this same structure, though in reverse. The missive originates with the son, ostensibly addresses the father, though never reaches him. For the son has enlisted the mother as medium of connection but simultaneously transforms her into the ultimate and alternate *destinataire,* establishing with her—at least on the level of pure form—the exclusive and horizontal bond that excludes the father. This demonstrates the typical Kafkan mode, as developed clearly in *The Trial* and *The Castle,* of procedure by alliance and affiliation

completely deprives the parents of their son.[48] "Justice" is no longer dispensed from above; nor is the death a mere punishment for sloth and incest, as moralizing and Freudian interpreters of Kafka have read into it. Death is rather, its reward.[49]

This scene then represents a *strategic* momentary recapture of Gregor's affective body by the institutional framework of the Law *(le propre)*. In a most uncharacteristically affect-charged moment, Gregor develops a sudden neurotic attachment to his furniture (and to his past—the [true] nightmare from which he is trying to awake). This simply makes of it a kind of "bad nourishment," like the fresh milk, bread, and fruit from the human world that Gregor had found so inedible earlier on:

> They were clearing out his room; depriving him of everything that he loved; they had already carried away the chest of drawers, in which he kept the fretsaw and other tools; were now budging the desk firmly embedded in the floor, the desk he had done his homework on when he was a student at business college, in high school, yes, even in public school. . . . (p. 35)

This invasion and pillaging of Gregor's room represents an undisguised attempt to conquer and reclaim; thus the mother's hesitation over the most expeditious use of the "territorializing" effects of the furniture.[50] The campaign is directed to an extensive domain—the space of Gregor's room—but the effects radiate throughout his entire temporal body; an assault aimed at intercepting him on the self-willed trajectory of his animal "becoming."

---

rather than confrontation in order to respond to and dismantle relations and forces of historical, temporal filiation. It also explains the predominant use of the mode of free indirect speech in Kafkan narration.

48 *The Metamorphosis,* p. 52.

49 "The child's happy exuberance is recovered in death's expression of sovereign liberty." Georges Bataille, "Franz Kafka," in *Literature and Evil,* trans. Alastair Hamilton (New York: Urizen, 1973), p. 138.

50 By "territorialization" one should understand a twofold process: that of capturing an element and drawing it away from one coherency or functioning ensemble and into a new one, as well as the secondary process of reinvesting this element with subjective essence based on the givens of the new context.

Milieu and Event

Indeed the most salient feature of this invasion scene is the clash of two worlds, which, like two regimes of meaning, struggle to gain control of the brute matter at their disposal. In the sister's eyes, ever sympathetic to Gregor's transformative adventure, furniture is but a useless sentimental obstacle *to movement,* and it is movement of a kind, that most deeply characterizes this animal world. But the furniture is caught up in another ensemble and takes on another meaning from the very moment that the (voice of the) mother is present (as part of the ensemble). It now reflects the shared historical processes of family life and economy, sedimentations of affectivity, living instruments inseparable from Gregor's *Bildung* as man, brother, and son. However, *Bildung,* or formation, is always a forming of finalities, that is, of a fixed and absolute Being. But the *Verwandlung* does not represent a changing or a "going over" merely from one self-identical Form to another. Rather, it describes an uncanny passage or slippage from the world of stable, individuated Being where a man (form) is ever identical with himself, to a monstrously unstable world of *becoming,* a world populated by an infinity of infinitesimal differences produced inexhaustibly at the heart of things, differences that risk at any moment to "swerve" into adjacent but tangential ensembles and worlds.[51]

These "swerves"—switchpoints for the sudden and indeterminate changes of state of Kafkan narrative—are rooted in the world of space (Being) but nevertheless represent anomalies, "singularities," that is, necessary departures from it. These swerves begin as microscopic events[52] that intervene in and mobilize an inert world of fixed relations by projecting into everything the aleatory flow of time. But it is not the global or linear time of a progress or *development,* which merely evolves and consolidates the identity of Forms in space (Being), but a time that destabilizes Forms, tearing them out of their fixed perches in Being and embedding them in the stochastic current of a (perpetual) *Verwandlung,* or Becoming. This is the Kafkaesque virtuality and the perpetual "flight" of things that was developed earlier. It is also the principle of the "explicatio" method, which discovers in every object, moment, or gesture a world to be unraveled, a road to be taken or not. The Kafkan universe reveals itself at this molecular level of bifurcations and events; in vain does one search for meanings, closure, or

---

51 On "slippage" and the clinamen, see the section below, "Death and the Double Turning Away."

52 See analysis of "A Little Woman" below, ibid.

signifying "spatial form" at the molar level of story, novel, or oeuvre. Events are always tear points in the tissue of Being, qualitative transformations of matter or destabilized essences. They are pragmatic, experimental; one does not know in advance where they will lead. Their purpose is neither to produce nor to arrive at preordained ends, but rather, blindly and without finality, to establish conduits and relays, as these nascent events domino outward pursuing their consequences back into the empirical and material world. The event does not reproduce; it burrows.[53]

The event, then, to return to the earlier discussion of Umwelt theory, is thus both an embracing and an excavation of a milieu. The milieu in turn is carved by the event and bears its shape. Every event is defined and exhausted by the production of a new milieu; it is a forcing to the surface of once virtual relations that have now become actual. Kafka's world is like a sea of indetermination on which float islands or clusters of determination unlinked among themselves, though no less internally coherent for that. This is because the event has two sides, depending on to which level it is related. On the one hand, it belongs to the undetermined, the chaotic, and the temporal, that is, it is a singularity; on the other, it seizes and constellates as much material as possible, it is worldly, spatializing, and persists in its being. One will immediately recognize in such a description the preconditions of the Kafkan universe, with its floating, disjunctive islands of space and time. It shares these Riemannian conditions[54] with Einsteinian and futurist space, for they alike derive their character and shape not from any preexisting substratum, but rather from the actual material content that fills it and its accompanying field of force.

53 Kafka's story "The Burrow" is paradigmatic of his method. The classic Kafkan predicament: a threat is posed *ostensibly* from the outside (the Law), whose tension is resolved in a different realm, within the "immediate givens" of the empirical world. The earth itself pantheistically embodies both the threat as well as the potential (though of course only partial) release from it. The animal ceaselessly excavates passages, exits, escape routes, gaps, cul de sacs, zones of invisibility, illegibility or problematic ontology, finding hope, or at least "indefinite postponement," within the same substance that simultaneously contains, multiplies, and expresses the threat (the "charges"). In this sense, the earth in "The Burrow," in Spinozist fashion, forms the infinite, expressive, and univocal substance, while at the same time acts as a concrete image of what exists above ground as human society and destiny in *The Trial*.

54 On Riemannian space, see Hermann Weyl, *Space Time Matter* (New York: Dover, 1952, orig. 1917), esp. p. 98.

To conceive of the field of *The Metamorphosis* in globalizing or strategic terms is inevitably to accept the interpretation of the story as one of unrelenting negativity and failure. Gregor's *Putsch* against Being, World, and Family would be seen as first contained, then repulsed, and finally extinguished altogether. On its own level and in its own terms such an interpretation is at least justifiable and, despite its triviality, would have to be accepted were it not for the fact that Kafka's narratives, individually and as a collective body, by virtue of their incomplete, episodic, heterogeneous, and open nature, belie not so much this specific interpretation as the underlying conditions that would make it follow inexorably. Of primary importance in Kafka is to give full recognition to the instant, to the role of the singular and to the isolated "problem." Again, in Kafka it is never a question of a global or permanent triumph; all advantage is momentary, fleeting, limited to the specific conditions at hand. In this sense, the same type of conflict or tension that determines the form of the content of Kafka's work—the antinomy of the two worlds— is also reflected in its form of expression: the very movement of narrative is continually molested by the exigencies and materiality of the event.[55]

There is certainly an apparent paradox embedded here. For it is simply not possible to argue that "narrative," because it involves a succession from one point to the next, is for that somehow excessively and illegitimately *spatial,* while on the other hand, the "event," because it is always associated with a concrete spatial correlative—a "milieu"—is somehow powerfully and subversively *temporal.* Nor is this what is being argued here.[56] It is not a question of opposing, according to the familiar neo-classical formula, a spatial to a temporal order, form, or regime, but rather, to oppose two different complex orders in which the same elements—spatial and temporal—are constellated in a different way to form separate aggregates with different regimes of effects. This is why it has been possible to oppose a classical or Euclidean "regime of narrative," in which time forms a substratum distributing and developing forms in space, to a modern—Riemannian, Einsteinian, Minkowskian—"regime of the event," which substitutes a "space-time" consistency in place of a substratum, yet maintains the true and irreducible materiality of nature through the concept of the milieu (field). The opposition of space and time is possible, in fact, only within the (neo-) classical model, whereas

55 See the discussion in chapter 4 on "Description of a Struggle," and note 10 above.

56 This does, however, seem to be the point argued by Worringer in his *Abstraction and Empathy: A Contribution to the Psychology of Style,* trans. Michael Bullock (New York: International University Press, 1980, orig. 1908). See also Joseph Frank, *The Widening Gyre,* p. 57.

the opposition constructed here concerns precisely the essential attribute of time—its capacity to make possible, or introduce, *change* (i.e., difference)—and this in relation to its two irreconcilable modes of appearance: (1) on the one hand, as a transcendent dimension determining through some magical medium events that take place outside itself (the classical or substratum theory of time); or (2) on the other hand, as a principle immanent to phenomena that can account for variation, diversity, and change from within. The first regime knows duration through development in *Time,* while the second, precisely because it is home to the "event," knows it only through the "untimely," that is, the sudden (catastrophic, singular, originless) and unexpected.[57]

Clearly an entirely new type of creature or being would be required fully and properly to inhabit such a world: creatures of pure unpredictability, creatures unable and disinclined to see themselves from outside the conditions of the *haecceitas* or point-moment (any point-moment whatever) in which their presence (individuality) is always fully given. Kafka's world indeed is replete with beings of just this type.

---

57 Nietzsche's concept of the "untimely" is such an example of an antihistorical temporality. Thought must act *against* time in order to act upon time, but as something arriving from outside of "time" itself . . . and thereby planting the seeds of a time to come. See the foreword to "On the Uses and Disadvantages of History for Life," in *Untimely Meditations,* trans. R. J. Hollingdale (New York: Cambridge University Press, 1983). For Nietzsche *qualitative* changes—e.g., the rise of the state or the origin of bad conscience—do not

> arise gradually through organic adaptations or social contracts but by breaks, leaps, or compulsions that wantonly defy linear historical processes, they come like fate *(Schicksal),* without *Grund,* reason, consideration or pretext, they appear as lightning appears, too terrible, too sudden, too convincing, too "different" even to be hated . . . wherever they appear something new soon arises, a ruling structure that *lives,* in which parts and functions are delimited and coordinated, in which nothing whatever finds a place that has not first been assigned a "meaning" in relation to the whole. They do not know what guilt, responsibility, or consideration are, these born organizers; they exemplify that terrible artists' egoism that has the gaze of bronze *(die wie Erz blickt)* and knows itself justified to all eternity in its "work" . . .

This (anthropomorphized) causeless cause which is the origin of all change, but which nonetheless always bears within it its own absolute inner *necessity,* is nothing else but the "untimely." (*The Genealogy of Morals,* in *Basic Writings of Nietzsche,* trans. Walter Kaufmann [New York: Modern Library, 1968], bk. 2, 17.)

Animality

As this first attack on his newfound autonomy grows, Gregor's reflections on his formative past give way to a desperation, a need to act, to affirm, in the tactical terms of his new form of being, an intensive modality (cathexis, animality) over and against an extensive domain (the territoriality of the furniture). Of all the room's "furnishings," however, only one is explicitly nonhistorical, antifamilial, and genuinely oriented to a true exteriority—and it is no coincidence that this object also represents a point of convergence (and bifurcation) of, among a great many other things, both the human and animal worlds. The object in question is the framed portrait of the woman in furs, which Gregor embraces now with a fervor and intensity unmatched in any scene of the story.

How might this gesture be understood? Does the depicted woman, introduced as early as the story's second paragraph, represent from the outset the promise of a successful *Verwandlung,* embodied in the form of a creature with one foot in the netherworld, full, mysterious, and eros-affirming, resplendent in her corporal and gestural animality? This woman most certainly comes from the same world as does, for example, Leni, the lawyer's nurse and cook in *The Trial,* whose webbed fingers and insatiable lust for accused men brand her with the necessary "defect" (singularity) and the univocity or singleness of affect that characterizes inhabitants of Kafka's animal world. To this world belongs also the never-ending procession of subalterns, those diminutive and almost paper-thin characters that appear so often (at least the men) in groups of two or three, nearly always as adjuvants, for they are in their deepest essences complementary beings, mirror images of themselves, isolated and purified fragments of a larger, more complex affectivity that never fully reveals its face.[58] These are beings steeped in play, they

58 Doubling is among the most consistent but also the most significant and structural of Kafka's leitmotifs. For these characters, insofar as they are double and essentially hybridized, are actually reflections of a doubled and therefore hybrid world: a world where two orders of being coexist and interpenetrate one another. For Lubomir Dolezel, Kafka's world consists precisely in having transformed the premodern oppositional schema of a natural vs. a mythological world into the modern schema of a visible vs. an invisible world. What is important here is that even though the relations between the invisible (institutional, organized) world and the visible one are maintained at best only tenuously by emissaries and messengers, these worlds are nonetheless entirely immanent to one another and no longer comprise separate domains as they did according to the earlier mythological vs. natural schema.

Now it is certainly only the creatures from this other world that are double—but they are so necessarily. They do not express formal or essential individuality as would any

ask few questions—they have an infallible instinct for the simple and useful answer, so fully and completely do they inhabit their worlds—they have the bodies,
the minds, and the faith of children. These creatures owe their animality more
than anything else to their perfect and radical immanence in the world. These
figures always appear conjugated with, or ancillary to, the filthy figures of the Law,
and they are themselves often sullied by this proximity.

But the important thing is that these creatures, even when subjugated or bru-
talized, are the embodiment of freedom, they are bodies first and foremost, almost
alarmingly plastic and without definitive form, innocent and pure like desire itself. Though they are often presented as subordinate to the figures of the Law, this
only more strongly marks their abject peculiarity: they have wills and desires of
their own that make them pathologically incapable of following orders properly.
Thus their mischievousness and deviance is not due to any corruption in a moral
sense, only to distractability, a chronic side effect of their being as creatures of absolute immediacy. They are figures of disorder and chaos (even of death itself),
though paradoxically they coexist side by side with, and sometimes even *as,* emissaries of the Law.[59] They wear bizarre bits of clothing—hats, aprons, bed clothes,
tight shirts—and as often as not are in a relative state of dishevelment or undress—often a bare neck,[60] a tear or a soiled spot in their clothing is a sufficient

creature in the natural, visible world, but rather express the indistinct, metastable complexity of mixtures of states and affects; they are virtual creatures, or as Benjamin observed,
ones who are incompletely formed. Their "individuality," insofar as they possess any, is reducible to an infintesimal and probably illegible difference. On indifferentiability, see note
4, chap. 4; on Titorelli's paintings, note 61, chap. 4. For the Benjamin citation see following note, and Lubomir Dolezel, "Kafka's Fictional World," *Canadian Review of Comparative Literature* (Mar. 1984), pp. 61–83. Ontologically, these creatures concern us and are
important first and foremost because it is their very similarity that testifies to their character as non-, or not entirely, individuated beings (Adorno, *Prisms,* p. 253).

59 That they are able simultaneously to inhabit both worlds is, of course, a necessary and constituent, rather than contradictory, factor of their being. I could not agree more with Walter Benjamin, who has compared them to the *gandharvas* of Indian mythology, celestial
creatures in an unfinished state. This undoubtedly is what makes them free, or at the very
least why "for them . . . there is hope" (Benjamin, *Illuminations,* pp. 116–117). Martin Buber has similarly compared them to licentious demons that are Gnostic transformations
of the archons in Pauline gospel. Martin Buber, *Two Types of Faith,* trans. Norman P. Gold-
hawk (New York: Harper, 1961), pp.162–169.

60 Bare necks as well as covered necks, as already mentioned, are a constant erotic leitmotif in
Kafka. For example, the baring of Gregor's mother's neck after her fainting spell in *The*

sign of their animal nature. Because they do not speak they are prone to extravagant and incomprehensible gestures and sounds.

It would be impossible to overestimate the importance of the woman in the framed portrait or, more importantly, the importance of the family of animal and doubled characters to which she belongs. To a deeper understanding of the ontological nature of this group of characters we must now to turn our attention, leaving a more detailed examination of the portrait until the following section. These characters are among the strangest and perhaps least understood characters in modern fiction.[61] To begin with, one might well argue that their very historical possibility did not even exist until, on the one hand, the advent of a more fully rationalized bureaucratic society that reduced the culture of the individual to a limited number of definable, market-oriented (quantifiable, exchangeable, abstractable), and utilitarian functions, and on the other, the advent in (literary) aesthetics of that "flatness" already discussed (of which Kafka was the prime innovator), which provided a kind of homecoming for those relatively indistinct, almost preindividual but profoundly happy characters of early Greek literature.[62]

Metamorphosis is followed immediately by the obscene doffing of her remaining garments and mounting her husband in an erotic embrace.

61 Though an entire study would be in order, a number of salient examples may be mentioned here: the Lulu character in Pabst's *Pandora's Box,* the protagonists of Chaplin's early films, virtually any Beckett character, the transformation of Kit in the third section of Paul Bowles's *The Sheltering Sky,* and perhaps preeminently, the figure of Robin Vote in Djuna Barnes's *Nightwood.* Seen from this perspective, *Nightwood's* final scene, which so scandalized, repelled, and perplexed its readers (including T. S. Eliot), appears logical by Kafkan standards, even overdetermined. Paul Bowles, *The Sheltering Sky* (New York: Ecco Press, 1978, orig. 1949); Djuna Barnes, *Nightwood* (New York: New Directions, 1937).

62 This is a question in itself of massive complexity and importance, for which an entire study would be inadequate treatment. It is raised here for the following reason: two of the magisterial works of literary history written in this century, Erich Auerbach's *Mimesis,* and Georg Lukács's, *The Theory of the Novel,* both attempted to ground their studies of the novel form (just then beginning to manifest irrefutable signs of moribundity) in Greek epic, which functioned as a model either of happy immanence (Lukács) or at least of a literary form whose dazzlingly flat surface perfectly approximated a full and unproblematic world where delight in physical existence was everything (Auerbach). Both works extended their studies through to the modernist period—Woolf for Auerbach, Dostoevsky for Lukács—and then failed egregiously to account for the anomalous nature of these works in relation to their respective *machines d'analyse;* witness: "In Tolstoy, intimations of a breakthrough into a new epoch are visible; but they remain polemical, nostalgic and

Second, once the status of these characters is granted, one immediately perceives to what extent *all* characters in Kafka are tainted to some degree with this kind of virtual animality. What character is free of the volatility of the children in "Children on a Country Road" or the protagonist of "Description of a Struggle," what figure of the Law does not either lapse periodically into strange fixed postures like Klamm's perpetually bowed head, Titorelli's hunched back, the weirdly restless contortions of the judges in the portraits he paints of them, or have food stains on their clothes, read pornography, spend their days skulking in attics or remain eternally in bed? And finally, what is "animality" after all, and what is its significance?[63]

---

abstract. It is in the works of Dostoevsky that this new world, remote from any struggle against what actually exists, is drawn for the first time. . . . Dostoevsky did not write novels . . ." (Lukács, p. 152). This observation is all the more striking when one considers that the precursors of Kafka's strange animal-like characters are unquestionably to be found in those inscrutable and perseverating characters of Dostoevsky, as much perhaps as in the most eccentric aspects—the tics—of those of Dickens.

The literature of Kafka is without doubt a literature of homesickness, but to relegate it to yet another reflection of "the age of absolute sinfulness" would be an unjustified reduction and a blind refusal to consider its true dynamic and its other, more essential side. Returning, with the advantage of hindsight, to the fundamental analyses of Auerbach and Lukács (and here one would certainly need to include Nietzsche's earlier study of the choral origins of character in his *Birth of Tragedy out of the Spirit of Music*), we must ask ourselves in all seriousness whether in fact, with the reappearance of these strangely uncomplicated and labile characters, whose being, unlike anything one finds in novels, is expressed in the fullness and immediacy of the instant, not to mention the peculiar narrative machine in which they find their home, we are not witnesses to an important historical phenomenon: the emergence of a new kind of world, and especially, of an entirely new kind of *epic* to express it.

If immanence is a primary quality of epic, an immanence that emphasizes the physicality and instantaneity of existence while reducing the distinction and individuation of forms, then the problem of the epic might well be re-posed today in light of the emergence of so many of these related themes in the most serious productions of modern culture. But this is precisely what Auerbach and Lukács fail to do.

63 Nearly all of the most interesting discussions of Kafkan animality, however much they differ, have in common the postulate that Kafkan animality posits a forgotten realm that is no longer accessible to man, even though it continues to exist right there alongside and within his world. The most powerful of these arguments sees animals as "receptacles of the forgotten," a category—first articulated by Benjamin but then taken up successively by

Let us begin by summarizing some of the ground already covered. We have already seen that there is a type of multiplicity—not necessarily "human" but *vital*—that may be conceived not from a transcendent but from an immanent perspective, and that from this perspective we should expect to find not individuals corresponding to forms or essences, but rather blocs of matter-moments or even function-circles (von Uexküll). We saw that the role of time in these two ontologies was very different. In the first we had to do with a monolithic, irreversible, and cumulative time, which corresponds perfectly to that mode of being which characterizes objects on this plane, that of *development*. In the second we saw how time, ceasing to serve as a substratum for objects, took on a full ontological materiality through its association with the aleatory but continually generated event. The Kafkan narrator (*not* the protagonist—for there is always a

---

Adorno, Emrich, Bataille, Stine, etc.—that includes childhood and freedom itself in its most abstract form, and which is as well intimately and inextricably connected to the body as though this were "the most forgotten alien land" of all. Yet for Benjamin animals are still sometimes associated with the family circle, are sometimes positions to which one has retreated from the human form out of shame, or are linked to a real distortion, insofar as they take on "the form things assume in oblivion." This, however, seems not to preclude the fact that only in animality can there be any hope whatever (Benjamin, *Illuminations,* pp. 116, 117, 132, 133, 144). Adorno sees animality as a possible salutary recollection or replacement for the bourgeois concept of human dignity. For Bataille it expresses an implicit defense of sovereignty: puerile exuberance over and a willful, even political, denial of efficient, rationalized activity.

Emrich's long (over 120 pages) though miscellaneous treatment also associates animality both with childhood and with purposelessness in general, as if it were only in first deinstrumentalizing the world that any type of freedom could even be posited. Animality is associated with a forgotten but recoverable totality (freedom, selfhood, etc.); it is opposed to work and rationality, and finally even defined as enigmatically embodying "man's true self" (pp. 206–207). Emrich seeks to identify animality with (positive) meaninglessness, and therefore with all strange and diminutive objects in Kafka, and with the entire mutinous, inaccessible objective world in general. The Benjaminian theme of "the forgotten" is meant to be the central theme of Stine's study, though he Christianizes Kafka's animals, seeing them less as prelapsarian than as "fallen" (p. 61); they are alternately ancestral and linked to what is both despicable and indestructible in us (p. 64), and as well function as a purely formal, heuristic element allowing Kafka an endless reflection on the modern present without ever presuming to grasp it (p. 79). Emrich, *Franz Kafka,* chap.3; Adorno, *Prisms;* Bataille, *Literature and Evil;* Peter Stine, "Franz Kafka and Animals," *Contemporary Literature* 22 1 (winter, 1981), pp. 58–80.

separation, and this difference provides the antinomial space through which Kafkan narrative unfolds) sees the world from the first perpective, yet the world he sees is nonetheless deeply rooted in the *other*.[64] Now the being of the animal differs from that of the human first and foremost because it is fully given in the instant and thus belongs to an undivided Being that to humans is lost forever. Thus Walter Benjamin was able to describe Kafka's animals as "receptacles of the forgotten": the animal world would have offered Kafka a means of developing, or at least approaching, realities that humans and human language can never finally attain.[65]

We then developed the question of corporality, or more simply, of the body, as a term opposed to and potentially replacing that of subjective essence. The body was seen as a surface or site, partly appropriated and partly shared, across which are effected the multiple practices of social exchange, that is, of community. The body furthermore was developed not as a discrete and autonomous entity but as physically continuous with its field or milieu of interaction: it is first and foremost a cluster of affectivity, a membrane that receives and imparts affects to its surroundings. We saw that gesture belongs to this world of immediacy and affectivity, and not to the divided world of language with which it is, in any case, always at odds. Corporality finally was linked to animality, as two related modalities of becoming, two inseparable forms of a radical immanence. What remains is to understand precisely what is the relation between animality and immanence.

A number of important approaches to this last question can be found in the philosophical anthropology of Georges Bataille, whose own career as writer and essayist began in the mid 1920s, almost exactly where Kafka's ended. Like Kafka's, however, Bataille's importance has grown since World War II and for the

---

64 In Kafka this is what structurally underlies and constitutes the theme of exile. It is also the tragic given: this other reality cannot be given in language. "Perhaps they did not even understand him . . . or perhaps they did understand him and with great self control answered his questions, but he a mere puppy, unaccustomed to music could not distinguish the answer from the music." "Investigations of a Dog," *Complete Stories,* p. 285.

65 This, to be sure, is a constant theme of Kafka criticism. Among Kafka's own works, "A Report to an Academy" is quintessential: language is constructed as the opposite of animality, first in the linguistic (illocutionary) circumstances of the original transformation, and then later when looking back: "what I felt then as an ape I can represent now only in human terms, and therefore I misrepresent it." *Complete Stories,* p. 253.

same essential, if vague, reason: they are both seen as having been the first, each in his own way, to have articulated a certain kind of experience, even a new space of thought, that arose out of the ashes of the old world—be it the world of Hegelianism or the bourgeois novel—and to mark the beginnings of a modern one.

It is sometimes said that Bataille's importance for twentieth-century thought was to have established the possibility of thinking outside of the Hegelian dialectic. Existence would no longer be conceived in terms of opposites resolving each other and overcoming themselves by means of a third term that would supplant them. For Bataille, opposites coexisted on the same plane, they fed each other, produced one another incessantly, with neither wish nor need to resolve themselves in a higher unity. For this reason, Bataille, like Kafka, could never have been interested in monolithic forms and metaphors like "development," and "depth," nor in the accompanying metaphysics of meaning, repression, and revelation. Bataille's anti-Hegelianism is, however, most strong in his demonstrations of how the true basis of life is to be understood *in the desire to destroy self-consciousness* rather than to attain it. The true impulse at the basis of life is the impulse towards indistinction, continuity, unconsciousness (notably the philosophical un-*self*-consciousness), and death. Humanity, in the deepest parts of our being, Bataille affirmed, does not desire the acute atomized state of transcendence and individuation in which the meaning and goal of history would be deposited; we long not to embody *Geist* but rather to be released from it by means of the violence that connects us to the night of our original "animality."

Bataille recovered the "negative" from its moral, psychological, aesthetic, even political exile within repressed modes of culture and restored it to the very heart of experience. The negative is now seen at once as the foundation of experience—it is the source of the sacred, of eroticism, of culture itself—and as the always proximate "Other" that experience *as such* (as experience of self, as the mode of being of self-transcendent, individuated subjects) cannot contain or know.

It is here in Bataille's work that the concept of animality finds its first, and to my knowledge its only, explicit philosophical elaboration. What is it, then, that an animal sees when it casts its indifferent and frictionless glance across the surface of the world? What this fluid and oblivious gesture fails to do—and this is the source both of humanity's fascination and horror—is to distinguish in the world anything resembling stable and distinct forms; it fails to separate even *itself* as distinct from this seamless continuity that it apprehends. The animal, in accordance with Bataille's famous formulation, "exists in the world like water inside of water."[66] For animality is immediacy (*l'immédiateté*) and immanence.[67] The animal, in other words, inhabits its world in pure and perfect continuity; its glance is totally devoid of "intelligence" (science) and self-consciousness—and yet the animal is neither a mere object nor does it belong to the world of the human. For Bataille the universe is contained between two poles: the world of animality, of immanence, source of the sacred, the realm of *indistinction* (undividedness) and continuity; and the world of the discontinuous (the distinct and individuated), the objectified, and the profane. If humankind eternally is fascinated by the animal's glance, this fascination amounts to little more than the simultaneous horror and ecstasy that we must experience in the presence of a being who is at once like us (that is, a nonobject and biologically discontinuous) and *yet continuous with the world.* It is here, in the animal's promiscuous and indifferent gaze, that we, in some fundamental way, experience our own death, first as the loss of the (self-) consciousness of our own living, and secondarily as that all-encompassing night in which the animal bathes (continuity with the not-I) and which we now apprehend as surrounding us too on every side. Animality (immanence) is an *écoulement,* or an uninterrupted flow of the outside to the inside and the inside to the out;[68] it is the eclipse of all oppositions or, in Bataille's terms, the absence of Negation.

For Bataille, experience forms a quasi-infinite surface—two-dimensional yet oceanic—on which humankind and humankind's activities (culture) form but an island whose solidity and stability is furnished solely by consciousness (i.e., language). But this solidity, this exile from the continuous, even if necessary to our existence, is nonetheless intolerable to us.[69] And so it is through religious experience that we have projected our longing for immanence into that realm which, for our discontinuous selves, has become an outside, a quasi-beyond by means of which we reestablish connection with our continuity.

The "beyond" to which I refer is not the same beyond that distinguishes the realm of transcendent objects. Insofar as one is discontinuous and self-conscious, he

---

66 Georges Bataille, *Théorie de la religion, Oeuvres completes* (Paris: Gallimard, 1976), vol. 7, p. 25.

67 Ibid., p. 23.

68 Ibid., p. 27.

69 Georges Bataille, *Erotism: Death and Sensuality,* trans. Mary Dalwood (San Francisco: City Lights, 1986), p. 15.

is already a transcendent object; he is already torn from the pure immediacy of his original animality, that "time" before the world was divided into distinct objects and before he had become a self-conscious and acting subject committing operations on them. Thus humankind is twice cleaved: first as a subject distinct from a world become an instrumental, exterior object; and then, once this exteriority has been introduced into our world, we are able to—and do—see ourselves from the outside as also distinct, that is, as an Other. I have used the word "time" above in quotation marks, for to say that the world of animality or immanence is the world of immediacy (*l'immédiateté*) is to elicit a world entirely given, *not in time* at all, but in the instant. For the original and happy plenitude of the instant gives way to the violations of time only through the operation of another type of transcendence, one that Bataille situates in humanity's first invention of tools. When one extracts an object from the world in order to fashion it, this object becomes subordinate to his or her will and desire—to humankind itself—a first but crucial step in the hierachization of Being. But more importantly, when a tool is fashioned, it becomes an object meant to act upon yet another; the tool itself is put into a relation of subordination insofar as it has become a *means* oriented toward an *end* that exists elsewhere or in another object. Transcendence is therefore introduced into humankind's being from the very moment that this split (discontinuity) between "means" and "ends" becomes conceivable. It is also in this means/end duality that one finds the definitive rupture of the instant (*l'immédiateté*), for it is in this relation that two events for the first time can be understood as simultaneously separate from one another *but also linked*. This eclipse of the instant means that events are no longer seen entirely from within—"like water inside of water"—but from *outside*. Time and humankind belong to this outside, and it is to this outside that they owe their irreducibly discontinuous beings.

From this discontinuity, from this outside, the underlying continuity of existence appears as a gulf, as the obliteration of the individual personality, in fact as a kind of nonbeing itself. Yet as humans, we long to be continuous with something beyond ourselves, we long to be connected with Existence, which is both deeper and broader than our own discontinuous, "random and ephemeral individuality."[70] Continuity is thus indissociable from death. But how can one approach this lost continuity, this "outside" that is really a pure insideness,[71] without inflicting a mortal wound to one's biological being? There is a particular

70 Ibid.

71 On the insideness of the outside, see Gilles Deleuze's concept of the fold in his book *Foucault*.

experience that Bataille calls "transgression" that can carry us momentarily across the line that separates the two fundamental forms of Being. Both erotic and religious experience (in the primal, ecstatic sense) as well as certain economic practices of pure unproductive expenditure (waste, *dépense*), are modes of approaching momentary continuity. They are both forms of forgetting and oblivion; they articulate that space that Bataille called the "limit," the region where our most intense experiences take us, but beyond which there is necessarily no "experience," no "time," and no distinction. This is the realm of death (remember "death" exists only for spatialized, discontinuous, self-transcendent humanity), the sacred, and of course, of animality.

In light of such a perspective it is possible to arrive at a richer, more nuanced and most importantly, more systematic understanding of these characters (i.e., the affects and processes that define them) that compose Kafka's world. First and foremost is the possibility of reconciling the erotic and economic themes with the religious. I have already spoken of a negative ontology in Kafka, the negative, subtractive, or evacuating method of many of the stories as they proceed toward emptiness, an emptiness that is totally unworldly *yet all the more full for that.* I have likened it to the apophatic methods practiced by early Christian mystics whose belief in the capacity of language to embody totality or infinity was as skeptical and problematized as Kafka's own. And of course we must take seriously Kafka's own personal view of his literature as a form of prayer.[72] Kafka's exile, like that of his central protagonists was categorical and irredeemable: "there is hope, plenty of hope . . . but not for us," he says on a number of occasions.[73] His protagonists, as has already been pointed out, are distinctly nonanimal, at least to the extent that they are identified with the perspective of the narrator. For these protagonists are in fact suspended forever, tragically and Gracchus-like between two worlds—a transcendent one whose rule would radiate from above, though whose power as origin has now receded beyond retrieval; and a purely immanent one in which everything coheres by the agency of a purely formal (empty) law, of which the goal is less to comprehend than somehow to come to reside or inhere within, and to which they attempt to gain entrance. For here literature is not only the last possibility—an incantation, a prayer—but this moment is also the last possibility for literature:

72 Erich Heller, "Punishments and Playthings *de Profundis*," in his *Franz Kafka.*

73 Janouch and Brod.

to the night of animality belongs only the happy but silent—gestural, corporal, musical—plenitude of the instant.

But it is also for this reason that deliverance, enlightenment, and "death" (silence) are not only *not* incompatible, they are complementary. A strange and empty peace accompanied by a clear light attends the last seconds of Gregor's wordly being, a scene that has echoes and variants throughout the stories.[74] But the obsessive themes of Kafka's work—the desire to gain admittance to the Law, to penetrate to its interior, or to establish at least some kind of material link with its otherwordly substance, to become one and continuous with even its most nefarious flows,[75] that is, to become willingly and profoundly guilty if only the Law would finally grant admittance and truly apply to him; plus the fundamental exile that neither Kafka nor his characters would ever overcome short of committing gestures of remarkable violence and self-destructive innovation—all this must now take on a new complexity and necessarily a new ambiguity. For the deaths that end yet do not resolve the narratives of "The Judgment," "In the Penal Colony," and *The Trial*, no different from that of Gregor in *The Metamorphosis,* are the hypothetical *consequences* of willed, positive, even happy solutions implicit in its narrative universe. This is not, however, to say that these death endings—with which Kafka, in the cases of *The Trial* and *The Metamorphosis,* was never satisfied anyway—are themselves merely and unproblematically affirmations of some felicitous and newly discovered mode of Being. But they are certainly a release from the pressures of exile in the individuated world; they are forms of artificial closure designed for narrative experiments that can never, on their own, embody the whole toward which they relentlessly and asymptotically move.

These narratives are thus truncated by the violent and final resolution that gains—for however much else it loses—admittance to the Law. Such contrived solutions were by no means foreign to Kafka's narratives. Their very cartographic, tactical, and piecemeal nature guaranteed that they would have the same nappe, flow, and shape as the world, and for this reason their endings were

74 The deaths of the protagonists of "The Hunger Artist," the parable "Before the Law," and the hypothetical victims of the punishment apparatus in "The Penal Colony" either are preceded by an enlightenment or function as a deliverance or passage into the embrace of a now immanent, maternally receptive, and almost bodily Justice.

75 "In the Penal Colony" and the ending of *The Trial* are two examples where admittance to the Law means leaving one's wordly body behind.

at best artificially imposed and at worst insoluble (narrative and ontological) dilemmas.[76] In one of his most philosophically sustained works, "The Great Wall of China," Kafka meditates on the three principles or guarantors of the divinely ordered cosmos (and classic narrative form): ground, center, and origin, and these in relation to an even more overriding question: What is it in fact that constitutes, for any given system, be it the world or a structure that would represent it, a principle of closure or totality? In the course of the narrative all of these "problems" ultimately ground in a single one: does there exist (in this world) an Emperor or not? Now the inquiry/narrative pursues this question with such unrelenting speculative rigor that soon the existence of the Emperor is brought so profoundly into question that "the very ground on which [the people] stand," in other words, the Empire itself, becomes threatened. The narrative is finally no longer able to conceal from itself the very ontological impossibility of closure, and with a suddenness that is almost dizzying is not so much ended as abandoned: "To set about establishing a fundamental defect here would mean undermining not only our consciences but, what is far worse our feet. And for that reason I shall not proceed any further at this stage with my inquiry into these questions" (pp. 247–248).

Only the most unnuanced and disingenuous reading of Kafka's works could see such impasses *merely* as finalities limited and determined by an all-encompassing negativity. Such a view, for example, would deny the two things that are most fundamental both to Kafka's work in general and to "The Great

---

76 In his essay "Kafka's Fictional World," Lubomir Dolezel remarks that it is structurally impossible to find an ending to the narrative of the haphazard, irregular hybrid world. Remarkably enough, he points to *The Metamorphosis* as the exception to this rule, specifically for its "final suggestion that the bizarre event might possibly recur, that it might affect any of the human inhabitants of the hybrid world." Gunter Anders has argued that any true ending to the works would only have misrepresented Kafka's view of life as a complete impasse. Life is too entangled to progress, thus there is no plot, no development, and no climax (Anders, pp. 56–57). Meanwhile for Adorno the novels could no more easily be ended than totalized, for they were meant more than anything else to approximate the serial adventure story (à la Dickens) that Kafka so admired (*Prisms,* p. 65). We have already characterized a Kafka story as a marquetry of embedded story fragments. According to Brod they were often referred to by Kafka himself as patchworks ("*Alles was nicht in solcher Selbstvergessenheit und Hingabe geschaffen wurde* [i.e., The Judgment] *heiss bei meinem Freunde 'Flickarbeit'*"), and it is this suggestion that is exploited so fruitfully by Malcolm Pasley. See especially his "Two Kafka Enigmas . . ." and Max Brod, *Franz Kafkas Glauben und Lehre* (Munich: Mondial, 1948), p. 19.

Wall of China" in particular: their segmentary nature as a linear "proceeding" of reprises, and their diagrammatic nature as a mapping of mobile forces or regimes.

Death and the Double Turning Away

It may be said of "The Great Wall of China" that it exemplifies a fundamental movement underlying all of Kafka's work: that it dramatizes the movement of *God turning away from humanity as humanity turns away from God.* Taking an overview of the entire body of Kafka's work, one notes the progressive eclipsing of the central despot figure, so literally and materially prominent in the early works (e.g., "The Judgment," "The Metamorphosis") as he begins, almost from that time on, to recede into the vague and murky depths of narrative space never to emerge again distinctly as such but only embodied within a more massive, diffuse, and immanent structure (e.g., *The Trial, The Castle,* "The Burrow"). This movement or passage is recapitulated in "The Great Wall" by means of the progressive descriptive obliteration of the Emperor's existence. Now this movement may be characterized qualitatively as that of a transformation of semiotic regimes. In *A Thousand Plateaus* Deleuze and Guattari set out a preliminary description of a number of regimes of signs (reality): the pre-, the counter-, and the postsignifying, as well as the signifying regimes.[77] In the following discussion we will be concerned primarily with relations between the latter two regimes.

The signifying regime is characterized as despotic and paranoid; it is organized into concentric circles of significance (tendency to produce and only to recognize signification or significance), and it deploys its signs (and power) always in relation to the full and central "faciality" of a paranoid, and therefore intensively interpreting, despot-god. This despot-god faciality has two primary functions: to convert all substance into signing material and to organize these signs into simultaneous, signifying, concentric circles, and continually to interpret and to reimpart to this system new significance or signifier. Now it is the proper function of the *post*signifying—also called the passional and subjectifying regime—to break the concentricity, simultaneity, and interpretance of the signifying regime by establishing within it its own characteristic if less global order. This order consists in establishing a single sign or cluster of signs that are detached or detachable from the irradiating apparatus of despotic signification, and which have the capacity to proliferate autonomously and by their own force, no longer in circular fashion but tangentially along a straight line (this is the by-product of subjectification that establishes the passional singularity or swerve). The forces of

77 Gilles Deleuze and Felix Guattari, *A Thousand Plateaus,* pp. 111–148.

proliferation here are no longer oriented to, nor susceptible of being caught by, the central, frontal faciality of the despot (nor are they entirely free and indeterminate), but remain in relation to their point of bifurcation, their process of (passional) "subjectification," and the tangential flow that ensued.

This subjectification in sum is made possible by a transformation of the role of the face. Deleuze and Guattari argue that this model of a postsignifying regime is strongly associated with the history of the Jewish people and for reasons of which only one can be treated here: it concerns the Abrahamic moment when God averts his face no longer to be seen by anyone, and humankind, in turn, either out of fear or an irrepressible need to betray the god who has betrayed it, averts its face as well. "The averted faces, in profile, replace the frontal view of the radiant face. It is this double turning away that draws the positive line of flight" (p. 123). What is important here is the difference between the linear, Mosaic, authoritarian, *proceeding,* of one step or bloc following another, and the absorbing, irradiating centripetality of despotic signifiance.[78] The "positivity" derives from the tangential movement *opened* by the turning (the averted gaze)—a passional discharge in which a subject's or a people's ethical being is elaborated concretely and breaks with the conditions of despotic signifiance. The turning always opens an infinite, linear, asignifying series of blocs, even if these blocs themselves are finite, catastrophic, and replete with betrayal (examples are Cain, Moses, Jonah, and Jesus). Death, it is true, belongs to the segment: "every consciousness pursues its own death, every love-passion its own end, attracted by a black hole, and all the black holes resonate together,"[79] but life and hope belong to the *openness* of the line: "the history of the Jews is punctuated by catastrophes after each of which there were just enough survivors to start a new proceeding . . ." (p. 122).

Any place, point, thing, or moment may serve as a point of subjectification so long as it bears the three traits of the subjective (postsignifying) semiotic: the double turning away, betrayal, and existence under (indefinite) reprieve.[80] The passional—open *and* doomed—line may bifurcate from any sign or point; almost any of Kafka's characters may be defined in relation to such a (desultory) singular point, and this condition characterizes both their exteriority and their ontological relation to a postulated signifying, despotic regime. Animality is also

78 Ibid., pp. 122, 128.

79 Ibid., p. 133.

80 Ibid., p. 129.

this passional turning and opening, just as destruction and death are inseparable from the possibility of a renewed "proceeding."

The present study has continually focused on the atomistic conditions of modernity in general and the theory of the *clinamen* or swerve in particular. That such infinitesimal deviations could produce holes in Being through which entire worlds may erupt, that one such minuscule or imperceptible detail could serve as a point of departure for a fully passional (e.g., delirious) proceeding is the very ontological firmament out of which Kafka's world unfolds. The event that is not an Event but only the site of an imperceptible slippage (based on a transformation of the relations of faciality) is the central (and not just the inaugural) theme of the story entitled "A Little Woman." Here, it is impossible to say *where* the slippage first occurs that imperceptibly transforms all the narrator's qualities into faults, just as the entire situation remains always *beneath the threshold* of Events, beneath the threshold of Formal, Essential individuation into culminating moments or decisive crises. Though the narrator's predicament is universally known—everyone, it seems is aware of it—it remains nonetheless but "a small affair" and, if not invisible, at least masterable: "if I keep my hand over it, even quite lightly, I shall quietly continue to live my own life for a long time to come."[81]

It is this same principle of a tiny event punctuating and inaugurating a totally transformative proceeding that is described by Benjamin in the story of a rabbi who, telling of the coming of the Messiah, explains that when finally he does arrive to save humankind, he will not proceed to recast the world in an entirely new image but will rather make only an infinitesimal adjustment. We have already seen how the *gestus* served for Benjamin as the break point or bifurcation point allowing the interpenetration or communication between two worlds. For Benjamin this was possible only and precisely because such gestures had "no symbolic meaning for the author from the outset; rather the author tried to *derive* such a meaning from them in everchanging contexts and experimental groupings"—in other words, they were implicitly postsignifying and virtually passional.[82]

In this light it is also possible to come to a more modulated understanding of the death-endings of Kafka's stories. "The Judgment," for example, may be seen as an archetypal case, and nonetheless so for the fact that it is the full faciality of the father, brutally represented by the uncovering of the genitals and the

81 *Complete Stories,* pp. 322, 323, and 323–324.

82 *Illuminations,* p. 120 (my italics). See also the mistaken ringing of the night bell and the tiny maladjustment or discrepancy as founding events in "The Country Doctor" (p. 225) and "Investigations of a Dog" (p. 278).

intrusive, despotic absorption and redeployment of communicative substance into significance (epistolary utterances originally destined not to him but to a distant friend) that constitutes the dominant signifying regime through most of the story. The passional regime is no less present in all its aspects—turning, betrayal (marriage, friendship), reprieve (condemnation)—and though it is twice blocked—along the epistolary and conjugal lines—it manages to capitalize on the father's sentence (in the double sense of "utterance" and "judgment") by transforming it into a pure illocutionary act, a point of postsignifying departure along a passional line or "proceeding." Thus the death it engenders has no particular finality about it but is associated with the superb ecstasy of flight and immersion in a new element (*Complete Stories,* p. 88):

> Out of the front door he rushed, across the roadway, driven toward the water. Already he was grasping at the railings as a starving man clutches food.

The appearance of the themes of water and food are by now, of course, less than surprising, but the final mysterious line—"At that moment [of the plunge] an unending stream of traffic was just going over the bridge"—had a powerful significance for Kafka. "Do you know," he wrote to Max Brod, "what the last phrase means? As I wrote it I thought of a violent ejaculation."[83] The same is true of the commander in the Penal Colony who similarly seeks, but does not actually find, a total orgasmic "immersion" of his own body into the no-longer signifying apparatus of the political machine to which he has become hopelessly and passionally external. To this may be added the scene at the end of part 1 of *The Metamorphosis* where Gregor, literally jammed at the threshold of two worlds receives from his father "einen jetzt wahrhaft *erlösenden* starken Stoss" that sends him flying deep into his new existence and out of the family domain (my italics).[84] In this sense, all characters in Kafka are already sentenced to "death by drowning," even though they continue to proceed under partial reprieve. Death exists for them at once as a compromise, a last resort, a spectacular and excessive fantasy of incorporation and continuity, but also as a turning and an opening and paradoxically as a reprieve. Kafka himself assiduously cultivated his cough into a full-blown tuberculosis, a cough whose advent was greeted with extraordinary elation

83 Michel Carrouges, *Franz Kafka* (Paris: Labergerie, 1949), cited in Georges Bataille, *Literature and Evil,* p. 137.

84 Franz Kafka, "Die Verwandlung," in *Das Urteil* (Frankfurt: Fischer, 1977), p. 36.

and relief, for he intuited immediately that in it, he finally had his "way out," and he called this cough, appropriately, "the animal."[85]

Pure Form

To consider Kafka's work story by story is to feel the weight of an apparent pessimism and a doom, the full immobility and horror of these impasses of death as they seem to spread back into the domain of the living. Yet when seen from greater distance, the frivolity, humor, and sanguinity of a certain *serio ludere* unmistakably emerges.[86] Here it is in the relentless and stoic reprise of the death and animal themes—like so many test runs of another, utterly new modernist machine, which, like the airplane itself, had all the science and physics of the ages pitted against it. In this sense Kafka's literature represents an entirely new mode of writing. For Kafka's stories are in fact *essays* in the deepest sense; they are attempts—trials—to find ways out (literally *in*), but in the process their task is first to attract and then force to the surface the relations of a certain (social, political, even historical) topography and make these palpable—in Kafka this often means to render them in language as literal—and so produce, in however piecemeal and provisional a fashion, schemas or diagrams of ambient force.

This, then, is why the stories never have an intrinsic "form": they are meant to *proceed* in tentative, experimental, and piecemeal fashion, spreading and multiplying at their edges like a crabgrass, absorbing more and more of the real as they insinuate themselves by pursuing the logical consequences of every detail ever more deeply into the same. *Their only form is the form(-lessness) of the world*—they are inseparable, both analytically and materially, from the actual terrain that they trace, so little do they actually empirically add or introduce into the world. Kafka's literary production is not really a "production" at all, but rather a redeployment of, an intervention in, a world of organized forces that already exist.

85 *Letters to Felice,* p. 545.

86 The crucial aspect of Kafka's work as a form of "play" has received intelligent, convincing and rigorous elaboration, yet has been ignored—to my mind, with catastrophic consequences—by the majority of criticism. See especially Malcolm Pasley, "Semi-Private Games," *The Kafka Debate,* pp. 188–205; "Two Kafka Enigmas: Elf Söhne and Die Sorge des Hausvaters," *Modern Language Review,* 59 (1964), pp. 73–81; Michel Dentan, *Humour et création littéraire dans l'oeuvre de Kafka* (Geneva: Droz, 1961); Erich Heller, "Punishments and Playthings De Profundus"; Georges Bataille, "Franz Kafka," *Literature and Evil;* Peter Hutchinson, "Red Herrings or Clues," *The Kafka Debate,* pp. 206–215.

Kafka's literary machine, then, is already at the level of its *form of expression* in a relation of continuity and immanence with the world, even if the *form of its content*[87] often appears to abort its mission—though this must be seen as nothing less than inevitable from the moment that one accepts that a story, no different from a life, continues its meander until a nonnegotiable impasse is reached—and terminates in a cul-de-sac or a compromise like death. Literature is and always was, for Kafka, the most dangerous game, because it is absolutely real, a "way out" that is simultaneously a way *into* life, a mode of being in relation to life "like water inside of water."

I have proceeded to situate, however idiosyncratically, the center of gravity or "navel," to use Freud's term, of *The Metamorphosis* in an object—the portrait of the lady in furs—and through it developed and emphasized a theme central to Kafka's entire oeuvre. But the meaning, or rather the function, of the woman's portrait is by no means exhausted by its association with doubleness and animality. The Kafka story or novel does not, I have argued, have distinct boundaries that delineate a well-rounded and autonomous Form, but rather "spreads" in a provisional, even improvisatory manner with constant reprises, adjustments, and variations. A brief glance at the table of contents of *The Trial* reveals the work's basic structure, and in this it is archetypal: a series of almost random forays or proceedings, one after another, into the "world," *ostensibly* in search of a hypothetical interior to the system (the search for a type of sense, coherency, or logic, the very type of legible system of which Kafka's oeuvre marks the historical impossibility)—an interior that was simultaneously a search for something "higher" (Higher judges, Higher Court).

I say *ostensibly*, for there is ample evidence showing that Joseph K. renounced any inquiry into the *content* of his charges and merely pursued the concrete channels—affiliations, alliances, pacts, relays—that determined their *form*. This full acceptance of the exteriority of the Law, that is, the complete and abiding indifference to the problem of its inside (interiority), seems to belie on a more profound level the sincerity of his ostensible search for a higher, that is, transcendent level of justice. In this respect one might note that Joseph K. opts for "indefinite postponement" (reprieve), not "ostensible acquittal"—a definitive sign that what he was searching for, and has perhaps now found, is a dwelling place—no matter how provisional or at how steep a price—inside the Law. What Joseph K. dis-

87 Louis Hjelmslev's refinement of Saussure's signifiant/signifié doublet in *Prolégomènes à une théorie du langage* (Paris: Minuit, 1968), pp. 65–80, taken up by Roland Barthes, "Eléments de sémiologie," *Communications* 4 (Paris: Seuil, 1964), pp. 91–135.

covers on these little visits and trips, is nothing more than the manifoldness and the ubiquity of the judiciary system. The offices and chambers of the court, for example, are never localized but exist virtually *nunc hinc nunc illinc* in every attic, broom closet, cathedral pulpit, or neighboring apartment. Similarly, all secondary, auxiliary, or derelict spaces—stairwells, ditches, attics, empty lots—are reclaimed as the seedy, somewhat shameful ground of the social, and of the Law that founds it. It is thus entirely understandable—no explanations need be, nor are, demanded—that Joseph K.'s charges are delivered to him in his bed by a trio of confused strangers in suits. What is in fact extraordinary is that from this point on, *justice itself is never explicitly sought,* that is, no recourse or appeal is made outside of the circumscribed realm in which the charges are made; everything is accepted and subsequently engaged at the level of pure form.

If animality characterizes the menagerie of strange duos and erotic women, it is in part because they are pure form, that is, pure connective tissue (*The Castle*'s Frieda is the extreme example here) without interiority, and because they inhabit pure form, for they constitute in their own mysterious and fleeting density the very substance and body of the Law. If Leni in *The Trial* finds all accused men attractive (just as the officials according to the decree are "drawn toward the guilty"), it is because their flesh too has become an expanded surface on which the collective desire (always impersonal and without content) has begun to propagate.[88] Her perpetual arousal expresses, in the deep sense, this new conjugation. It is clear that if Kafka's books are replete with animals essentially free of interiority and in perfect continuity with the matter and forces of their worlds, almost none of the main protagonists can be said to belong fully to this species. But it is their migratory efforts that mark them, and which is the "becoming" that they all so tortuously attempt. To become immanent is to become "pure form," and this specifically is the magisterial theme of *The Castle*. For the object of the castle itself, insofar as the work's title has a referent, is a social and political institution of pure form and voided of all content—though it is made only the more powerful, material, and nefarious for that.

This concept undoubtedly finds its original expression in the Nature Theatre of Oklahoma depicted in the last chapter of *Amerika*. This work is no exception to the structural rule governing all of Kafka's novels: it is little more than a series of reprises or renewed proceedings within a variable system in which the

88 "Attraction" and "negligence" are twin determinations that precipitate passage to the "outside" in the work of the preeminent philotypic Kafkan, Maurice Blanchot. See Michel Foucault, "Thought from Outside," *Foucault/Blanchot*, pp. 27–32.

protagonist's movements are but an excuse to repertory and map the different configurations of power that each chapter represents. And each chapter is associated with an unfathomable and labyrinthine object whose global plan or diagram far exceeds the protagonist's powers of conceptualization: thus the labyrinth of corridors and the densely stratified bureaucratic structure of the ship in "The Stoker," the deliriously compartmentalized desk at the uncle's house, the vast communications room that makes up his place of business, Pollunder's strangely porous and unnavigable house, the colossal Hotel Occidental with its panoply of elevators and army of uniformed information givers, even the bizarre quasi-familial and certainly animal grouping represented by the Robinson-Delamarche-Brunelda trio. The Nature Theatre is but a final and uncharacteristically felicitous response to all these political/institutional machines and the social apparatuses they engender. The Nature Theatre of Oklahoma is the Law itself—the categories, subcategories and bureaus—become absolutely continuous and coextensive with the world, and with no asperities, excess, or external parts. It is also an assemblage of pure form, there being no distinguishable theater other than the world itself as it already exists. There is, however, a place for everyone, even for Karl Rossman. This final image is the one closest to the classic, Christian form of salvation that Kafka would ever produce.

The present study has everywhere tried to maintain, rather than compensate for, the imprecise boundaries that surround any of the given works,[89] proposing to see in Kafka's oeuvre no more unity, yet no less coherence, than pertains to any consistent though dynamic *field* of relations. This field draws its consistency not from a schema in which the individual story units fit together as do parts in a jigsaw, but rather through the filiating series of elements and the relations, repetitions, and resonances they set up while wending their way through the overall work. These series seize the work like so many filaments woven into a continuous fabric, surfacing now here and now there to release their effects. To turn now to the examination of the portrait, it follows that its full significance will be graspable not at the second-order level of meanings—for its problem, precisely, is its meaninglessness—but at the formal level of associated elements or series to which it belongs, in other words, with what other blocs or movements it can be put in relation.

The obvious step is to situate the portrait within the series of photos and portraits that appear elsewhere throughout the works. This certainly includes the

89 This imprecision is further confirmed and exacerbated by the fact that so many of the works and all of the novels remained unfinished, and that the letters and diaries have entered, justifiably, and in no secondary way, into the canon of Kafka's works.

portraits in Titorelli's studio, the photo Kafka himself solicits and finally receives from Felice, the family portrait that Rossman carries with him through most of his travels in *Amerika,* those in Fraulein Bürstner's room and the obscene illustrations in the tribunal notebooks from *The Trial,* and so on. We have seen how the Titorelli portraits also form an independant, proliferating, postsignifying series of their own. In addition to this, one must ask what relation this series of portraits and landscapes has to the series or pack of lascivious and squealing little girls that haunt Titorelli's studio and Titorelli's own egregious state of dishevelment and undress. The inherent eroticism (animality) associated with the portrait/photo series is further attested to in the arrest chapter of *The Trial,* where the three clerks hover like bees around Frau Bürstner's collection of photos. These photos too are clearly associated with an image of intimacy and undress: a white blouse dangling from the latch of an open window, as well as the general aggressive invasion of Fraulein Bürstner's privacy—a transgression for which Joseph K. is later moved to apologize, and an occasion that he does not fail to exploit in order to seize her himself, shower her with kisses "like some thirsty animal," and finally plant a kiss on her neck and "keep his lips there for a very long time." It is easy to recognize in Fraulein Bürstner, who lives in an immediately adjacent room, at least a structural analogy with Gregor's sibling Grete in *The Metamorphosis,* and not least in the symmetrical repetition and eroticism of the prolonged kiss on the neck.

Most important, however, is the other photograph that appears in *The Metamorphosis,* the one "of Gregor in his army days, in a lieutenant's uniform, his hand on his sword, a carefree smile on his lips, demanding respect for his bearing and his rank."[90] Earlier we were forced to reject the thesis of Deleuze and Guattari for whom the photographs in Kafka's work always constitute blockages of affect, reduction of connection, submissiveness, and a cooptation through memories. On the contrary, photographs, like all else in the Kafkan universe, are commutation points, that is, *pure form* first and foremost, and only later—through time and the trial of experimentation—might they take on regressive interiority and meaning, and this only in the worst of cases.[91] As instances of pure form, we characterized them as composing "nothing less than a concrete plane of the real . . . site of a potential

90 *The Metamorphosis,* p. 15.

91 If photographs seem to play the same role as gestures (à la Benjamin) this is not altogether a coincidence, for photographs and images in general seem to depict, however paradoxically, movements and gestures more so than fully subjectivated figures. Consider Titorelli's portraits of barely distinguishable figures of the Court who squirm and posture in their seat

transformation of states" while affirming that "every image implies a world." Every photograph is in fact a bifurcation point or crossroads: a door, a gateway, an opening outward or a regressive return; they are rather sites of high affectivity, potential connection, and are just as likely to be *anti*memories (the woman in furs) or antifamilial, antisubmissive memories of liberation and escape.

In the terminology developed in relation to the double turning away, one would say the photograph commonly functions as a point of detachment and subjectification giving birth to an openness and a potential linear proceeding. It must not be forgotten, however, that there is equally—and perilously—a signifying and a postsignifying regime of photographs. The task of the Kafkan work is to achieve "indefinite postponement" by blocking the emergence of the latter two regimes in any material organization and to propagate the passional line of the asignifying regime. It may be said, then, that in Kafka the photograph bears the same relation to the real as rumor does to knowledge, animality to self-conscious humanity, and the gesture to individuated language—they are emblems and stations of hope because they are still connected to the fullness of their virtuality, they are as yet incompletely formed, and they are the embodiment of *pure expression,* that is, an expression so fully realized that it is without content.[92] "Demanding respect for his bearing and his rank," then, plainly does not conjure up an image of subjugation, while such phrases as "army days" and "a carefree smile on his lips" unquestionably denote a highly charged memory of life outside the familial and conjugal circle.

Jean Starobinski has written that no one in Kafka really has his own place to live,[93] though perhaps no character suffered from this condition so much as Kafka himself, who, for reasons no biographer could even begin to unravel, never completely left the Oedipal nest. The humiliation and submission that this situation engendered is unquestionably the central, manifest (though obvi-

rather than dignifiedly pose or repose, not to mention the preeminent examples of the two photographic images under examination here, i.e., with regard to their pronounced and remarkably similar gesturality.

92 On the spontaneous unreflected gesture as pure expression *(der reine Ausdrück),* Jorgen Kobs, *Kafka: Untersuchungen zu Bewusstsein und Sprache seiner Gestalten* (Bad Homburg: Athenaum, 1970), p. 412; and Stanley Corngold's discussion, "Recent Kafka Criticism," *The Kafka Debate,* pp. 60–64.

93 Jean Starobinski, "Le rêve architecte," *Cahiers de la compagnie Madeleine Renaud–Jean Louis Barrault,* no. 50, Paris (Feb. 1965).

ous and overhashed) theme of *The Metamorphosis*. From the original inherited debts to the intolerable physical abuse Gregor must endure at his hands, and the perverse symbiosis of strength and vigor that inextricably links him bodily and ecologically to the older man, it is clear that Gregor has never not lived in the shadow of his father—except, perhaps, in the idyllic time of the photograph in question, when the mythical brotherhood of the army might have replaced the subjection and petty indignities of familial and professional life. The "carefree smile" places the depicted scene on an affective register wholly outside of the world of "The Metamorphosis," which, itself, is utterly saturated with fretting and anxiety. Uniforms, too, appear throughout Kafka as signs—again purely material, formal ones—of being connected to the Law, or of being connected tout court.[94] Gregor's father, for example, doffs his bathrobe and now wears his renewed vigor and social standing as a tight suit of clothing with gold buttons and high, stiff collar.

The photo also depicts a gesture, perhaps finished, perhaps not yet begun: Gregor has "his hand on his sword." Can this gesture be read as a response to the woman in the corresponding photo who raises "up against the viewer a heavy fur muff in which her whole forearm had disappeared?" How much farther can we get beyond, without denying, the Freudian cliché that would see each figure in a ritual presentation and mutual offering of genitalia—the Father/Law forthright, invasive and sovereign, the Sister/Animal mysterious, dissembling and erotic? In what follows, the portrait's multiple participation in several series or systems of objects is developed, with a view less to reducing the portrait to a fixed system of textual meaning than to embedding it, along with the story itself, within a larger general economy or regime of desire. The particular "economy" I have in mind here is one whose explicit historical task it may be said was to forge a counterproduction and a countermemory designed to subvert every tendency to form out of the flux of the world, discrete totalities and stable meanings, while at the same time ceaselessly generating its own immanent web of proliferating *relations*.

An Isomorphism: The Bachelor Machine

The last decades of the nineteenth and especially the first of the twentieth century produced a plethora of works whose obsession with machine culture and

---

94 These are as likely as not to be ridiculous or utterly inappropriate, such as the tourist outfits of the warders in *The Trial* or the "close-fitting silken-gleaming jacket" that Barnabus wears in *The Castle*.

whose fascination with the new possibilities and models it offered for the expression and diagramming of desire gave birth to a hybrid form of cultural object that has been called the "Bachelor Machine."[95] Foremost among those who produced these strange objects, and originator of the term itself, was the artist Marcel Duchamp. In 1911 he produced a series of paintings in a Cubo-futurist style depicting the progressive stages of a woman—her unclothed body resolved into individual geometrical blocks and lines of force—making her way down the stairs in a blurring sweep of angles and lines. These paintings were called "Nude descending a staircase." Another painting executed in the same style and part of the same series, showed the same blur of geometrical components rendered with the same reduced pallette (shades of brown with a few regions of greyish green) in which was depicted another figure, this time male, as he is projected forward by the movement of a train (i.e., he is also moving down a corridor) but also jostled from side to side. The title of this painting is "Sad young man in a train." In the first painting, the woman arriving from above and behind a wall approaches the viewer;[96] in the second painting, the young man is masturbating, his genitals in full view.[97]

Nothing links these paintings together except their style, the time they were painted, and the strange mixture of eroticism, movement, and the technical equipment (train, stairway) with which the figures are put in relation, and into whose bodies their respective rhythms are imposed. Yet a few years later Duchamp started work on his master oeuvre, "The Large Glass," conceived in a certain sense I suggest as a combination of these two images—the "Nude . . . ," now transformed into "The Bride," and the "Sad young man . . ." together become the ejaculating Bachelor Apparatus. The entire work, officially known as "The Bride Stripped Bare by her Bachelors, Even," deploys both male and female elements, but keeps these radically apart—the bachelors never succeed in inseminating the bride, the bride never deigns to descend fully to the bachelors' domain. The unconsummated sexual act is never seen as an absence or lack but as the positive production of incompletion, as a metaphysical putting into place of an infinite delay. Duchamp even offered as an alternate title for the work "Delay in Glass." The work is born of, and continues to inhabit in the deepest possible way, this radical incompletion.

95 See the concluding discussion of chap. 3, and note 54.

96 This is most apparent in the 1911 variant, "Nu descendant un Escalier no. 1."

97 This observation, as far as I know still undocumented, was first made by Joseph Masheck.

The work not only is deliberately unfinished, it also embraces both chance and the most invasive influences from the outside in a total and uncompromising way. When the work fell from a truck en route to its owner in Philadelphia and was smashed to pieces, Duchamp welcomed the "collaborative" intervention of chance and chose to reconstruct the work, at an enormous cost of time and effort, and to display it, shatter marks and all. Even the use of transparent glass is "meant" to attract to itself, like a screen receiving centripetal momentary projections, the images of every object or event that may ever find its way into the work's vicinity. Onto its inscrutably rich and elaborated surface has also been projected a myriad of the most involved and complex meaning systems and cosmologies perhaps ever devoted to any single artificial object in history.[98] The work has found a point of convergence in so many discourses—it itself arose out of, and is indissociable from a discursive work, "The Green Box"—that its already tenuous and ethereal materiality is almost completely dissolved in them. The work has no intrinsic meaning of its own; its role rather is to multiply meaning and to produce through a kind of *embouteillage* a perpetual interference—cancellation, migration, and hybridization—of meanings. For if all meaning is desire made manifest, then the Large Glass is nothing but a machine producing and tracing desire, accelerating it and making it circulate.

Duchamp's lifelong obsession with the pun is nothing other than an ontological generalization of this embouteillage or interference, that is, the extension of an epistemological category to the realm of Being. The Readymades—"puns in three dimensions," as he called them—are the prime examples. For the pun is nothing more than a vehicle or site—this may be a sign, an image, a word, an object—in which two or more "meanings" overlap or coincide. Yet for Duchamp "meaning" was no more than an artifically constructed *effect* reducible to the circuit, series, or assemblage in which a given element takes up its place. Thus the "pun" is quite simply a place marker across which two or more systems are simultaneously articulated. By transferring the importance perennially associated with the object to the large-scale and often abstract systems of which it is a part, Duchamp effectively transformed, or marked the transformation of, twentieth-century metaphysics.[99] For this reason Duchamp did not so much create objects as displace them; he rarely intervened materially inside an object but

98 These include the cabalistic, the onanistic/erotic, the literal marriage rite, the alchemical, the violent, the demonic, the machinic, the social-economic.

99 We have seen how futurist thought was proceeding, by other means, in this same direction.

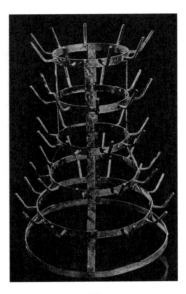

5.2
Marcel Duchamp, *Bottlerack,* 1914

used objects to intervene within social, economic, cultural, etc. systems of articulation.[100]

A urinal, for example, combined with a signature explodes with "signifying" traffic: the signature draws it into the aesthetic realm of "authentic creation" just as surely as its flawless surface and geometric contours connect it to the social realm of "industrial mass production." The effect of this destabilizing undecideability is to force to the surface a manifold of other virtual relations (systems) that articulate it at the same spot: the hydraulic-conjunctive in which human biology—the urinary tract—is coupled with industrial engineering—plumbing, drainage; the conjugal-erotic that valorizes the receptacle as female (the male genitalia are ritually placed inside it), but this also forges a union with the signature valorizing it as male—and this by extension becomes true of *writing* generally—

---

100 Of course Duchamp often "assisted" his readymades—here a dab of paint, there a signature or heteroclite conjugation of forms—transforming them indeed into something else, but these transformations—and herein lies Duchamp's modernity—are *incorporeal* in essence and are due to the forced convergence of series or systems. They seize and address the object *from outside*—a kind of transvaluation through transmigration of milieus or realms.

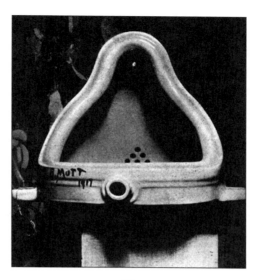

5.3

Marcel Duchamp, *Fountain,* 1917

thus likening in its turn micturation/ejaculation with (sterile?) inscription; then on to the themes of hygiene, onanism, the laboratory (urinal as alembic), hermeticism (R. Mutt), vase painting, and so on. For Duchamp, and certainly for the rest of us since Duchamp, social (cultural) space could no longer be understood in terms of private or discrete realms of uncontaminated univocal articulation, that is, of individual and independent instances. For every instance is already multiple. Duchamp's work, like that of Kafka, demonstrates the central epistemological break in modern culture, that (1) systems are not parallel, they are immanent; and (2) systems are real even if abstract, not because they are actual but because they are virtual. Objects do not bear meanings, but rather a shifting battery of thresholds that may be triggered by any act whatever, no more of art than those of life.[101]

Let us now consider another work, a collaborative photograph made with Man Ray in 1921, more than six years after work on the Glass had begun, but at least

101 Ihab Hassan has described the delirium of Kafkan multiplicity more succinctly than perhaps anyone else: "The rage for absurd analysis leaves no unity intact; all things multiply and are multiple." "Kafka: The Authority of Ambiguity," *The Dismemberment of Orpheus* (New York: Oxford University Press, 1971), p. 119. See also, e.g., *The Metamorphosis,* p. 19: "The voice behind Gregor did not sound like that of only a single father."

5.4

Marcel Duchamp, *Rrose Sélavy par Man Ray,* 1921

two years before its completion. The photograph depicts Duchamp himself in drag, wearing a hat, wig, and what seems to be a coat with a large fur collar. It is no longer the male Duchamp at all but a woman, an alter ego, named Rrose Sélavy (eros, c'est la vie). Her ringed hands simultaneously clutch and offer coquettishly outward to the viewer something—exactly what is not clear, perhaps the collar or its wearer herself, or perhaps it expresses a simple "me voila!" presenting the astonishing transformation of the artist into womanly eros. As in nearly all of Duchamp's work autoerotic themes proliferate, their prodigality limited only by the reductiveness of psychoanalytic readings. Both male and female genitalia are continual presences in Duchamp's work, and the gesture of half-drawing-open, half-closing the fur collar is certainly consonant with this series of images (the hands, incidentally, belong to a female friend of Picabia). What persists as complex and interesting in this photo, however, is the combination of address—Rrose's glance is deliberately intent and arresting—and the utter self-sufficiency of an erotic creature who embodies both male and female "systems" in a single being. In yet another typically gender-paired Duchampian work, the "Couple de tabliers" of 1959, a pair of "aprons" are fashioned from fabric from pot holders modified to resemble "his and her" crotches with open flies and with genitals exposed. The woman's genitalia again are represented by a sewn-on patch of fur.

5.5
Marcel Duchamp, *Couple de Tabliers,* 1959

It is possible to recognize in these Duchampian bachelor and bride figures certain hypersophisticated and sublimated versions or attributes of Kafka's own promiscuous animal creatures. In Kafka, bodies are never personal, intimate objects but always public property; they are the surfaces through which so much communication and therefore social bonds are articulated. They are there, by and large, for the mere taking. The indifference and impassivity that accompanies sexual acts in Kafka merely literalizes the fact that the most intense bonds of connection and conjugation have already, historically, begun to take place less at the expressive level of the human organism but to an ever greater degree at the level of the much more complex and global political and bureaucratic systems, of which individual men and women are mere points or relays.[102] Likewise, eroticism is no longer limited (in conception) to an intrinsic quality of individual activity but is now a central aspect of the collective and extrinsic forces that constitute the impersonal and supraindividual machine of social exchange and communications.[103] To conceive in this way of the *socius* as an erotic mechanism englobing human

102 Sex acts are no more easily nor satisfyingly consummated than telephone calls or dispatched messages.

103 Among the great number of principal themes shared by Kafka's and Duchamp's work are the common preoccupation with temporal/spatial problems: distanciation, concealment, demultiplication, detotalization; substitution of allegorical significance by proliferative machinic and surface connections; desire developed in terms of frustration, (closed-) circuitry and continuous remapping on a cartographic/machinic model; and of course, the affirmation of exteriority as the element *par excellence* through which all meaning-effects are constituted. See also below, note 110.

relations, conditioning them and articulating them, is to conceive of the human organism too, insofar as it is a social entity—and in Kafka it is this above all that the human must strive to be—as a mechanism regulating and distributing flows that originate outside it (the Law, like guilt itself we are told, is fundamentally *an attraction*). Desire is no longer born from the depths of bodies but rather adheres to their promiscuous and highly valent surfaces, and is translated there into a form of social communication and worn as signs—clothing, uniforms, gestures, deformities.[104] The so-called hollowness of Kafka's characters and the rhetorical sterility of those of Duchamp are but the negative formulation of what is in fact a radical—and radically modern—commitment to exploring phenomena in the element of their exteriority, the irreducible communicative medium of social organization, that is, of power and desire.[105]

Thus the two portraits of *The Metamorphosis* belong to a similar, complex relation of autoerotic complementarity joining a Bride and a Bachelor, a kind of wedding that results not in the climax of a union, but in a machinic coupling of autonomous devices incessantly producing desire and turning it outside, rather than fulfilling or completing it. In a certain sense the story's two portraits may be said to stand at opposite poles between which the universe of the story is suspended: on its near side, the dark animality of the woman in furs, the night of chthonic continuity and nonindividuation, and on the far side, the sovereign sword-bearing embodiment of the Law, the *principium individuationis* itself. Yet in another, more important sense, they are poles that are irrepressibly attracted to one another: as soon as Gregor has extracted himself from his sticky perch against the cool glass that both weds him to and separates him from his bride, the filthy[106] and dreaded conjugal scene is enacted in front of him by proxy.

104 On the subject of the personality and eccentricity and clothes, see Georg Simmel, "The Metropolis and Mental Life," in *Georg Simmel on Individuality and Social Forms,* ed. Donald Levine (Chicago: University of Chicago Press, 1971), and Walter Benjamin, *Charles Baudelaire,* particularly the recurrent theme of the phantasmagoria.

105 Kafka's protagonists in *The Trial* and *The Castle,* intent on establishing a maximum of affiliative (lateral) alliances and connections to help gain ground in their cases, are invariably and repeatedly drawn into "purely formal" sexual encounters.

106 Kafka's obsessive antifiliality manifested itself in a great many symptoms of which some have already been listed in these notes. Among them was his visceral revulsion when confronted with the evidence of his own conception, for he could not bear to see the disorder of sheets and bedclothes. Citation provided below, p. 203.

As the scene is left at this point—Gregor's sudden coupling with the photo-Bride—the mother has fainted, leaving only Gregor and Grete to care for her. As already noted, the entire scene leading up to this point takes place in the conspicuous and explicitly noted absence of the father, so that Gregor's bedroom has become accessible to the mother only for the first time. The fatherless world that this scene opens up is one populated by three women: mother, sister, and quasi-Bride. The fact that they all congregate in Gregor's room, in explicit transgression of the decrees of the father's will (the scene is fraught with anxiety about the father's return),[107] underscores the polarity that the photo itself introduces: that between conjugality (Oedipal family)—love and sex under the sign of the Father/Law—and anticonjugality—the erotics of the Bachelor Machine.[108] The essential difference from this perspective is that the former is rooted in reproduction and representation, that is, *dynasty*, while the latter is concerned with channeling desire and incarnating it in a mechanism that is necessarily "perverse" because unaffiliated with either history—the perpetuation of lineage; or genitality—the extremely limited biological gesture, that is, more simply, with the Law.

Now the "bachelorhood" in "Bachelor Machine" denotes the principle of non-affiliation only in a very specific sense. The constant presence of a Bride is only a decoy (this is why she remains necessarily and forever in abeyance), for the Bachelor is a citizen not of the world of institutions and Forms, but of the continent

107　The image of the mother and daughter ever so busily, naughtily, and chaotically trifling about in Gregor's room is one that resonates powerfully with many similar erotic, animal- or childlike scenes throughout Kafka (the attics of the Court in *The Trial*, the hallways in *The Castle*, etc.), and this is all the more clearly underscored by its opposition to the story's final image of the neatly restored threesome family (triangle) after the *rappel a l'ordre:* the story-closing threeway embrace before the window.

108　It seems that sex for Kafka was virtually impossible within the context of conjugal life. He continually warned fiancées of some terrible problem requiring medical attention and which, under ordinary circumstances, precludes the possibility of marriage, and certainly of any hope of ever having children. And yet there is no sign that Kafka lived anything less than a normally active sex life with a great enough variety of women not of the marriageable category (i.e., prostitutes, singers, very young women, already married women, etc.). Kafka did not want a conjugal life, he only wanted to want it. The only truly happy periods in Kafka's life, from this point of view, were the days spent in utter serenity at his sister Ottla's country house, and of course, his final days spent living common-law with his nineteen-year-old lover Dora Dymant. On the themes of conjugality and anticonjugal eroticism and love in Kafka's life there is no better study than Ernst Pawel's biography, *The Nightmare of Reason*.

of pure desire itself, *a desire without an object.* The Bachelor neither exists outside of the desire whose very organization gives him his "form," nor is oriented to a beyond, that is, anything that transcends this desire itself. There are no objects *of* desire, only objects *in* desire. For desire is little more than an affective or intensive transmission, a passing from one object to another in an openended circuit that links these objects together, incorporates them in a common function. The Bride does not complete the Bachelor's desire, nor does she receive it; she extends it, accelerates it, and "attends" it. She is not a counterpart but an integral part of the desire mechanism (even in abeyance).[109] The Bachelor's mode is nonaffiliation because his desire does not posit a field or object external to himself that would in turn complete him. This radical nonaffiliation places the bachelor in a field where everything is connectable in manifold ways on the same plane and in a common dimension, namely, that of desire.

Thus the Bachelor's pure *exteriority* comes to replace both progeny and forbears.[110] The Bachelor Machine is always a socially nonsanctioned form of desire because it is nonproductive and fundamentally outside of the Law.[111] The entire scene, then, concerns the triangle of the Law—this includes but is not exhausted by the relations of the Oedipal triangle—and the potential, even if only fantastic, ways to subvert, dismantle, or pass outside of it. Gregor, the traveling salesman bachelor—how Duchamp himself would have reveled in the onanistic possibilities of such a construction![112]—after further disaffiliating himself (indeed, *disfiliating* himself as well) from the "propre" domain of the Law by becoming an insect—an antiprogeny without forbears—conjugates himself with the photo-

109 For an excellent, but diametrically opposed argument see Octavio Paz's neo-Platonist reading of the "Glass" in Octavio Paz, "The Castle of Purity," *Marcel Duchamp,* trans. R. Philips and D. Gardner (New York: Viking, 1978).

110 One can certainly see in such an arrangement a strong similarity to that of Kafka's own oeuvre—the flatness of Being, the infinite extendability of relations, the absence of signifying oppositions, the deferment of closure, in a word, the radical immanence of the act (event) in the substance to which it is oriented.

111 There is no better example of this relation than the terrifying apparatus of "In the Penal Colony," which has become a Bachelor Machine by virtue of its recent separation from the State apparatus to which it once belonged—connected now only in the most tenuous way by legend, by the unreadable script that constitutes its divine (or despotic) "program."

112 See below, note 120.

Bride as an act affirming perversity (nonreproductive, dissipative, and polymorphous desire) over history (reproduction and patrilineal filiation). The embrace of the portrait is of course postsignifying and passional, prelinguistic and gestural/corporal, but also *machinic* in that it constitutes an assembly of independent but mutually functioning mechanisms. It is constructive in the deepest sense because it creates, or opens up, an entire alternative world.

This world, however, is no sooner posited than it is smashed by the arrival of the father-despot and with him the return of the Law. The father, splendid and formidable both in his renewed vigor and in the gold-buttoned uniform that celebrates it, reestablishes the old order in a series of recuperative gestures, the first of which may be seen in his embrace of the sobbing Grete while reaffirming to her the eminent *raison* of his own privileged intuition or interpretance: "I kept telling you, but you women don't want to listen." Second, it is in the stalking and wounding of Gregor with an apple that becomes lodged in his back and then forcing him back into his room and once again to the periphery of the family domain. The third gesture is the public enactment of the (primal) conjugal scene. This scene, already alluded to—the final one of the section—throws into greatest relief the earlier coupling act of Gregor with the portrait of the woman in furs. Here the mother, already partially unclothed especially at the neck—Grete has loosened her chemise and petticoats so that she might breathe more easily—precipitates herself toward and onto the father, "embracing him, in complete union with him . . . her hands clasping the father's neck," while her undergarments continue to fall from her body.

Kafka's own reaction to scenes of this nature as well as his acute awareness of their temporal implications was once described without ambiguity in a letter to Felice:

> Yet, I am my parents' progeny. . . . Sometimes this too becomes the object of my hatred; at home the sight of the double bed, of sheets that have been slept in, of nightshirts carefully laid out, can bring me to the point of retching, can turn my stomach inside out; it is as though my birth had not been final, as though from this fusty life I keep being born again and again in this fusty room; as though I had to return there for confirmation, being—if not quite, at least in part—indissolubly connected with these distasteful things; something still clings to the feet as they try to break free, held fast as they are in the primeval slime.[113]

---

113 *Letters to Felice*, p. 525.

In the story itself, the witnessing of the parental embrace is accompanied by a definitive dimming of Gregor's sight, a diminution of his powers and a final demoralization from which he will never recover. This threefold return of the Law is a return with a vengeance, the Bachelor Machine is all but destroyed, though more by the brutal affirmation of conjugality with the imposed constraints of lineage and progeny than by the wound that marks, like a circumscision rite, the transmission of this legacy.[114]

There is yet another formal series with which the portrait must be put in relation, and it is here that we will see the Bachelor Machine make a final futile attempt to assemble itself. Both of these instances find their focus in the scene that furnishes the climax of the third and final section of the story, the scene in which Grete performs an impromptu violin concert for the three bearded roomers that the family has taken on. These men, it is worth noting, are unmistakeably animal-like in their hirsuteness,[115] their childish movements, their huddling and synchronized gestures, their uncanny self-resemblance, and their inscrutable, laconic natures, while their absurd officiousness and obsession with cleanliness and order link them also to the Law, as does their most important feature, their existence as a shadowy threesome, yet another sinister sign of the Law's and animality's consistently triangular nature.[116] In the same vein they constitute a

114 This theme, which is Nietzsche's, is taken up explicitly by the anthropologist Pierre Clastres: "No one is meant to forget the severity of the law. *Dura lex sed lex.* Various means have been devised, depending on the epoch and the society, for keeping the memory of that severity ever fresh." One of the oldest and most common ways is in the tribal marking of the body. The mark says: "You are one of us and you will not forget it." In *Society Against the State* (New York: Zone Books, 1987), pp. 177, 184.

115 Hirsuteness is a common theme among Kafka's court and animal characters. One of Titorelli's portraited judges is described as "a stout man with black bushy beard which reached far up on his cheeks on either side" (*Trial*, p.145), while thin, sparse beards either stroked pensively or twisted (the voyeur threesome across the courtyard from Burstner's room, that of the student Berthold, K's beard-pulling audience in the courtroom during his speech, that of Huld which is stroked while he contemplates the spot on the floor where K. had lain with Leni, that of Block, and so on) have been noted for their sexual and erotic overtones. See Wilhelm Emrich, *Franz Kafka,* p. 331, and Karl Kuepper, "Gesture and Posture . . . ," pp. 147–148.

116 The crucial story in this context is "Blumfeld, an Elderly Bachelor." Blumfeld's ontological bachelorhood is the story's dominant theme: he embodies the very principle of the "guilty singular" by being presented as in some way unpairable, for he has neither a child,

kind of antifamilial and anticonjugal bachelor cell, for a certain time even displacing the Samsa family triangle itself to the apartment's antechambers.[117] They are, however, far too distractible and impatient to have much use for Grete's violin playing, which nonetheless has a notably powerful and mesmerizing effect on Gregor. So moved is he, in fact, that he forgets himself entirely,[118] and slowly begins to inch out of his room toward her in an extended—though mostly anticipated and fantasized—vertiginous embrace, one that is consummated with the prolonged kiss on her neck.[119] It is impossible to ignore the startling isomorphism that this scene represents by means of the sheer contiguity and interchangeability of elements through which this gesture itself embodies and seizes the true "unknown nourishment." In other words, it is no coincidence that the sister's violin playing reproduces physically the same gesture assumed by the woman in furs, both in the relationship to the covering up of the neck while

---

a wife, nor even an assistant. He thus literally considers buying an animal to compensate for this fundamental uncomplementarity and un-unifiability of his being. What ensues in fact is a medley of encounters with doubleness: the janitor's two children that flank him on either side, the two attendants that flank the czar in the french magazine, the two assistants he is given in place of the single one he requests (that he may not be admitted to any communal pairing himself?), and of course the pair of enigmatic balls that follow him wherever he goes. The triangular, open, and proliferative "1+2" replaces the closed, totalizing "1+1=2=1" of conjugal unity. Blumfeld is as exiled from this latter formula as he is from history and (patri-) lineage itself. His lack of biological offspring translates at work into the impending moribundity of his department and the "lack of a younger generation to carry on" (p. 199). Instead his bachelor machine seems to spawn a proliferative horizontal series of children-animals-doubles, which he consistently fails to recongnize as spin-offs of his own being, so obsessed is he with efficiency, history, and work.

It is also perhaps worth registering here that for Nabokov "threeness" is the dominant theme of *The Metamorphosis* as well, though he is unwilling to offer any reason or idea of why this should be so. See Vladimir Nabokov, "Franz Kafka: 'The Metamorphosis'," *Lectures on Literature,* New York: Harcourt Brace, 1980).

117 Kimberly Sparks has argued that together they form an insectlike *tripelganger* counterpart to Gregor himself. "Drei Schwarze Kaninchen: Zu einer Deutung der Zimmerherren in Kafkas 'Die Verwandlung,'" *Zeitschrift für Deutsche Philologie,* 84, Special Issue (1965), 73–82.

118 Recall that it is self-forgetting that characterizes animal continuity and immanence for Bataille.

119 The Fraülein Bürstner–Grete analogy receives here, perhaps, its definitive expression.

applying a piece of seductive equipment to it and in the outstretched gesture of the arm, it too employed simultaneously in an act of address and in an act of relation to a piece of erotic equipment.

There is still a third element belonging to this series. This image occurs quite a bit earlier in the narrative and concerns that first and only gesture of address that Grete pays her brother after his metamorphosis. We must return now to the scene in Gregor's room just as Grete and her mother are reentering it to find Gregor obscenely perched against the portrait. The mother proceeds immediately to faint, correctly intuiting perhaps the very level on which this gesture of Gregor's explicitly concerns and addresses her.[120] It is the sister's turn now to respond, and we find her frozen once again in yet another version of this same gesture: "'You Gregor!' cried his sister with raised fist and piercing eyes."[121] That the sister is not herself scandalized by the action but only angry at the way it has upset their mother seems to betray some form of tacit understanding between them. When later she explodes hysterically upon discovering that her mother has trespassed on the terrain shared, however unequally, by her and Gregor, without permission having entered his room to clean it herself, the sense of a profound but concealed and now violated intimacy is undeniable. The anticonjugal and perhaps even perverse love between a brother and a sister is certainly a central experiment/fantasy that it is this story's function to express.[122]

The violin-playing scene is a clear reenactment of the scene with the portrait. The momentary conjugation, however, takes place this time not through the surface of the portrait but through the pure sonorous medium of the music,[123] which

120 It is surprising that an interpretation of *The Metamorphosis* based on a shame and guilt fantasy at having been discovered masturbating (among the story's primary themes are violated privacy, self waste, and even blindness, not to mention the intimate metonymical association of the action of the fretsaw work and the sexy magazine clipping, Gregor's perpetual exudations, the themes of seediness, filth, etc.) seems never to have been suggested.

121 This gesture of a raised fist is, by Kafka's own admission, one of the most common in his work.

122 To call this an incest fantasy, and to end analysis there, would be a hollow reduction of simple, straightforward facts to a secondary and at best speculative readymade schema. As Deleuze and Guattari's *Kafka* seems to imply, if Kafka's work is important it is not least for offering not so many examples but rather a systematic *corrective* to the essentially moralizing and normalizing Freudian theory of the family.

123 Just as in "Josephine the Singer" there is a powerful discrepancy between those who find the music beautiful and those, though they know that it is not, appreciate it all the more for its aspect as "pure form" and connectivity.

in its own way brings the neck area again into prominent relief. Here again this imminent coupling is broken up by the intervention of the father and the violent *rappel à l'ordre* that reestablishes normalized household relations. The ambiguous roomers, themselves forming a strange, self-constituted and usurping bachelor mechanism (i.e., a passional linear proceeding), are evicted so as to allow the family members once again to resume their rightful dominion over the apartment and its furniture. Gregor is relegated again to his room, this time to die.

Yet this final death, cannot be a sign only of abjection and defeat. If it is a defeat on one level, it is also a compromise, a kind of petty triumph nonetheless.[124] The vector of becoming—here, a becoming animal[125] is also a becoming not-of-this-world; it implies the embrace of an immediacy and a continuity so profound that ideally it erases not life itself, but all consciousness of life or consciousness *tout court*.[126] In this sense both the music from the sister's violin and the mute

124 Even critics as conservative as Wilhelm Emrich have been unwilling to elide this aspect of Kafka's work. Emrich casts the death ending alternately as "abortive," "redemptive," or as liberatory breakthrough. See Emrich, *Franz Kafka,* pp. 363–364, 132, 145, 163.

125 Animality is itself a form of pre-being, nonbeing, or pure becoming. Yet true becoming is not embodied in a thing becoming something else, but in forming a bloc with that other thing's "becoming":

> A becoming is not a correspondence between relations. But neither is it a resemblance, an imitation, or, at the limit, an identification. . . . Becoming produces nothing other than itself. . . .What is real is the becoming itself, the bloc of becoming, not the supposedly fixed terms through which that which becomes passes. Becoming can and should be qualified as becoming-animal even in the absence of a term that would be the animal become. . . . *This is the point to clarify: that a becoming lacks a subject distinct from itself; but also that it has no term, since its term in turn exists only as taken up in another becoming of which it is the subject,* and which coexists, forms a bloc with the first. This is the principle according to which there is a reality specific to becoming (the Bergsonian idea of a coexistence of very different "durations," superior or inferior to "ours," all of them in communication). [Deleuze and Guattari, *A Thousand Plateaus,* pp. 237–238; emphasis mine]

The kitten-lamb from the story "A Crossbreed" is paradigmatic here: it too has no pedigree, no descendants or filiation, no particular forms that it must realize, yet it does continue incessantly, and unpredictably to metamorphose. See Kafka, *Complete Stories,* pp. 426–427.

126 "The lament at the deathbed is actually a lament that dying in its true sense did not take place there." *Hochzeitvorbereitungen auf dem Lande und andere Prosa auf dem Nachlass* (Franfurt: Fischer, 1953), pp. 122–123, cited in Emrich, p. 364.

gesturality of the portrait were each in their own way a passage toward a certain ecstatic form of "death." And in this we saw eroticism in its purest and most fundamental aspect: "the assenting to life even into death."[127]

The Metamorphosis is nothing if not an exploratory device, an experiment, an essay, and at the limit, a machine to dismantle the stultifying mega-architectures of family and Law. If it is this very positivity that I have sought to reclaim for Kafka's work, I have expressly avoided searching it out at the literal level of what appears to be the story's explicit content. For *The Metamorphosis,* it cannot be denied, both cosmologizes and topologizes the family as a universal field of relations. We know from Kafka's best biographers, both Klaus Wagenbach and Ernst Pawels, as well as Gustav Janouch,[128] to what extent the family in early twentieth-century Prague was considered by Kafka to be little better than yet another technological relay in a burgeoning system of bureaucratic modernization.[129] Yet there were affects, even unspeakable ones, that exceeded such institutionalization, and which Kafka sought to recover wherever he could find them—the eastern European Yiddish theater, Zionism, women—and which he sought to develop, or try out, if not always in the world of literal flesh then in that of literature. Kafka's analytic isolation of this unit—the family—from the historical continuum in which he lived was virtually overdetermined, especially when one considers that in an almost identical context—bourgeois, Jewish, middle European society at the turn of the century—Freud himself was led to posit the psyche as a mirror of this same pseudo-universal group of relations. If in Kafka we find an attempt to violate these relations by rendering them perverse or casting them into continuous experimental variation, or by merely rehearsing them in a grotesque mode as in a child's puppet theater, we have here nonetheless a positivity that humbles Freud's own sad pessimism as it is reflected in virtually all of his concepts and most notably in that of the "cure." To have oriented practice around something else than the "strategic" cure, is indeed, I am arguing, why

127 Bataille, *Erotism,* p. 11.

128 Klaus Wagenbach, *Franz Kafka, Eine Biographie;* Ernst Pawels, *The Nightmare of Reason;* Gustav Janouch, *Conversations with Kafka.*

129 This did not, to be sure, prevent him from being deeply fascinated by technological relays within the burgeoning system of bureaucratic modernization. See *Letters to Felice,* pp. 166–168.

Kafka is important. In Kafka, (positive) experimentation replaces (negative) reconciliation.

What we share with Kafka—our shared modernity—is the predicament of inhabiting a world whose forces of coercion and evil have spun around us a web so tight and dense that its totality has passed well beyond measure. There is no longer an outside to which one might escape or from which an attack might be launched nor even an enclave within or from which a clear image of this monstrous, burgeoning new reality might be forged. But then this is only a problem of optics. For life naturally must seek to discharge itself, must seek to engage, seize, and make terms with the element that serves as its milieu. It is a fundamentally neurotic assumption (and much in our critical culture depends on such an assumption) that man cannot live without an *image* of Being.[130] (Not for nothing did philosophical modernity begin with Nietzsche, nor scientific and aesthetic modernity with a series of breaks from "optical naturalism.") Kafka himself was undeniably difficult and often morose, though by no means excessively so, certainly not for someone as reflective and deeply concerned as he about the tendencies of the age in which he lived. From the moment we move beyond the baseless clichés of his Olympian angst, dilapidated self, and pathological imagination,[131] we discover a personality armed and endowed with an abundance of energy, irony, and especially humor, one who chose to write—more as an everyday practice of living than as a fully self-conscious vocation—as a way of negotiating reality, testing and prodding its obstacles, counterpressures, and resistances, working out its arguments and counterarguments, modeling it and inserting hypotheses, test runs, and documenting—especially documenting—its various properties and results. What lies behind all of Kafka's work is the echo of an exhausted and no longer possible worldview: the clear image of a happy, apprehensible totality.

130 All of Kafka's work, though *The Castle* especially, resides in the tension produced by a false equivalence: that between the Infinite and the Absolute. The Infinite is capable of producing an image, albeit a false one, and when this image is mistaken for the Absolute, man is plunged into an ancestral repetition of the curse of idolatry. On the unattainability of the image *qua* image and its relation to unity, see Blanchot, *Espace Littéraire,* pp. 96–98.

131 Ernst Pawel's recent biographical study *The Nightmare of Reason* goes far in dispelling such myths.

What is it then that constitutes Kafka's reality in its direct and irreducible materiality? Relations, fragments, complex and impure mixtures—a peculiar lack of reassuring *Zusammenhalt*. Kafka's sentences and stories weave bits and pieces of this world-material together, producing occasional fits of vertiginous momentum, chains of astonishing musical assemblage, other times stalling to become mired in infelicitous combinations, wrong turns, lanes of gravity and immobility, dead ends. This does not make it sad literature. And if this alone is not enough to make it happy literature either, it nevertheless does make it *affirmative*. This is the positivity I have tried to describe. Just as it must be part of Kafka's optics—and that of any other modern (in the sense I am using the word),—practitioners to identify shards, pieces of world for experimental recombination, so too must we use the same lens to scrutinize these new objects and moments that make up his fiction. Indeed I have argued that its very structure begs us to do so; the effects exist at this micrological level and no other, so that a critical method that recognizes only story units is certain to be humiliated by what is now the legendary recalcitrance of Kafka's oeuvre.[132] In other words, one must *read the relations and the movements*, not the image, the totalities.

132 I have shown, with a variety of examples and in relation to very disparate modes, how a Kafka story is constructed as a field of multiple, contradictory, and centrifugal movements rather than as a unity of either dissonant or harmonious fragments. I have for the sake of exposition maintained the two-world theory that is a mainstay of at least one stream of traditional Kafka criticism, proposing to fix different objects and relations at different levels of actuality, or within different systems of distribution. There is no better example of the mechanics of Kafkan narrative (this example is a refinement of the story-, wall-, and world-building technique referred to earlier) than the following excerpt from the *Fourth Octavo Notebook:*

> Foreign workers brought the blocks of marble, already hewn and ready to be fitted together. . . . No building ever rose into being as easily as this temple did, or rather, this temple came into being in the true manner of temples. Only on every block—from what quarry did they come?—there were clumsy scribblings by senseless childish hands, or rather, entries made by barbaric mountain-dwellers in order to annoy or to deface or to destroy completely, scratched into the stone with instruments that were obviously magnificently sharp, intended to endure for an eternity that would outlast the temple.

> There can be no question that for Kafka writing was caught simultaneously in a futile attempt to erect temples from individuated prehewn bloc(k)s as well as a process of giving

Kafka most certainly did not turn away from life, even though he did turn away from God (the Law, the Father, signifiance). And as I have tried to show, this "turning" is the powerful central motor of his work, and can be understood either in its positivity or not at all.

body to the incessant, undivided, and continuous murmuring or scribbles of barbaric (animal) or childlike being whose "magnificently sharp" instruments molest equally the mute surface of the stone as well as the hubristic vainglory of temple makers. The point here lies in the different relations of parts to wholes: the *meaning* of the blocks depends on the existence—past, future, mythic, or possible—of the totalizing, signifying temple of which they are patient, hopeful parts, whereas the "writing" is eternal and fully realized at every moment and at every level of cutting *(découpage)*.

Kafkan immanence is always bound to a movement toward this micrological field. The eminently binding and social nature of the *asignifying* stone inscriptions links them in no uncertain way to music, and to the prelapsarian in general, in the "Investigations of a Dog" and "Josephine the Singer," but also to the delirious calligraphy of the blueprints in "The Penal Colony" and the cacophonic telephone transmissions of *The Castle*. Citation from the *Fourth Octavo Notebook,* quoted in E. Heller, *Franz Kafka,* pp. 100–101. For the views of another critic who, in attempting to explain the multiple and indeterminate movements in Kafka's narrative structure, has come all but to the point of positing a notion of field, see Michel Dentan, *Humour et création.*

6.1
Bobsled course, Oberhof

6   Conclusion

THROUGHOUT THE PRECEDING ARGUMENTS one theme has remained constant, albeit in a variety of forms: that of movement and its relation to the problem of time. More explicitly, perhaps one should say it is the theory of time that is here treated, in relation not just to space, as most conventional formulas would have it, but in relation to movement itself conceived as primordial and *creative,* as the principle itself of individuation. This positive, materialist approach to time and movement characterizes a central feature of modernity that for the most part (outside of the sciences) continues to be overlooked. This approach necessarily owes a certain debt to ancient materialist philosophy, especially for the concepts of immanent cause and univocal substance (it matters not what this latter might be, only that it be dynamic and serve as a principle of infinite potential or virtuality), whose combination gives rise to what I have called an ontology of the "event."[1] Different arrangements of these elements can be found at the heart of many of the most significant bodies of modernist works, from Nietzsche through Foucault, from Medardo Rosso and Van Gogh through Robert Smithson and Robert Ryman, from Joseph Conrad to Thomas Pynchon.

It is unusual perhaps to admit to having been inspired in one's approach to modernist cultural artifacts by the spirit of physics treatises considered "discredited" for over two millennia. On the one hand, many historians have already called attention to the sudden renewal of interest (today's is but the most recent of a long periodic series of such renewals) in antique physics and cosmology[2] for practitioners in these and related fields today. This type of "return" is at any rate a common strategic feature of many modernizing philosophical movements.[3] But much more than this, such philosophical/cosmological systems that are essentially physical and concrete provide probably the clearest examples of the type of analysis that I have attempted to undertake. This type of analysis proceeds by

---

1 Especially the Epicurean atomism adumbrated in Lucretius's *De Rerum Natura* and the legacy of these ideas in later thinkers such as Scotus, Cusanus, Bruno, Spinoza, Nietzsche, and Bergson. On univocity in Scotus, see David Knowles, *The Evolution of Medieval Thought* (New York: Vintage, 1962).

2 Prigogine and Stengers, *Order our of Chaos;* Serres, *Hermes IV: La Distribution.*

3 See chap. 2, note 5.

working back from the object toward the system of mutual implications, the system of regularities, and the coherent network of conditions of possibilities that give the object its body and its sense.

But that such a method should have any success when applied to a literal solid body such as a sculpture or building seems unremarkable; that it should yield any result whatever when confronting a literary text, such as one of Kafka's, for example, is perhaps less obvious. Yet it may be said that any truly great body of work—literary or otherwise—derives its unique power (if this is not categorically true of the work in relation to the specific epoch in which its is created, it is certainly so of any subsequent epoch in which the work survives) from the global universe of relations that it expresses (*actualizes*, in the perpetual and dynamic sense), not the individual local meanings it manifests. The totality of these virtual relations—the universe expressed—determines, in a purely pragmatic sense, what one can call the capacities of a work, that is, what it is capable of affecting, transforming, or *doing* in the world.

It is this aspect that places a "work" on an equal footing with "world"—for what are either of these but flows of matter encountering one another and actualizing—here and there—various aspects of their virtuality in singularities or *haecceity*-events? Indeed what is traditionally called "eternal" in a work is not its meaning—for this is necessarily contingent and historically bound—but rather everything else in it that overspills the meaning, an internal dynamism that engages the perpetual coming-to-be of the world with its own ceaseless, creative (because always oriented to an outside) coming-to-be.[4]

This method has in its favor, I believe, an ability to describe in identical terms the *effective* nature of any cultural object, and ultimately even the relations between several such objects, without recourse to metaphysical notions or discipline-specific concepts that immunize and isolate a work from its fundamentally *conductive* role and immanent position within the concrete, historically evolving world. If this is indeed a type of materialism it is one that I have tried not to let stray too far from those of Nietzsche's *Genealogy of Morals*, Bergson's *Matter and Memory*, Foucault's *Archaeology of Knowledge*, and Deleuze and Guattari's *A Thousand Plateaus*.

As stated in the introduction, the attempt in this study was to establish neither causal nor analogic relations between events clearly separated from one another

---

4 The claim here is not that all instances of art or literature, any more than all instances of "the world," are equally dynamic, productive, and disruptive of identity and fixity, but merely that works—or real phenomena—in which these relations are either no longer, or are very incompletely dominated by transcendent codes, are often deemed "modern."

either through time, space, or the analytic divisions between disciplines. Rather, it sought to discover, then describe, a level of relations common to these disparate practices, which shared at their empirical level perhaps nothing more than an iconoclastic or groundbreaking status with regard to the respective histories of their own disciplines. Yet, beyond this, there was discovered in each case a clear and fundamental challenge not only to their own specific histories but to the concept of historical time itself. Out of this deeper, transverse rupture was seen to evolve a series of secondary problems, both specific and general. Among the general ones, common to all of the phenomena examined was a new relation to the "outside"—the constitutive or worldly milieu—which became either a constitutive plenum or a mobile stratum in which all "individuals" (entities) were embedded or linked. "Actuality" emerged, or, let us say, became intelligible, only within complex ensembles that formed on and within individuating events. These "events" bore time along within themselves (and therefore all "effects") as singularities. This "immanent time" was seen as a principle of creation, novelty, and becoming.

Fundamental transformations within Western scientific and cultural disciplines often embody returns or revivals of classical "heterodoxic" texts or ideas. Such works are deemed heterodoxic because at one point or another they are seen either to contradict or to be of no intelligible use to an orthodox religious-scientific regime. Though far from homogeneous, it is still safe to say that Western religious and scientific cultures have seldom if ever wavered on two basic questions: in religion, on the existence of a transcendent cause and its accompanying independent world, and in science, on the discrete and timeless nature of phenomena. Undoubtedly these two affirmations have always been, and remain, deeply linked, yet frictions, even cataclysmic ones, have nonetheless resulted from momentary incompatibilities produced by the incessant shifts and fluctuations that afflict these two, only partially distinct regimes. But do "paradigm shifts" or "epistemological breaks" occur merely on the basis of colliding asperities originating in these two orthodox series? Or do changes of this order only come, as Nietzsche has said, from elsewhere—from an *outside?* Clearly what is at stake here is a theory of phenomenal—social, historical—*change.*[5]

The present study suggests, at least as a preliminary hypothesis, that significant atomist and Lucretian tendencies are present almost anywhere modernity in general, or modernisms specifically, seem to erupt. Clearly these philosophies bear an

5 See Michel Feher and Sanford Kwinter, "Foreword," *ZONE 1/2* (New York: Zone Books, 1986), pp. 10–13.

intrinsically antagonistic relation to the late Greek and early Christian cosmologies that serve as the foundation of Western religious/scientific orthodoxy—a relation that might well merit further scrutiny especially in relation to its putative, continued transmission throughout Western history. Already in Giordano Bruno's proto-scientific and philosophical modernity, for example, it is possible to trace Lucretian (vs. Christian and Platonic) themes. Can a similar relation to be discovered in Spinoza, Newton, Vico, and later in some of the most cataclysmic intellectual developments of our own century?[6] It would seem clear in any case that from this perspective twentieth-century modernism is at once exemplary and far from over, first because the revolution in intellectual models is still so dramatically incomplete, and second because it is just possible that from the customary (religio-scientific) epistemological viewpoint, the so-called phenomena, for the first time ever, can simply no longer be saved.

6 Such relations, for example, could and ought to be compared to the phylum of technical modernizations—e.g., the stirrup, the clock, double-entry bookkeeping, analytical geometry—whose progression clearly entails successive suppressions or conjurations of dynamic or fluid phenomena.

ILLUSTRATION CREDITS

Chapter 1

1.1 Courtesy of Dr. Don James

1.2 Basel: Basilius Presse AG. Courtesy of Mrs. Maria Jenny

1.4 Reprinted, by permission, from Michel Foucault, *Surveiller et Punir: Naissance de la prison* (Paris: Editions Gallimard, 1975)

1.6 Courtesy of the Corbis/Hulton-Deutsch Collection

1.7 Reprinted, by permission, from Standish Meacham, *A Life Apart: The English Working Class, 1890–1914* (Cambridge, Mass., Harvard University Press, 1977), p. 145

1.8 Photo by Kenneth Libbrecht, Caltech

1.9 Courtesy of Simon Carter/Onsight Photography

Chapter 2

2.1 Photo by Igor Kazus

Chapter 3

3.1 Courtesy of the Paride Accetti collection, Milan

3.2 Umberto Boccioni. *Unique Forms of Continuity in Space* (1913). Bronze (cast 1931), 43 $\frac{7}{8}$ × 34 $\frac{7}{8}$ × 15 $\frac{1}{4}''$ (111.2 × 88.5 × 40 cm). The Museum of Modern Art, New York. Acquired through the Lillie P. Bliss Bequest. Photograph © 2000 The Museum of Modern Art, New York.

3.3   Courtesy of Musei Civici, Como

3.4   Courtesy of Musei Civici, Como

3.5   Courtesy of Musei Civici, Como

3.6   Courtesy of Musei Civici, Como

3.7   Courtesy of Musei Civici, Como

3.8   Courtesy of Musei Civici, Como

3.9   Courtesy of Musei Civici, Como

3.10   Courtesy of Musei Civici, Como

3.11   Courtesy of Musei Civici, Como

3.12   Courtesy of Musei Civici, Como

3.13   Courtesy of Musei Civici, Como

3.14   Courtesy of Musei Civici, Como

3.15   Courtesy of Musei Civici, Como

3.16   Courtesy of Musei Civici, Como

3.17   Courtesy of Musei Civici, Como

3.18   Courtesy of the Paride Accetti collection, Milan

3.19   Courtesy of the Paride Accetti collection, Milan

3.20   Courtesy of Musei Civici, Como

3.22   Umberto Boccioni. *Development of a Bottle in Space* (1912). Silvered bronze (cast 1931), 15 × 23 ¼ × 12 ⅞" (38.1 × 60.3 × 32.7 cm). The Museum of Modern Art, New York. Aristide Maillol Fund. Photograph © 2000 The Museum of Modern Art, New York.

5.2   © 2000 Artists Rights Society (ARS), New York/ADAGP, Paris/Estate of Marcel Duchamp

5.3   © 2000 Artists Rights Society (ARS), New York/ADAGP, Paris/Estate of Marcel Duchamp

5.4   © 2000 Artists Rights Society (ARS), New York/ADAGP, Paris/Estate of Marcel Duchamp

5.5   Marcel Duchamp. *Couple of Laundress' Aprons* from Exposition Internationale du Surrealisme, Boite Alert. (Paris, Galerie Daniel Cordier, 1959). Supplementary multiple for grand deluxe edition of exhibition catalogue: cloth and fur, composition: (male), 8 ¹⁵⁄₁₆ × 6 ¹⁵⁄₁₆" (22.8 × 17.7 cm); (female) 9 ¼ × 7 ¹³⁄₁₆" (24.8 × 19.8 cm). The Museum of Modern Art, New York. Gift of Arthur A. Goldberg. Photograph © 2000 The Museum of Modern Art, New York.

Chapter 4

4.1   © Michal Rovner. Courtesy of Pace/MacGill, New York

4.2   Courtesy of the Museum of Modern Art, New York

4.3   Courtesy of the Museum of Modern Art, New York

Chapter 5

5.1   Courtesy of the Museum of Modern Art, New York

INDEX

References to illustrations are in italics.

Fiction. *See also* Kafka's fiction; Novels
animal and doubled characters in, 173
Kafka's work compared with traditional,
125
Field. *See also* Milieu; Social field
concept of, 67
of consistency, 68
continuity of, 66
in Kafka's oeuvre, 190
notion of, 59, 60
problem of, viii
Fielding, Henry, 108
Field phenomenon, motion of liquid as, 60
"First Sorrow, The" (Kafka), 148
Flatness
of being, 202n.110
in Kafka's stories, 173
modernist, 129–130
richness of, 138
Flaubert, Gustave, 96
Fluidity of movement, in sports, 29
Food
fasting, 156, 156n.28
in Kafka's stories, 154–156, 155n.25, 157,
161
in *The Metamorphosis,* 160
refusal of, 155
Force, and movement, 38, 40
Force-lines
Boccioni's, 97
in field, 68
of object, 66
Form
H. Bergson on, 33
in Kafka's fiction, 142, 187
Formal, term, 6n.2
Formalisms, modernist, 39
Formation, *vs.* emergence, 109
Forms
actualized, 26
apodictic, 40

development of, 109
in Kantian doctrine, 137
patterning processes in, 6n.2
theory of participation of Ideal, 37
time and, ix
Foucault, Michel, 11, 15, 18–19, 21, 115n.18,
131, 134n.55, 214, 215
on mechanics of language, 131n.48
on subjection, 124
"Foundation Manifesto" (Marinetti), 54–
55, 61
Fountain (Duchamp), *197*
Fourth Octavo Notebook (Kafka), 210n.132
"Fractal dimensions," 130
Fractal object, 129
Fragmentation
vs. multiplicity, 36–38
polyvocality of, 38
Fragments
vs. forms, 37–38
and function, 136
in Kafka's stories, 142
"Frame and mesh" construction, 88
Freud, Sigmund, 108n.6, 134, 208
"Function-rules," 136
Futurism
and field and event, ix–x
Italian, 54
Futurist Campari Pavillion (Depero), 92
Futurist movement, 70
Futurist theory
architecture in, 73–74
epistemology in, 72
proponents of, 69
space in, 69

Galilean principle of relativity, 56
Genealogical method
in history, 41
post-Nietzschean, 122n.28

Industrial building, Sant'Elia's study for, *82*

Industrialization. *See also* Capitalism

and bureaucracy, 105

and human experience, 96–97

and social organization, 25

Infinity, in Kafka's works, 115–116

Information, time as, 46–49

Information dissemination processes, in urban continuum, 90, *91, 92*

Inmixing, in Kafka's fiction, 148

Innovation. *See also* Technological innovations

in sports, 29

unmasterable, 5

Instrumental culture, 4

Intensity, notion of, 111n.10

Intensive, realm of, 110

Intentionality, E. Husserl's, 39n.7

Interconnection, functional, 113, 137

Interference, in modern art, 43

International Style movements, 44n.20

Interpenetration

and continuity, 66

idea of, 64

in Kafka's stories, 185

in Sant'Elia's sketches, 80

In the Penal Colony (Kafka), 107, 181, 181n.75, 202n.111

Intuition, in sports, 29

Inventions

and plasticity of space, 56

time and, 8

"Investigations of a Dog" (Kafka), 154n.23

Irreversibility principle, viii

Irruptions, and tactics, 123

Jameson, Frederic, 98n.55

Janouch, Gustav, 208

Jewish people, history of, 184

Joyce, James, 39, 97, 125, 143

"Judgment, The" (Kafka), 145, 165, 181, 185

Juxtaposition, 42

Kafka, Franz, ix, x, 49, 97, 99, 104

"animal stories" of, 144–145n.6

antifiliality of, 200n.106

apparent stasis of, 114n.16

bureaucratic universe of, 106

cartographic element associated with, 134

compared with Freud, 108n.6

descriptive techniques of, 117

figures of indifferentiability of, 107n.4

literary production of, 187

mapping of, 130

negative ontology in, 180

personality of, 209, 211

on photography, 114–115n.17

politics of, 124

sex life of, 201n.108

theology of, 121, 124

tuberculosis of, 186

"Kafkaesque," the, 143

Kafkan universe, Cusan notions of, 116n.20

Kafka's fiction. *See also specific stories*

bifurcation points in, 146

characteristics of, 210n.132

characters in, 139, 186

doubling in, 171–172n.58

family in, 208

fragments in, 142–144

gesture in, 144

hirsuteness in, 204

narrative in, 111, 114, 118, 119, 126–129, 143, 147n.13, 149, 167, 169, 182n.76, 210n.132

organization of character in, 137

principal themes of, 199n.103

sexual acts in, 199

universal theme in, 145